2016 Annual Competitiveness and Growth Slowdown Analysis for Sub-National Economies of India

NUS National University of Singapore

Lee Kuan Yew School of Public Policy
ASIA COMPETITIVENESS INSTITUTE

In 2016 and 2017, ACI was ranked 13th globally, 2nd in Asia and 1st in Singapore amongst 90 think tanks worldwide under the "Best University Affiliated Think Tank" category by the Think Tanks and Civil Societies Program at the University of Pennsylvania, USA.

About ACI

The Asia Competitiveness Institute (ACI) was established in August 2006 as a research centre at the Lee Kuan Yew School of Public Policy (LKYSPP), National University of Singapore (NUS). It aims to build the intellectual leadership and network for understanding and developing competitiveness in the Asia region. ACI seeks to contribute to the enhancement of inclusive growth, living standards and institutional governance through competitiveness research on sub-national economies in Asia. It identifies mitigating issues and challenges for potential public policy interventions through close collaboration with regional governments, business corporations, policy think-tanks and academics. ACI's three key research pillars include (i) sub-national economies level competitiveness analysis and city-level liveability analysis, (ii) firm-level competitiveness analysis in 16 Asia economies, and (iii) Singapore's long-term growth strategies and public policy analysis.

ACI's value propositions may be encapsulated in its acronym:
Analytical inputs to initiate policies for policy-makers and business leaders in Asia
Capacity building to enable others through improvement in productivity and efficiency
Intellectual leadership to create pragmatic models of competitiveness and inclusive growth

The institute's core research competencies can also be encapsulated in this acronym describing our evidence-based assessments conducted on public policies for ASEAN in the context of the rise of China and India.

Vision and Mission

- ACI's over-arching vision is to build up its research credibility with policy impact, contributing as a professional, world-class think-tank.
- ACI's mission is to establish our niche as a leading policy think-tank by identifying competitiveness trends, opportunities and challenges, as well as promoting competition and synergising complementarities amongst Asian economies and business corporations.
- ACI endeavours to articulate sound recommendations, entice discourse, and shape agenda in the arena of public policy amongst Asian governments.
- ACI undertakes evidence-based analysis of public policy issues and decisions, in order to provide assessment of their effectiveness as well as economic and societal impact.

Research Initiatives and Collaborations

I. Identify trends of competitiveness and policy analysis on trade and investment of ASEAN, within the regional context of competition and complementarities with China and India.
II. Identify competitive strengths and conduct policy analysis on Singapore within the context of regional economies with international benchmarking.
III. We are regularly releasing three indices on liveability ranking including 64 Global Cities, 100 Greater China Cities and 17 Shandong Cities.
IV. We have established an Ease of Doing Business Index on Attractiveness to Investors, Business Friendliness and Competitive Policies for 21 sub-national economies of India and 33 sub-national economies of Indonesia.
V. We have signed Memoranda of Understanding with The World Bank (2015), SPRING Singapore (2014) and European Central Bank (2014). The Memorandum of Understanding between The World Bank and National University of Singapore, coordinated through ACI, was signed in 2016.

VI. We have signed Memoranda of Understanding with various institutions in Greater China economies, including Shanghai Academy of Social Sciences (2016), Shandong Academy of Social Sciences (2015), Chongqing Municipal People's Government (2015), China Institute for Reform and Development, Haikou (2015), Counsellors' Office of the People's Government of Guangdong Province (LOI, 2014) and Chung-Hua Institution for Economic Research, Taiwan (2015).

VII. We have signed Memoranda of Understanding with six Chief Ministers' Offices in Andhra Pradesh (2015), Bihar (2015), Chhattisgarh (2015), Madhya Pradesh (2015), Odisha (2015) and Punjab (2015).

VIII. We have signed Memoranda of Understanding with Committee for Acceleration of Priority Infrastructure Delivery at Coordinating Ministry for Economic Affairs, Indonesia (2016), Indonesia Investment Coordinating Board (2014), Indonesian Agency for Agricultural Research and Development at Ministry of Agriculture (2014), Indonesian President's Delivery Unit for Developing Monitoring and Oversight (2013) and Employer's Association of Indonesia (2013).

IX. We have signed Memoranda of Understanding with ASEAN think-tanks and institutions, including Vietnam Chamber of Commerce and Industry (2016), Centre for Strategic and International Studies, Indonesia (2015), Institute of Strategic & International Studies, Malaysia (2015), Philippine Institute for Development Studies (2015), Thailand Development Research Institute (2015) and Central Institute for Economic Management, Vietnam (2015).

About ACI's Research Pillars

ACI has consciously engaged in economic research that has significant relevance to Singapore and the Asian region. Over the years, ACI has focused on our expertise in quantitative competitiveness analysis and simulation, spinning off volumes of research output in the applications of our methodology and regional insight. At this stage, ACI has identified three core research pillars that will guide and define its research efforts moving forward. The three research pillars are as follows:

Pillar I. Sub-national Economies Competitiveness Analysis

ACI engages in systematic and methodical competitiveness analyses of the *sub-national economies* by using an evidence-based, empirical approach involving a comprehensive list of relevant indicators, which are categorised under multiple layers called the 'environments'. A number of our projects, including competitiveness analyses of Greater China, ASEAN-10, India, and Indonesia, as well as other thematic research projects, were conducted by adopting this common methodology, with potential variations in the specific environments and indicators. ACI's competitiveness analysis of Asian economies goes beyond the usual ranking to offer constructive policy recommendations on how individual member states can improve their rankings vis-à-vis their sub-national or regional peers through the application of the 'what-if' simulation, which provides the projected improvements of each state's ranking whereby the bottom one-fifth of its indicators are enhanced.

Pillar II. Micro-based Firm Level Competitiveness Analysis

Micro-based firm level competitiveness analysis is ACI's second research pillar that has been developed in view of the intrinsic importance of firm-level competitiveness in terms of productivity, efficiency, and governance. In the context of globalisation, mobility of economic activities, and blurring of borders, an understanding of the determinants and dynamics of firm-level competitiveness is paramount, in order for policy makers to make adjustments and prepare their industries for an increasingly competitive economic landscape. To this end, ACI has partnered with the European Central Bank to carry out research in this area, possessing a solid foundation in firm-level productivity research in the form of European Competitiveness Network database and methodology. ACI envisaged the expansion of CompNet into Asia, thereby pioneering the Asia CompNet research network encompassing 16 economies in Asia.

Pillar III. Singapore's Long-term Economic Growth Strategies and Public Policies Analysis

The third and imminent research pillar focuses on Singapore's long-term economic growth strategies in the context of changing circumstances, future trends, and emerging opportunities for Singapore in the decades ahead. In particular, ACI will take on the task of critically examining Singapore's public policy strengths and areas of improvement by assessing policy successes of the past, identifying new issues to address and the current policy gaps, through a systematic and evidence-based research inquiry using quantitative methodology and empirical data, leveraging on our network of policy experts.

Founding Patron and International Advisory Panel

Founding Patron

Mr George Yeo
Visiting Scholar, Lee Kuan Yew School of Public Policy, National University of Singapore & Former Minister of Foreign Affairs, Singapore

International Advisory Panel

Co-Chairs:

Professor Michael Porter (2006–2010)
Bishop William Lawrence University Professor

Ms Marjorie Yang (2006–2012)
Chairman, Esquel Group

Members:

Professor Kishore Mahbubani
Dean, Lee Kuan Yew School of Public Policy, National University of Singapore

Dr Kuntoro Mangkusubroto
Head, President's Delivery Unit for Developing Monitoring and Oversight (UKP4), Indonesia

Mr Narayana Murthy
Chairman, Infosys Technologies Limited

Mr Philip Yeo
Chairman, SPRING Singapore

Mr Loh Khum Yean
Permanent Secretary, Ministry of Trade and Industry

Ms Yong Ying-I
Permanent Secretary, Public Service Division

Professor Chan Kam Leung Alan
Dean, College of Humanities, Arts and Social Sciences, Nanyang Technological University

Asia Competitiveness Institute

Co-Directors:

Associate Professor Tan Khee Giap (2011 till now)
Professor Tan Kong Yam (2011 till now)

Asia Competitiveness Institute - World Scientific Series

(ISSN: 2424-9912)

Series Editor: Tan Khee Giap (*Lee Kuan Yew School of Public Policy, NUS, Singapore*)

In the tradition of the Asia Competitiveness Institute (ACI) at the Lee Kuan Yew School of Public Policy, National University of Singapore (NUS), our research publications make a distinctive contribution to the understanding of economic development in Asia. These books, first published in 2013, in the Asia Competitiveness Institute - World Scientific Series evaluate and track competitiveness for the sub-national economies of China, India, Indonesia and ASEAN annually through combining leading-edge methodologies with an extensive dataset. The study covers four environments of competitiveness: (1) Macroeconomic Stability, (2) Government and Institutional Setting, (3) Financial, Businesses and Manpower Conditions, and (4) Quality of Life and Infrastructure Development. It also conducts "what-if" policy simulations to propose policy suggestions.

2016

2016 Annual Competitiveness Analysis and Growth Slowdown Analysis for ASEAN-10
by Tan Khee Giap, Nguyen Le Phuong Anh & Luu Nguyen Trieu Duong (Lee Kuan Yew School of Public Policy, NUS, Singapore)

2016 Growth Slowdown Analysis by Income Thresholds and Annual Update of Competitiveness Analysis for 34 Greater China Economies
by Tan Khee Giap, Wang Peng & Xie Teleixi (Lee Kuan Yew School of Public Policy, NUS, Singapore)

Inaugural 2016 Ease of Doing Business Index on Attractiveness to Investors, Business Friendliness and Competitive Policies (EDB Index ABC) for 21 Sub-National Economies of India
by Tan Khee Giap, Sasidaran Gopalan, Jigyasa Sharma & Tan Kong Yam (Lee Kuan Yew School of Public Policy, NUS, Singapore)

2016 Annual Competitiveness and Growth Slowdown Analysis for Sub-National Economies of India
by Tan Khee Giap, Sasidaran Gopalan, Anuja Tandon & Tan Kong Yam (Lee Kuan Yew School of Public Policy, NUS, Singapore)

2016 Growth Slowdown Analysis, Ease of Doing Business Index, and Annual Competitiveness Studies of Indonesia's Sub-National Economies
by Tan Khee Giap, Mulya Amri, Nursyahida Ahmad & Tan Kong Yam (Lee Kuan Yew School of Public Policy, NUS, Singapore)

2016 Annual Competitiveness Analysis and Development Strategies for Indonesian Provinces
by Tan Khee Giap, Mulya Amri & Nursyahida Ahmad (Lee Kuan Yew School of Public Policy, NUS, Singapore)

2015

2015 Annual Competitiveness Analysis, Agricultural Productivity and Development Vision for ASEAN-10
by Tan Khee Giap, Nguyen Le Phuong Anh, Sasidaran Gopalan & Luu Nguyen Trieu Duong (Lee Kuan Yew School of Public Policy, NUS, Singapore)

*More information on this series can also be found at http://www.worldscientific.com/series/aciwss

(Continued at end of book)

Asia Competitiveness Institute - World Scientific Series

2016 Annual Competitiveness and Growth Slowdown Analysis for Sub-National Economies of India

Tan Khee Giap
Co-Director, Asia Competitiveness Institute
Lee Kuan Yew School of Public Policy, National University of Singapore

Sasidaran Gopalan
Research Fellow & Deputy Director (Administration), Asia Competitiveness Institute
Lee Kuan Yew School of Public Policy, National University of Singapore

Anuja Tandon
Research Assistant, Asia Competitiveness Institute
Lee Kuan Yew School of Public Policy, National University of Singapore

Tan Kong Yam
Co-Director, Asia Competitiveness Institute
Lee Kuan Yew School of Public Policy, National University of Singapore

Reviewers

Pulapre Balakrishnan
Professor, Ashoka University, India

Sun Jingying
Assistant Professor, Institute of World Economics and Politics,
Chinese Academy of Social Sciences, China

Darwin Marcelo
Infrastructure Economist, The World Bank

Lee Kuan Yew School of Public Policy
Asia Competitiveness Institute
NUS National University of Singapore
World Scientific

Published by

World Scientific Publishing Co. Pte. Ltd.
5 Toh Tuck Link, Singapore 596224
USA office: 27 Warren Street, Suite 401-402, Hackensack, NJ 07601
UK office: 57 Shelton Street, Covent Garden, London WC2H 9HE

British Library Cataloguing-in-Publication Data
A catalogue record for this book is available from the British Library.

Asia Competitiveness Institute – World Scientific Series
2016 ANNUAL COMPETITIVENESS AND GROWTH SLOWDOWN ANALYSIS FOR SUB-NATIONAL ECONOMIES OF INDIA

ISBN 978-981-3226-81-4

Desk Editor: Jiang Yulin

Typeset by Stallion Press
Email: enquiries@stallionpress.com

Printed in Singapore

Contents

Foreword

Asia Competitiveness Institute (ACI) started producing their flagship analysis of competitiveness covering the sub-national economies of India on an annual basis since 2013. This book entitled *2016 Annual Competitiveness and Growth Slowdown Analysis for Sub-National Economies of India* is their fourth annual update. I am quite impressed by the extensive, rigorous and robust analysis undertaken by the ACI research team. The book produces a lot of valuable policy insights that further our understanding of both competitiveness and growth at the sub-national level in India, which is a refreshing addition to the existing body of knowledge, particularly seen in light of the versatility and heterogeneity present in a large country such as India.

ACI's competitiveness ranking and scores are a welcome departure from the popular aggregate nature of competitiveness analysis produced by multilateral organisations like the World Economic Forum (WEF) and the International Institute for Management Development (IMD). By virtue of shifting the unit of analysis to the sub-national level, the insights gleaned from such a disaggregated analysis proves immensely useful for policymaking, especially in a federal setup like India. This year's book has two dedicated chapters analysing competitiveness in a holistic way both at the state and regional levels. The empirical findings support the notion of widening incongruence among the competitiveness profile of the sub-national economies. However, the book also goes on to show some patterns of convergence in various competitiveness indicators between the sub-national economies ranked at the bottom and middle *vis-à-vis* those at the top, suggesting the seriousness with which sub-national governments are working towards addressing the growing imbalances.

Furthermore, one of the distinguishing features of this year's book is the comprehensive analysis on the prospects of a growth slowdown in India's sub-national economies. It is common knowledge that despite the growth strides that India has made ever since it opened its economy to economic liberalisation in 1991, the resultant patterns of economic growth have been asymmetric at best. While there have been several policy initiatives taken to achieve an equitable distribution of the benefits of economic growth and development, the country still has a long way to go to meet such a goal. Viewed in this context, it is absolutely critical for India to keep finding new sources of growth and ensure that lagging sub-national economies stuck at specific income-levels catch-up with those that have done remarkably well. Understanding these growth dynamics at the sub-national level is a difficult analytical and policy exercise which ACI has undertaken in this book. In particular, to compute the probabilities of a growth slowdown in India's sub-national economies, which may be responsible for delaying the country's transition to the upper-middle-income and high-income groups, is not only fascinating but also generates invaluable insights to policymakers. I also find the execution of this exercise empirically strong and robust.

Overall, as someone who continues to believe in India's tremendous growth potential, studies such as this are quite refreshing as they contribute greatly to furthering our understanding of the complex set of issues that the country grapples with, especially at the sub-national level.

Professor Tommy Koh
Ambassador-at-Large, Ministry of Foreign Affairs, Singapore

Preface

Global economic growth is still struggling to reach its pre-global financial crisis levels. Eight years and counting, the ripple effects of the crisis still seem to haunt the world economy. A significant part of this struggle is due to the continued stagnation in the advanced economies that have not yet completely figured their way out of the woods. While emerging markets in general and those in Asia in particular are relatively better off, the nature of global integration dictates that they also take a hit when the advanced economies struggle.

While the global economy is struggling to be back on its feet, the stunning election victory of Mr. Donald Trump as the President of the United States seems to be jeopardising the recovery prospects of the global economy. With serious concerns about 'de-globalisation' trends in both trade and capital flows taking root in the world economy, emerging markets in the Asian region now face an uncharacteristic threat in this day and age of a reversal in the economic gains brought about by global interconnectedness for decades. This will likely have negative repercussions on the growth sustainability of large Asian emerging markets like India. It is imperative that policymakers are cautious in their economic policy management and brace themselves to deal with such uncertainties, moving forward.

India is a vital player in the Asian region and has grown to be a formidable economic force in recent times. However, one of the striking features about the complexity of the Indian economy stems from its vast heterogeneity owing to its federal structure that strings together 36 sub-national economies. This makes it imperative to grasp the dynamics of growth and competitiveness of what the country is going through at the sub-national level. This is where the research conducted by Asia Competitiveness Institute (ACI) of Lee Kuan Yew School of Public Policy on sub-national competitiveness in India assumes immense significance and policy relevance. ACI's research provides a platform for understanding the strengths and weaknesses of each sub-national economy in a vast country like India. This book takes a step in that direction and is the Institute's fourth competitiveness ranking exercise for the Indian sub-national economies.

The timing of the book is interesting. It is coming out at a time when India just attempted an incredible experiment by demonetising 86 percent of its high-value currency notes in circulation in order to tackle the growing menace of black economy, counterfeit notes and terrorist financing. The macroeconomic effects of this shock are yet to be seen and it will be interesting to see how this plays out in terms of its effect on economic growth and competitiveness. Further, a series of commendable policy initiatives have been floated by the Narendra Modi-led government aimed primarily at attracting domestic and foreign investment, from facilitating the ease of doing business at the sub-national level to the "Make in India" initiative targeted at boosting foreign direct investments in manufacturing. Despite these various initiatives, one can see that the country is still characterised by a weak investment environment which threatens the growth potential of the country in the near-term. In this context, this book undertakes a timely and robust piece of research dealing with the prospects of an economic growth slowdown of the sub-national economies in India.

Overall, this book empirically tackles several economic issues and policy concerns relating to growth and competitiveness of India's sub-national economies. It goes beyond just presenting a technical exercise and packages it in a way that is useful for policymakers. I hope that the rich insights found in the book would not only contribute to a greater understanding of dynamics of competitiveness at the disaggregated level, but also provide an intellectual platform for relevant policy interventions to be undertaken that will in turn enable India to sustain its growth dynamism.

Professor Kishore Mahbubani
Dean, Lee Kuan Yew School of Public Policy
National University of Singapore

Acknowledgements

Asia Competitiveness Institute (ACI) at the Lee Kuan Yew School of Public Policy (LKYSPP), National University of Singapore (NUS) has been tracking the competitiveness of the all the sub-national economies of India both individually as well as regionally since 2000. Analysing the strengths and weaknesses individually for large and diverse countries is best done when the policymaking process and outcomes are assessed effectively at the sub-national level.

In this book, *2016 Annual Competitiveness and Growth Slowdown Analysis for Sub-National Economies of India*, we update our previous sub-national and regional competitiveness studies with the latest available data. Our comprehensive approach to measuring competitiveness takes into account different factors that collectively shape the ability of a nation or region to achieve substantial and inclusive economic development over a sustained period of time. Furthermore, ACI analyses the dynamics of growth slowdown of the Indian sub-national economies against the backdrop of other developing Asian economies including the Association of Southeast Asian Nations (ASEAN), the Greater China economies and the sub-national economies of Indonesia to inform policy directions.

This book has benefitted immensely from the ACI–World Bank Greater China–India Economic Forum held in LKYSPP, NUS on 2nd September 2016 where ACI received tremendous support from various experts on India and China representing academia as well as regional policy think-tanks. We appreciate the effort and time taken by the reviewers in evaluating our papers presented during the forum whose constructive comments have helped us improve our study significantly. The valuable comments offered to us have also been included in this book to enrich the discussion. We therefore would like to thank the following experts and academic reviewers including:

Professor Pulapre Balakrishnan
Professor of Economics, Ashoka University, Kundli, Haryana, India

Dr Sun Jingying
Assistant Professor, Institute of World Economics and Politics, Chinese Academy of Social Sciences, China

Professor N.R. Bhanumurthy
National Institute of Public Finance and Policy, New Delhi, India

Professor Wang Jiann-Chyuan
Vice President, Chung-Hua Institution for Economic Research, Taiwan

Dr Gilberto M. Llanti
President, Philippine Institute for Development Studies, Philippines

Dr Marife M. Ballesteros
Acting Vice President, Philippine Institute of Development Studies, Philippines

This book would not have been possible without the support of our research and administrative colleagues. In particular, we would like to extend our sincere thanks to an able and dedicated administrative team at ACI including Yap Xin Yi, Cai Jiao Tracy, Nurliyana Binte Yusoff, Qian Yuwei, Nurul Ashikin Bte Adjeman, and Yip Fung Yi Estelle. We would also like to note with great appreciation the high team spirit and contributions from ACI research staff including Professor Ramkishen S. Rajan, Mulya Amri, Tan Beng Kai Evan, Sangiita Yoong Wei Cher, Lian Xiao, Luu Nguyen Trieu Duong, Jigyasa Sharma, Nguyen Duy, Nursyahida Binte Ahmad, and Xie Teleixi.

We place on record our appreciation for the encouragement from Dean Kishore Mahbubani, Associate Professor Eduardo Araral, Vice Dean (Research), Mr Donald Low, Associate Dean (Research and Executive Education) and other colleagues in LKYSPP for making this effort possible.

Tan Khee Giap
Sasidaran Gopalan
Anuja Tandon
Tan Kong Yam

Asia Competitiveness Institute
Lee Kuan Yew School of Public Policy
National University of Singapore

About the Authors

Tan Khee Giap is a Co-Director of the Asia Competitiveness Institute (ACI) and Associate Professor at the Lee Kuan Yew School of Public Policy, National University of Singapore. He is also the Chairman of the Singapore National Committee for Pacific Economic Cooperation. Upon graduating with a PhD from University of East Anglia, England, in 1987 under the Overseas Research Scheme awarded by the Committee of Vice-Chancellors and Principals of the Universities of the United Kingdom, he joined the banking sector as a treasury manager and served as secretary to the Assets and Liabilities Committee for three years, thereafter he taught at the Department of Economics and Statistics, National University of Singapore, 1990–1993. Dr Tan joined Nanyang Technological University in 1993 and was Associate Dean, Graduate Studies Office, 2007–2009. He is now with Lee Kuan Yew School of Public Policy, National University of Singapore.

Dr Tan has consulted extensively with the various government ministries, statutory boards and government-linked companies of Singapore government including Ministry of Finance, Ministry of Trade & Industry, Ministry of Manpower, Housing & Development Board, Civil Aviation Authority of Singapore, Singapore Tourism Board, Trade Development Board, Maritime Port Authority, Ministry of Information, Culture & Arts, Economic Development Board, Ministry of National Development, Media Development Authority, Ministry of Environment and Water Resources, Singapore Design Council, Ministry of Community Development, Youth & Sports, Singapore Press Holdings, Mendaki, StarHub, CapitaLand and Great Eastern Life on policies concerning financial, fiscal, trade, tourism, public housing, labour, telecommunication, tourism, liveable cities, creative industry, media, community development, airport and seaport activities. He has also served as a consultant to international agencies such as the Asian Development Bank, Asian Development Bank Institute, United Nations Industrial Development Group, World Gold Council, ASEAN Secretariat, Central Policy Unit of Hong Kong, Kerzner International, Las Vegas Sands and Marina Bay Sands.

Dr Tan is the lead author for 27 books, serving as journals editor and published widely in international refereed journals. His current research interests include econometric forecasting, Cost of Living Index, Global Liveable Cities Index and competitiveness analysis on 31 provinces in China, 35 states in India and ASEAN-10 economies.

Dr Tan was Deputy President of the Singapore Economic Society, 2004. He served in the 2002 Economic Review Committee (ERC). He has also served as Chairman of the Task Force on Portable Medical Benefits (PMB), as the Deputy Chairman of the IPS Forum for Economic Restructuring (IFER) in 2003 and as a member of the Resource Panel of the Government Parliamentary Committee for Transport, Government Parliamentary Committee for Finance and Trade & Industry and Government Parliamentary Committee for Defence and Foreign Affairs since 2007.

Dr Tan has extensively advised and guided multinational corporations leading to public listings especially those companies from Mainland China and Taiwan. He is also currently an Independent Director of the publicly listed BreadTalk Group, Boustead Projects, TEE Land and Chengdu Rural Commercial Bank.

Sasidaran Gopalan is a Research Fellow and Deputy Director (Administration) at the Asia Competitiveness Institute (ACI) at the Lee Kuan Yew School of Public Policy (LKYSPP), National University of Singapore (NUS). Prior to joining ACI, he was based in Hong Kong as a Post-Doctoral Fellow at the HKUST Institute for Emerging Market Studies and HKUST Jockey Club Institute for Advanced Study at the Hong Kong University of Science and Technology (HKUST).

Dr Gopalan completed his PhD in Public Policy, specialising in International Finance and Policy at the School of Public Policy, George Mason University, USA. He obtained his Bachelor's and Master's degrees in Economics from Loyola College (Chennai, India) and Madras School of Economics (Chennai, India), respectively. He spent a year at the Indian Institute of Management Bangalore (IIMB) post-graduation as a Research Associate and was subsequently based at the Institute of South Asian Studies (ISAS) at NUS for two years undertaking research on international economic policy issues concerning South Asia.

He has extensively published in the broad fields of financing for development and international macroeconomic and financial policies with respect to emerging and developing economies in Asia. Specific topics include an empirical analysis of financial openness and international capital flows, financial development, financial inclusion, foreign aid and remittances. His research has a heavy empirical and policy flavour. He is the author of several books, which include publications with leading publishing houses such as Oxford University Press and Palgrave–Macmillan. He has also published several academic articles to his credit in refereed international journals including top-tier field journals. His other publications include contributions to book chapters in edited volumes, policy briefs as well as op-eds for leading global financial dailies.

At ACI, he is the lead coordinator for the flagship projects on India relating to competitiveness analysis and ease of doing business for India at the sub-national level. In addition, he is also the co-coordinator for thematic projects such as exchange rates on foreign direct investment and trade as well as productivity tracking and efficiency monitoring of small and medium enterprises spanning the economies of ASEAN and sub-national economies of India, China and Indonesia. He also supervises and contributes to the formulation as well as implementation of several empirical research projects, targeted towards journal publications and broader policy outreach.

Anuja Tandon is a Research Assistant at the Asia Competitiveness Institute at the Lee Kuan Yew School of Public Policy, National University of Singapore. She completed her Master's degree in Applied Economics at the Department of Economics, National University of Singapore and her undergraduate degree with Honours in Economics at the Shri Ram College of Commerce, University of Delhi. At ACI, she has worked on the research project in collaboration with the

World Bank on understanding the impact of Master Plan for ASEAN Connectivity (MPAC) on the ASEAN region. She has also been involved in working on the sub-national and regional competitiveness project on India as well as on developing the Ease of Doing Business Index on Attractiveness to Investors, Business Friendliness and Competitive Policies for India. Her research interests include applied econometrics, business economics and development economics.

Tan Kong Yam is presently the Co-Director of the Asia Competitiveness Institute. He is also Professor of Economics at the Nanyang Technological University. From June 2002 to June 2005, he was a senior economist at the World Bank office in Beijing where he worked on issues of macro stabilization, integration of the fragmented domestic market, banking reform, international trade and investment, energy security as well as regional inequality. In 2004, he was a member of the World Bank expert group on the eleventh five-year plan (2006–10) for the State Council in China. The expert group provided analysis and policy recommendations on urbanization, regional inequality, innovation policy, energy and water policy as well as strategy on banking reform to the Chinese government.

Prior to that, he was the chief economist of the Singapore government (1999–2002), and Head, Department of Business Policy, Faculty of Business Administration at the National University of Singapore (NUS). He is a graduate of Princeton (1975–79, class of 1931 scholar, Paul Volcker Thesis prize) and Stanford University (1980–83), where he completed his Master's and PhD in three years. Prior to joining NUS, he worked at the Hoover Institution at Stanford University, World Bank, Monetary Authority of Singapore, and was the Director of Research at the Ministry of Trade and Industry in Singapore.

His research interests are in international trade and finance, economic and business trends in the Asia Pacific region and economic reforms in China. He has published ten books and numerous articles in major international journals including *American Economic Review*, *World Bank Economic Review*, *Long Range Planning*, and *Australian Journal of Management* among others on economic and business issues in the Asia Pacific region. He served as board member at the Singapore Central Provident Fund Board (1984–96) and the National Productivity Board (1989–90). He has also consulted for many organizations including Temasek, GIC, Citigroup, IBM, ATT, BP, ABN-AMRO, Ikea, Bank of China, China Construction Bank, People's Bank of China, EDB, Areva, CapitaLand, Guangdong provincial government, Samsung, Mauritius government, Ministry of Trade and Industry, Mobil, Singapore Technology, etc.

List of Abbreviations

ACI	Asia Competitiveness Institute
ASEAN	Association of Southeast Asian Nations
ATM	Automatic Teller Machine
BMA	Bayesian Model Averaging
CII	Confederation of Indian Industry
CMIE	Centre for Monitoring Indian Economy Pvt. Ltd.
CUI	Catch-Up Index
EDB	Ease of Doing Business
FBMC	Financial, Businesses and Manpower Conditions
FDI	Foreign Direct Investment
GCI	Global Competitiveness Index
GCR	Global Competitiveness Report
GDP	Gross Domestic Product
GDPPC	Gross Domestic Product per Capita
GFC	Global Financial Crisis
GFCF	Gross Fixed Capital Formation
GIS	Government and Institutional Setting
GNI	Gross National Income
GRDP	Gross Regional Domestic Product
GSDP	Gross State Domestic Product
GST	Goods and Services Tax
GVA	Gross Value Added
IMD	International Institute for Management Development
IMF	International Monetary Fund
LKYSPP	Lee Kuan Yew School of Public Policy
MOSPI	Ministry of Statistics and Programme Implementation
MS	Macroeconomic Stability
NUS	National University of Singapore
OECD	Organisation for Economic Co-operation and Development
PIP	Posterior Inclusion Probability

PPP	Public–Private Partnership
PSTD	Posterior Standard Deviation
QLID	Quality of Life and Infrastructure Development
RBI	Reserve Bank of India
RCA	Revealed Comparative Advantage Ratio
REER	Real Effective Exchange Rate
SEZ	Special Economic Zone
TOT	Terms of Trade
UNCTAD	United Nations Conference on Trade and Development
US	United States
WCY	World Competitiveness Yearbook
WEF	World Economic Forum

List of Tables and Figures

Figures

Chapter 1

Chapter 2

Chapter 3

Chapter 4

Chapter 5

Tables

Chapter 2

Chapter 3

Chapter 4

Chapter 1
Introduction

1.1 Introduction and Motivation

One of the flagship research areas of Asia Competitiveness Institute (ACI) pertains to studying the dynamics of competitiveness in India at the sub-national level. A unique feature of ACI's research comes from an effort to recognise the heterogeneity of India and how the variations in the dynamics of competitiveness pan out at the sub-national level. More generally, ACI's niche comes from contributing to a better understanding of the complexity of competitiveness of fast growing emerging market economies in the broader Asian region including India, Indonesia, and China at a disaggregated sub-national level as well as the national economies of the Association of Southeast Asian Nations (ASEAN).[1]

Recognising the diversity inherent in these economies is of prime importance because such an understanding gives rise to a varied set of policy implications at the disaggregated level instead of a one-size-fits-all approach to policy. Thus, one of the cornerstones of ACI's research strategies is to factor in the diversity of these sub-national economies and undertake rigorous research that will inform policymakers in these economies.

Now into its fourth edition, this book entitled *2016 Annual Competitiveness and Growth Slowdown Analysis for Sub-National Economies of India* presents our annual update of competitiveness analysis of India's sub-national economies. Further, the book delves deeper into understanding the dynamics of economic growth of the various sub-national economies in India. This is a significant value-addition to the related literature as the book has a comprehensive and dedicated discussion on the prospects of and determinants of growth slowdown at the sub-national level. By undertaking such an empirical exercise, in this book, we attempt to complement and further our understanding of competitiveness at the sub-national level with an in-depth analysis of their economic growth performance and trajectories, which arguably remains one of the most important priorities for policymakers.

One of the distinguishing features of ACI's research on competitiveness is that it introduces a novel research tool in the form of the *What-if* simulation analysis which assists policymakers in identifying the areas that need improvement in order to enhance their respective competitive environment. Through the *What-if* simulation analysis, ACI goes beyond just constructing a ranking exercise of the sub-national economies and treating it as an end in itself. Instead, the aim of the simulation analysis is to demonstrate the degree of improvement that sub-national economies can achieve upon remedying their identified weaknesses. Such an analysis produces

[1] ACI's flagship research publications also include a competitiveness analysis of the economies of ASEAN-10 and sub-national economies of Indonesia and Greater China. See for instance, Tan *et al.* (2017a, 2017b, 2017c) for a detailed competitiveness analysis of the economies of ASEAN-10, Indonesia and Greater China, respectively.

invaluable policy advice and beneficial effects to these economies, as it not only assists low-ranked sub-national economies to strategically mitigate their weaknesses but also serves as a warning signal to the relatively better-performing counterparts to avoid complacency, as others can play catch-up by implementing appropriate policy prescriptions. The results generated from a unique simulation tool such as the *What-if* analysis tend to facilitate the creation of a situation whereby sub-national economies outcompete each other while at the same time earn a positive reputation for themselves by taking corrective policy steps in the right direction.

Meanwhile, it is also important to not lose sight of the potential opportunities for collaboration that such research tends to open up among the sub-national economies, which eventually leads to the pooling of resources, learning of best practices, and harnessing of each other's potential. A peer review among sub-national economies is a better alternative than learning from the world's best, as it provides contextualisation for sub-national actors to undertake improved measures based on local conditions. Of equal importance is the fact that it also allows sub-national actors to build confidence upon hitting attainable targets from their domestic counterparts. Thus, this facilitates and triggers the development of more sustainable economic fundamentals in these economies.

ACI also recognises the rapidly emerging role that public–private partnerships (PPPs) are playing in these economies along with the greater trends towards decentralisation that has resulted in according a prominent role for sub-national actors in spurring and facilitating economic development. In fact, considering that sub-national governments appear to possess more autonomy in policymaking and have set precedents in enacting forward-looking policies, well ahead of their respective national governments, it is imperative that any endeavour to empirically study the dynamics of competitiveness in the Asian region must factor in the prevalent heterogeneity of the sub-national economies.

Finally, undertaking a holistic and comprehensive competitiveness study at the sub-national level enables ACI to achieve its founding organisational principle of promoting inclusive growth and enhancing living standards in the broader Asian region. A study such as the one undertaken in this book identifies challenges for every sub-national economy and prescribes appropriate policy interventions. The results thus generated in turn also present an opportunity for a variety of state and non-state actors including national and sub-national governments, business corporations, policy think-tanks and academic institutions to forge effective partnerships in designing and implementing tailor-made policies to attain the desired outcomes. An inclusive and prosperous Asia allows every individual in the region to enjoy the fruits of economic success, a noble objective to which ACI's research contributes.

With this background in mind, the remainder of the chapter proceeds as follows. In Section 1.2, we first begin the discussion by providing a comprehensive stock-taking of India's recent developments in the macroeconomic domain. The section highlights the trends and patterns in key macroeconomic variables running up to 2016 by way of setting the context for the discussion in the rest of the book. In Section 1.3, we conclude the chapter by previewing the roadmap for the remainder of this book. This section offers a synopsis of the discussion in all the remaining chapters of this book.

1.2 India: A Macroeconomic Overview

A watershed in the recent history of Indian policymaking occurred on November 08, 2016 when India undertook a radical monetary experiment. Narendra Modi, the Prime Minister of India, in a televised address to the nation announced that currency notes denominated in ₹500 and ₹1000 would lose their legal tender status. This was a riveting policy measure that sent shockwaves across the country (and to some extent took the world by surprise as well) because the notes that were demonetised or delegalised overnight constituted 86 percent of currency notes in circulation in the economy at that time.[2] Furthermore, considering the importance of cash in the Indian economy, with about 90 percent of transactions conducted in cash, this bold policy was understandably greeted with a lot of excitement and trepidation.

There were multiple objectives behind the currency swap experiment that India undertook. Arguably, the most important reason given by the government at the time of announcing this decision to demonetise was that the move was intended to deal with the "black money" circulating in the economy. The size of India's black economy or shadow economy, typically referring to income gained but undeclared to the tax authorities, has been noted to be significant ranging between a fifth and a quarter of India's Gross Domestic Product (GDP) (Schneider *et al.*, 2010).

Yet another important reason cited as a rationale for demonetisation pertained to concerns about counterfeit currency notes circulating in the economy which were reportedly used for several anti-social activities such as terrorist acts. A study by Indian Statistical Institute in Kolkata in 2015 suggested that the value of Indian currency notes that were counterfeit was worth ₹4 billion with the old ₹500 and ₹1000 accounting for about three-quarters of these fake notes (Economic Times, 2016). Interestingly, banning such high denomination currency bills is not an isolated policy idea experimented by India alone. This proposition has been advanced by several notable Western economists such as Larry Summers and Kenneth Rogoff, who have recommended demonetising US$100 bills which they believe will help significantly reduce criminal activities such as money laundering and tax evasion (Sands and Summers, 2016; Swanson, 2016). There are also instances in other countries such as Singapore which stopped issuing S$10,000 notes to combat financial crime.

In addition to the above-mentioned objectives of curbing black money and terrorist financing, an implicit objective of this move also appears to be the possible long-term benefits accruing from improved financial inclusion and greater digitisation of financial services in the economy. Considering the urgent need to bring a significant amount of unbanked population in India under the formal banking system and the policy push that India has been giving to enhance financial inclusion in the country, the demonetisation experiment could be regarded as an instrument that would push the country in this direction in the long term.

However, it must be reiterated that the macroeconomic implications of the demonetisation exercise are unclear as yet for two reasons. First, it is too early to assess whether the expected long-term benefits would outweigh the expected short-term costs. Second, there is not enough

---

[2] It is worth noting that India has experimented with such a policy twice before, once in 1946 and again in 1978.

data even to assess how the short-term macroeconomic costs are panning out except various estimates and projections that anticipate short-run adjustment costs. In addition to the several logistical bottlenecks faced by the people in the immediate aftermath of demonetisation, as was seen in the long lines in front of automatic teller machines (ATMs) and banks which appeared to be inadequately prepared to handle a transition of this magnitude, there are two possible consequences of demonetisation at least in the short run that are expected to affect the country's macroeconomic numbers moving forward.

The first relates to short-run economic growth. Given that 86 percent of the currency notes in circulation were taken out of the system, the slow pace of remonetisation and the logistical difficulties associated with it has affected the bulk of the informal sector which survives on cash transactions. This is especially applicable to many small and medium enterprises which are cash-dependent for running their businesses. This cash squeeze resulting in lower money supply in the economy leading to a decline in short term economic activity might be reflected in lower growth numbers in the next fiscal year.

The second related point is the expected decline in consumption demand. As the cash squeeze could lead to consumers postponing their planned purchases, prices may experience a downward pressure eventually leading to a disinflationary environment in the short term till confidence is boosted and normalcy is restored.

In fact, anticipating these developments, the International Monetary Fund (IMF) has downgraded India's growth forecasts to 6.6 percent in 2016–2017, as against an estimate of 7.6 percent provided earlier before demonetisation (Livemint, 2017). The grounds of such a revision were a possible "negative short-term consumption shock". Similar views were also echoed by India's 2016–2017 Economic Survey. To quote the Economic Survey (Government of India, 2016–2017, p. 53):

> "*Demonetisation has been a radical, unprecedented step with short term costs and long term benefits. The liquidity squeeze was less severe than suggested by the headlines and has been easing since end-December 2016. A number of follow-up actions would minimize the costs and maximise the benefits of demonetisation. These include: fast, demand-driven, remonetisation; further tax reforms, including bringing land and real estate into the GST, reducing tax rates and stamp duties; and acting to allay anxieties about over-zealous tax administration. These actions would allow growth to return to trend in 2017–18, following a temporary decline in 2016–17.*" (p. 53).

While the detailed macroeconomic growth impacts of this policy shock will be clear only in the coming years with the emergence of more data, it is important to acknowledge that India's overall economic growth trajectory since the turn of the millennium has averaged over 7 percent annually between 2000 and 2016. Interestingly, before the global financial crisis struck in 2007, India's average growth was a little over 7 percent. The immediate aftermath of the global financial crisis produced a significant dip in the economy's growth in 2008 when it hit a low of 3.9 percent before it bounced back to reach an average growth of 9.5 percent in 2009 and 2010. However, for three consecutive years after this phase of robust recovery between 2011 and 2013, the average growth in India was only about 6 percent. Although the post-global financial crisis phase saw the economy re-emerge, strongly buoyed by a surge in domestic demand, the momentum slipped due to a combination of external and domestic structural factors which dented the average growth of the Indian economy.

Figure 1.1: Annual Real GDP Growth and Inflation (Percent)

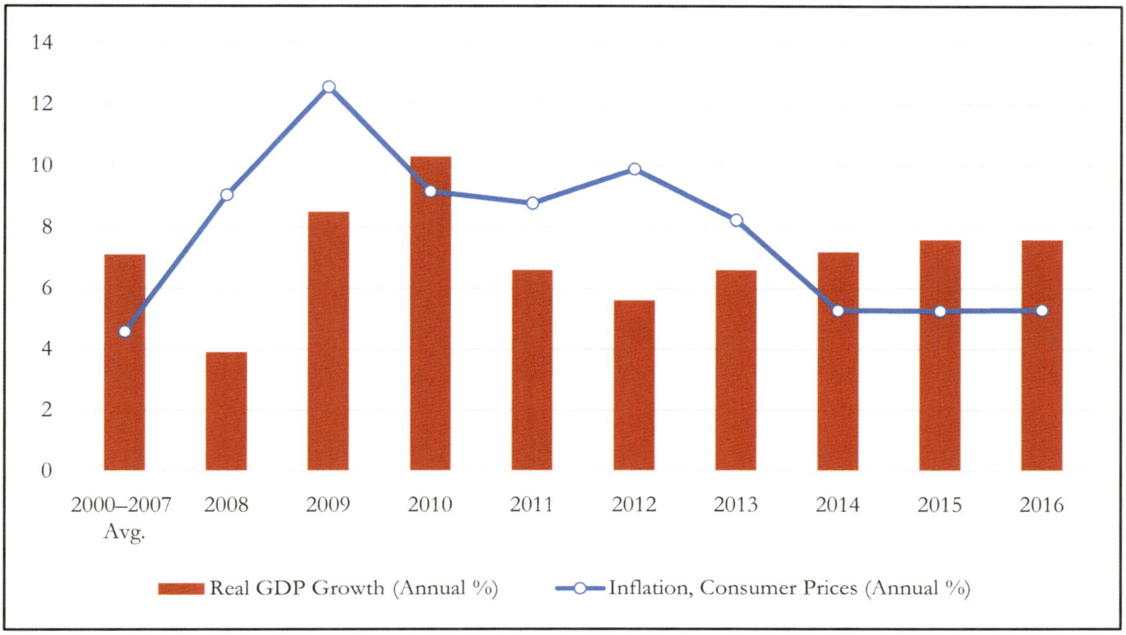

Source: Asia Competitiveness Institute based on International Monetary Fund's World Economic Outlook Database.

However, as Figure 1.1 shows, India seems to be back on its high and stable growth path. The average growth rate stood at 7.5 percent for the period covering 2014–2016, which is not only comparable to the pre-global financial crisis performance but also suggestive of the robust feature of this growth trajectory.

It is also evident from Figure 1.1 that those years when India's growth was dented, the country also suffered from a bout of high inflation, with inflation rates exceeding growth significantly between 2011 and 2013. On average, inflation rates have hovered around 4.5 percent during the pre-global financial crisis era from 2000 to 2007. It skyrocketed in the years following the global financial crisis with annual consumer prices touching a peak of 12.5 percent in 2009. The trends continued to be persistent till 2013 with average inflation rates still above 9 percent between 2010 and 2013, before the price pressures eased starting 2014. The average growth in inflation has moderated significantly and been consistent around 5 percent between 2014 and 2016. This period marked by stable economic growth has also helped overcome the persistent higher inflation-growth differential that characterised the five years following the global financial crisis where average inflation exceeded growth (Figure 1.1).

Zooming in on the supply-side contributions to India's economic growth over the last five years, we can observe that overall economic growth has largely been driven by a robust growth in services sector followed by a strong resurgence in manufacturing growth (in value-added terms) despite weak industrial production (in terms of volumes). As Figure 1.2 shows, services sector consistently has had an average contribution of over 4.5 percentage points to aggregate growth since 2012. While the overall contribution of the industrial sector has hovered around

Figure 1.2: Supply-Side Contributions to Growth (Percentage Points)

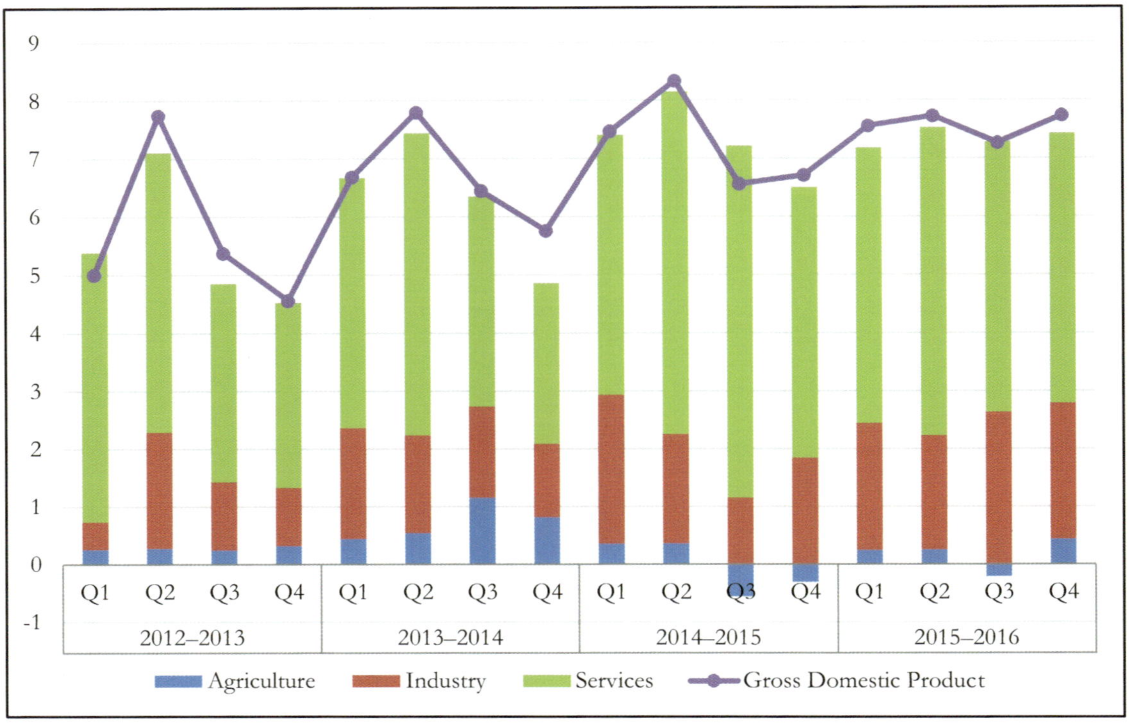

Source: Asia Competitiveness Institute based on Asian Development Outlook 2016 Database.

1.7 percentage points to aggregate economic growth during the corresponding period, there has been a notable resurgence in the last two years running up to 2016 with the contribution exceeding 2 percentage points on average. As the World Bank India Development Update (2016, p. 5) notes, "… while services were as usual the largest contributor to Gross Value Added (GVA) growth, the acceleration in industrial activity was noteworthy, accounting for nearly one-third of overall growth (one-quarter in FY15). Manufacturing picked up, while the performance of the electricity and mining sectors appeared to improve, possibly reflecting a more conducive policy environment in these sectors." The contribution from agricultural sector still continues to be marginal to overall economic growth (Figure 1.2).

Looking into the sources of growth in terms of whether external or domestic demand has been the driver of economic growth in India over the last few years, we find that in aggregate, the components of domestic demand have outweighed the contribution of external demand to overall growth. However, this aggregate picture masks significant variation in the components as India's economic growth has largely occurred at the back of private consumption expenditure instead of gross fixed capital formation signalling a relatively weak investment environment (Figure 1.3). As Figure 1.3 clearly shows, private consumption expenditure on average between 2013 and 2016 has made about a 4 percentage point contribution to India's aggregate economic growth

Figure 1.3: Demand-Side Contributions to Growth (Percentage Points)

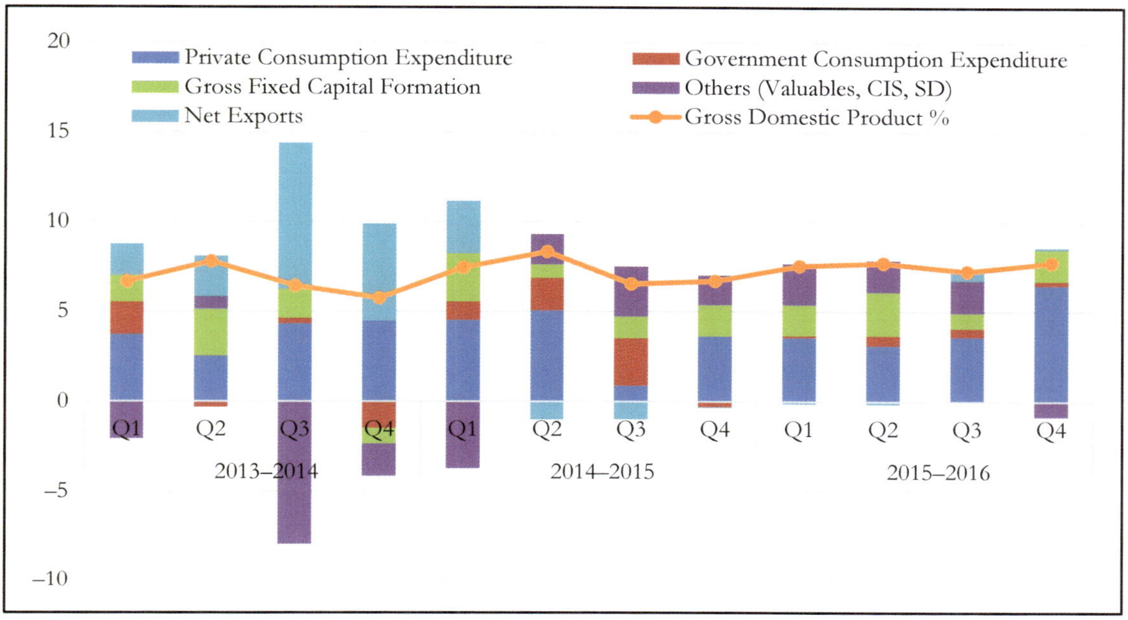

Source: Asia Competitiveness Institute based on Asian Development Outlook 2016 Database.

during the corresponding period. The other component of domestic demand, namely government consumption expenditure, has remained fairly subdued as any boost in capital expenditures were offset by a concomitant reduction in current expenditures (Asian Development Outlook, 2016).

Looking more closely into the weak investment environment, it has been noted that private investment has remained weak largely on account of a combination of overcapacity or low capacity utilisation and weak financial position of India's corporate sector which has been affected by debt overhang (Organisation for Economic Co-operation and Development (OECD), 2016). Figure 1.4 shows how growth rates of gross fixed capital formation capturing domestic investments have seen a precipitous decline since 2015, which actually reflects the broader trend in declining investments since 2011 (barring occasional spurts). Further, the weak investor confidence and the slack that prevails in the firms can be best captured in the declining proportion of managers expecting an increase in capacity utilisation (Figure 1.4).

Although the weak investment environment is a serious cause for concern for the policymakers as far as sustaining India's growth potential, on the flip side, India has experienced not only lower inflation but also a drastic decline in its current account deficit (Figure 1.5). The decline has been notably marked since 2012 when the current account deficit stood close to 5 percent of GDP raising concerns about the country's ability to handle external vulnerabilities. In stark contrast to the average of close to 3.5 percent of GDP in the aftermath of the global financial crisis between 2008 and 2012, India's current account deficit stood at close to 1.5 percent of GDP in 2016. It has hovered around 1.3 percent on average between 2013 and 2016 and a notable

Figure 1.4: Investment Environment

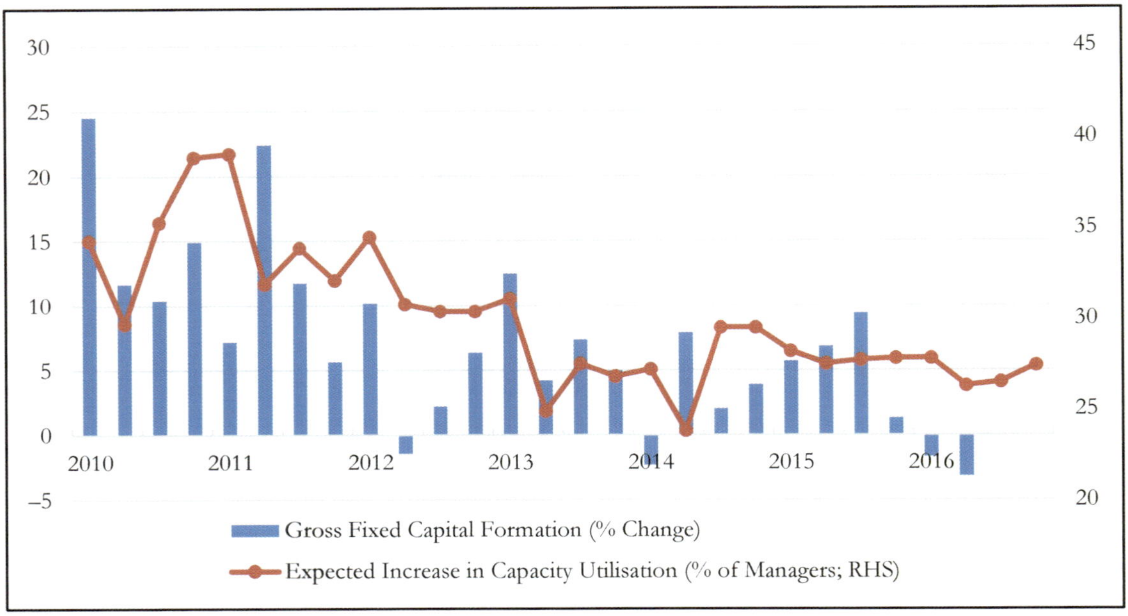

Note: Percentage of managers interviewed by expecting an increase in capacity utilisation by Reserve Bank of India.

Source: Asia Competitiveness Institute based on Organisation for Economic Co-operation and Development Database.

Figure 1.5: Domestic Savings, Investment and Current Account Deficit (Percent of GDP)

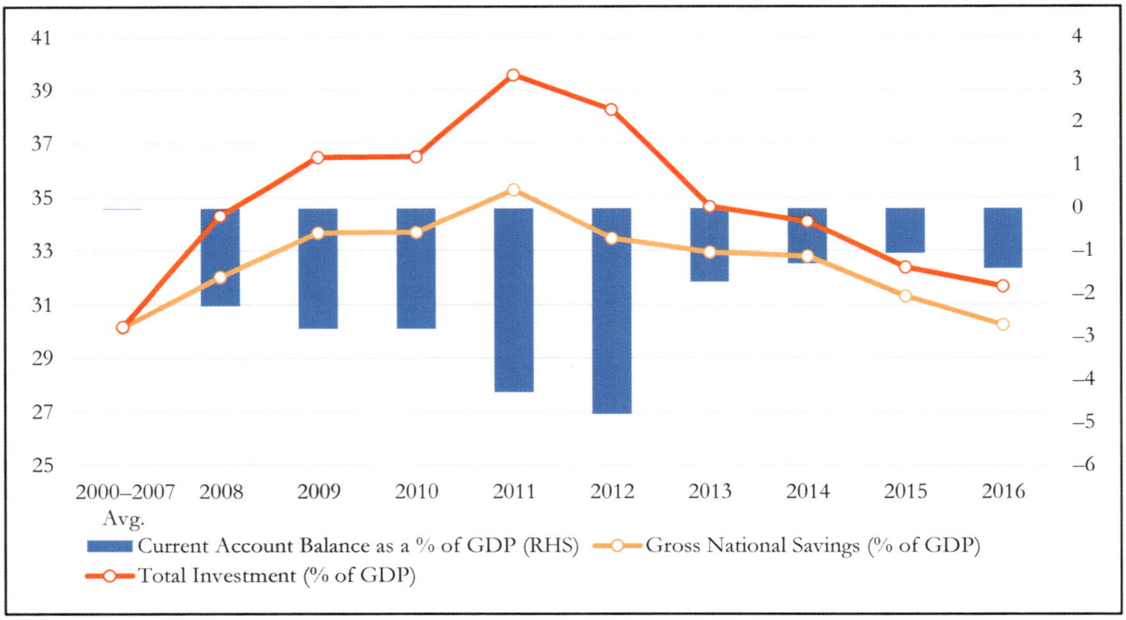

Source: Asia Competitiveness Institute based on International Monetary Fund's World Economic Outlook Database.

reduction in merchandise imports as well as lowering of gold imports have been important factors driving this phenomenon.

An intuitive way to understand the shrinking current account deficit is to consider the trends in current account from a savings–investment standpoint. As Figure 1.5 clearly shows, India's current account deficit widened right after the global financial crisis largely because there was a sharp increase in domestic investments from about 34 percent of GDP in 2008 to a peak of 39.5 percent in 2011. Concomitantly, while national savings as a share of GDP also registered an increase during this period from 32 to 35 percent, it was much more modest relative to the increase in national investments that in turn fuelled the current account deficit.

However, from 2011, there has been a sustained and precipitous decline in national investments which have contributed to the reversal of current account deficit (as a percentage of output). Although savings have also been on a declining trend, the relative decline in investments have been steeper which have primarily driven the reduction in current account deficit to pre-global financial crisis levels. These trends are also consistent with the weak investment environment that appears to be prevailing in India right now, highlighting the need for policymakers to focus on kick-starting the economy through augmenting investments.

The trends in current account balance as viewed from the prism of trade flows reveal that there have been a sharp contraction in India's total imports of goods and services since 2011–2012 with the value of imports dropping from US$490 billion to US$380 billion in 2015–2016 (Figure 1.6). Interestingly, while the immediate few years post the global

Figure 1.6: Exports and Imports of Goods and Services and Trade Balance (US$ Billion)

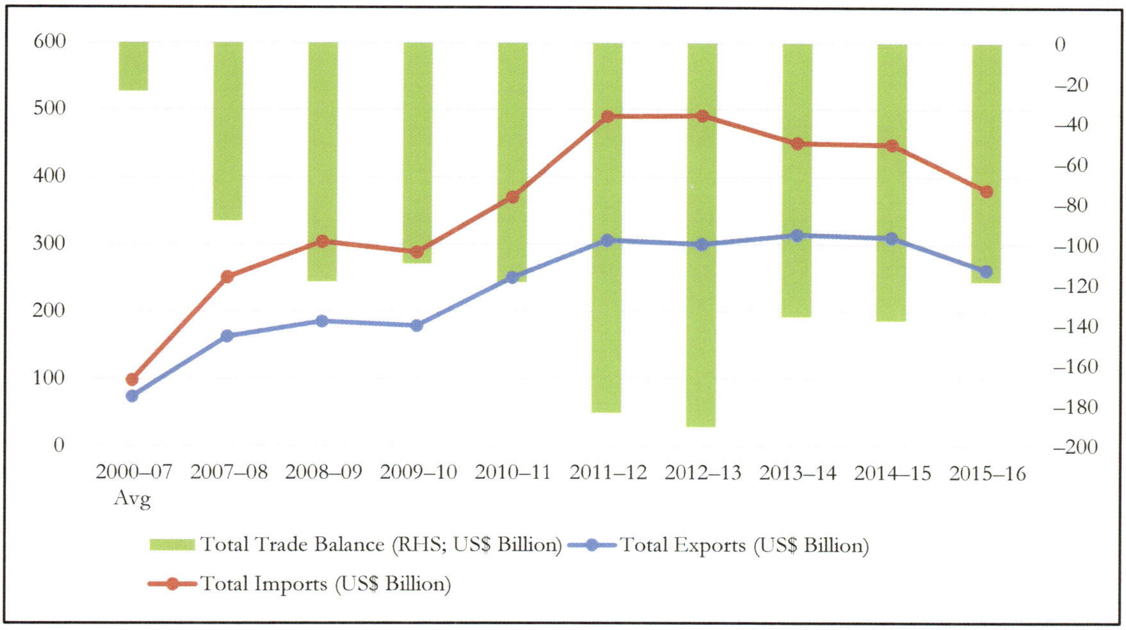

Source: Asia Competitiveness Institute based on Reserve Bank of India Database.

Figure 1.7: Volume of Trade in Goods and Services (Percent of GDP)

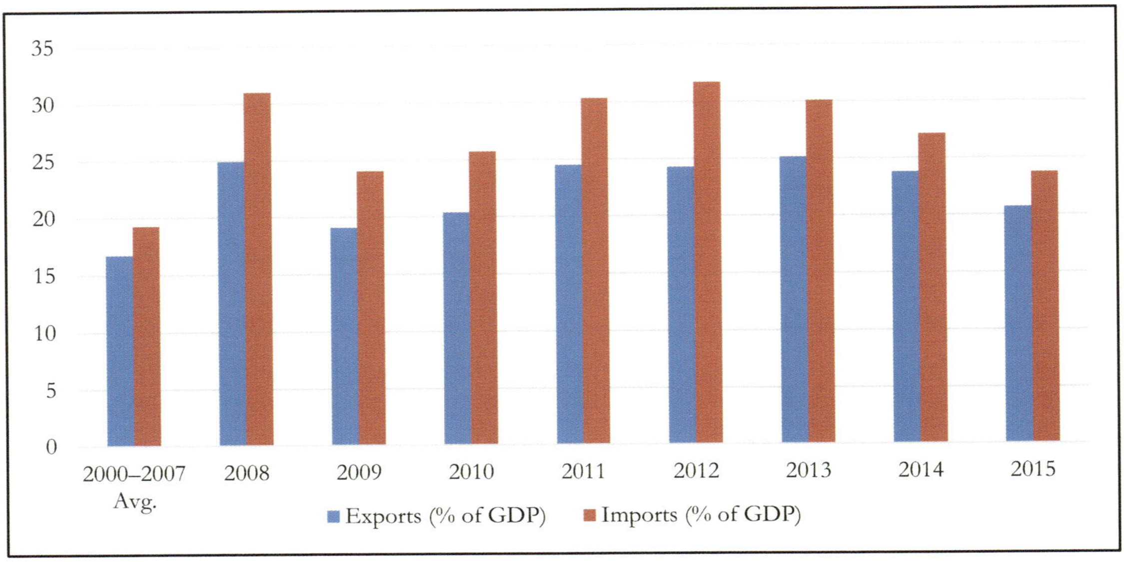

Source: Asia Competitiveness Institute based on International Monetary Fund's World Economic Outlook Database.

financial crisis saw imports picking up, specifically between 2009–2010 and 2011–2012, there has been a steep decline since then. Overall exports of goods and services have followed a similar pattern by and large, although the imports have contracted much more sharply than exports. Asian Development Outlook (2016) notes that imports contracted by over 15 percent in 2015–2016, driven mainly by a reduced oil import bill.

Figure 1.7 expresses the volume of trade in goods and services for India as percent of GDP to place the trade patterns in perspective. As the figure clearly shows, the contraction is evidently larger for imports relative to exports, with total imports as a proportion of GDP declining from 31 percent in 2008 to 23 percent in 2015 while the corresponding figures for exports fell from about a quarter of India's GDP to 21 percent during the same period. However, it must be noted that on average, both exports and imports as a share of India's GDP exceed the corresponding share that prevailed before the global financial crisis.

On the fiscal side, India has been gradually seeing a turnaround in its public finances with a sustained effort to consolidate its fiscal deficit over the years. In 2015–2016, India met its fiscal deficit target of 3.9 percent of its GDP, a reduction from 4.1 percent in 2014–2015 (Figure 1.8). Despite the fact that the combined deficit and debt of the central government and states are high compared to its emerging market peers, it is remarkable that India is firmly committed to be on a sustainable path to fiscal consolidation.

The reduction in fiscal deficit was driven mainly by a reduction in current expenditures of the government offset by significant growth in tax revenues, in particular, the revenues from excise duties and taxes (Asian Development Outlook, 2016; OECD, 2016). Other revenue components like non-tax revenues also grew at a healthy pace. On the expenditure front, India faced a growth

Figure 1.8: Key Fiscal Indicators (Percent of GDP)

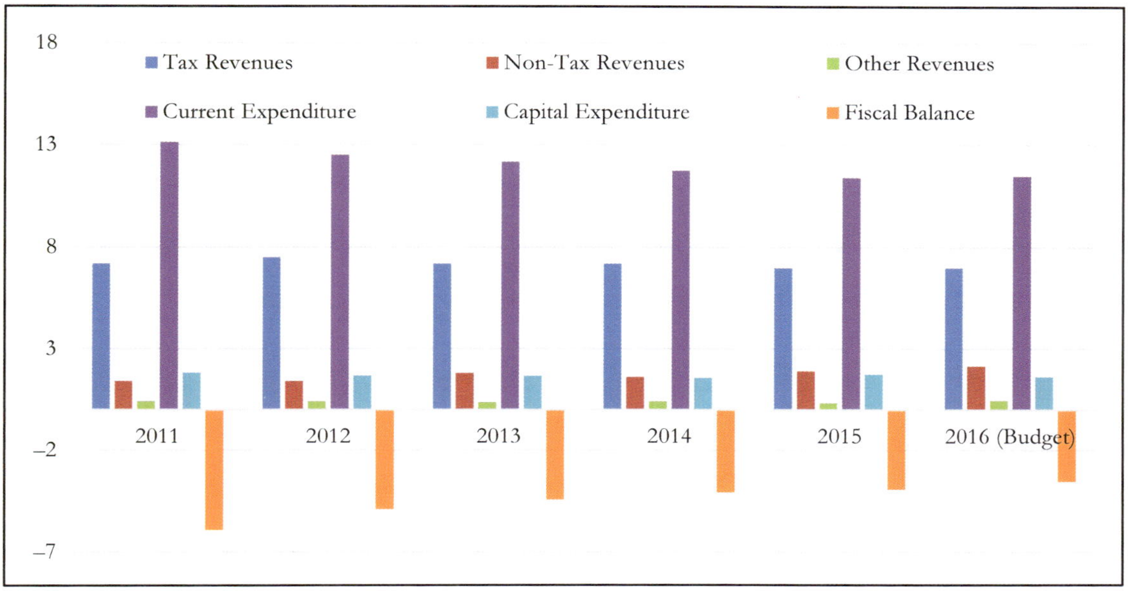

Source: Asia Competitiveness Institute based on Asian Development Outlook 2016 Database.

of over expenditures over 7 percent in 2015–2016 which was slightly higher than the budgeted target of 6.8 percent. This was mainly due to a sharp increase in capital expenditures as opposed to current expenditures, which was a departure from the previous years (Figure 1.8). The broad trends of consolidation of India's fiscal deficit appear to have laid the path for the economy to motor ahead in the desirable direction.

Finally, turning to external sources of financing, India has continued to maintain its attractiveness to foreign direct investments. In 2015, for instance, India ranked among the top 10 recipients in the world for global foreign direct investment (FDI) inflows. The country's share of world FDI inflows stood at close to 3 percent in 2015, up from a negligible 0.3 percent in 2000. Within Asia, about 8 percent of FDI inflows were destined to India in 2015, a marked increase from around 3 percent in 2000.

FDI inflows into India as a share of the country's GDP also experienced a gradual but sustained increase during this period, from about 0.5 percent in 2000 to close to 2 percent in 2015, with this share peaking at approximately 4 percent in 2008 just before the global financial crisis. In absolute terms, United Nations Conference on Trade and Development (UNCTAD) data suggest that India experienced a sharp surge in FDI inflows in 2015, with the magnitude of such flows touching about US$45 billion almost reaching its previous peak of US$47 billion in 2008 before the global financial crisis (Figure 1.9).

To sum up, India appears to be on the right track, with several key macroeconomic indicators supporting such an optimistic outlook. However, as was emphasised in the discussion earlier, despite positive sentiments about the country moving forward in the right direction, there are

Figure 1.9: FDI Inflows to India (US$ Billion and Percent of GDP)

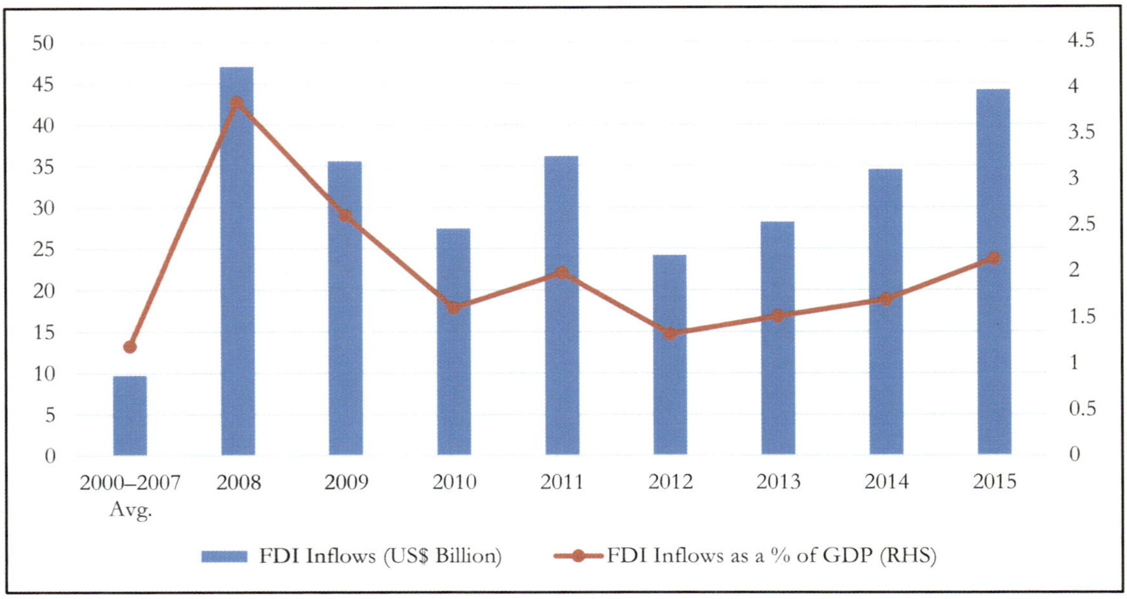

Source: Asia Competitiveness Institute based on United Nations Conference on Trade and Development Database.

legitimate downside risks to such an optimistic growth outlook which mainly stem from the weak investment environment that prevails in the country. There is an urgent need for policymakers to overcome the slack in the economy. As the World Bank India Development Update (2016, p. 13) summarises succinctly:

> "*Despite the acceleration in overall economic activity, including the manufacturing sector, evidence suggests that the Indian economy continues to operate below potential, and manufacturing firms still have idle installed capacity. Excess capacity domestically is partly a reflection of excess capacity globally. The decline in growth in China and weakness of recovery in advanced economies has been greater than anticipated when manufacturing facilities were built in the recent past. Investments in the manufacturing sector are further constrained by weak external demand. Rising non-performing assets in the banking sector, which weakened monetary policy transmission and dampened credit growth, have also hampered private investments.*" (p. 13).

While the unfavourable external environment is not something that Indian policymakers can do anything about, there is certainly a lot of scope to fix the domestic structural issues that will remove the slack and help accelerate as well as sustain the growth momentum. The government at the centre led by Prime Minister Narendra Modi has rightly been placing a significant degree of emphasis on fostering inclusive growth and economic development through increasing investments (both domestic and foreign direct investments) as well as channelling them effectively to develop a robust infrastructure base that will in turn provide the much needed enabling environment for such investments to yield high returns. The strong policy push towards encouraging the sub-national economies to compete with each other to enhance their ease of doing business is a case in point.

Further, notwithstanding the demonetisation episode, the landmark implementation of the Goods and Services Tax (GST) is likely to occur later this year. Although the transition to such a regime will be marred by administrative difficulties, the promise that such a tax regime brings to the economy are substantive. The push once again is to recognise the importance of forging a systematic, strong and cohesive relationship between the central and state governments that would facilitate "cooperative and competitive federalism" among the various sub-national economies.

With the global economic growth still weak, a combination of 'deglobalisation' threats after the electoral victory of Donald Trump in the United States (US) presidential elections, the gradual normalisation of monetary policy in the US coupled with concerns of secular stagnation, it becomes imperative for India to fix domestic economic policy issues that would allow the country to achieve higher growth and development in a sustainable way.

Given this background, the next section concludes by offering a roadmap for the rest of the book through a brief synopsis of the remaining chapters.

1.3 Roadmap of the Book

As noted earlier, this book presents the 2016 annual update on competitiveness for 35 sub-national economies of India.[3] Chapters 2 and 3 are dedicated to an understanding of competitiveness both at the sub-national and regional levels. These chapters will first provide the rationale for undertaking such an analysis and then outline the methodological nuts-and-bolts of ACI's competitiveness framework that enables an analysis to be carried out at the sub-national and regional levels. Following this discussion, the chapters will present the empirical research findings of the competitiveness analysis for 35 sub-national economies. In addition to providing a detailed multi-dimensional analysis of competitiveness embedded in ACI's framework which will be discussed in detail in the next two chapters, the chapters will also furnish the results of the unique *What-if* simulation exercise which identifies the policy strengths and weaknesses of the different sub-national economies and regions in India, allowing policymakers to have a targeted approach to policymaking.

Following the discussion of competitiveness, as indicated earlier, we turn to the crucial issue of economic growth in Chapter 4. This chapter offers a dedicated discussion on growth slowdown analysis in India's sub-national economies. Despite the stellar growth trajectories posted by India in the last 25 years ever since it opened its doors to economic reforms in 1991, and successive governments trying to sustain the growth momentum while enabling all segments of

[3] It is important to clarify at the outset that the analysis in our book makes use of 2013 data due to lags in availability of the indicators at the sub-national level for later years. Further, we would like to clarify that our analysis is confined to 35 sub-national economies which does not include Telangana because of data constraints. Telangana came into existence on June 2, 2014.

society to reap the benefits of economic development, the notion of equitable economic growth still remains a work in progress. Going forward, continuous efforts in pushing through reforms are vital as India's future economic growth may be challenged by both domestic impediments and external risks. It is in this context, we assess India's growth trajectories and investigate the risk of growth slowdown for India, which may delay the country's transition into the upper-middle-income and high-income groups. The key contribution of our analysis stems from the fact that we make a significant departure from the traditional growth literature that has largely focussed on analysing the country as a whole entity. In ACI's tradition, with the firm belief that national aggregates mask the remarkable diversity within the country, we look closely into the growth performance of the sub-national economies. It is important to recognise that the sub-national economies in India are at different stages of development, as reflected by the great variations in their Gross State Domestic Product (GSDP) per capita. As a result, they are likely to face dissimilar growth problems and challenges, which can only be accounted for through an analysis at the sub-national level.

In this light, ACI aims to fill this gap in the literature by providing a comprehensive assessment of growth slowdown of the Indian sub-national economies *vis-à-vis* other Asian developing economies such as the national economies in ASEAN, the economies in the Greater China region as well as the provinces in Indonesia. The analysis will cover economies at all income groups, including low-income, lower-middle-income, upper-middle-income and high-income economies as it intends to reveal relevant determinants of growth slowdown specific to each level of development. Further, based on the empirical findings, the study generates statistical predictions for each sub-national economy in India about the probability of it experiencing a growth slowdown in the near future. This probability can be interpreted as preliminary caution for national and local governments so that they may implement targeted policy interventions to minimise the chances of an economic slowdown.

Chapter 5 offers concluding remarks and discusses the agenda for future research. Considering the importance of investments (both domestic and foreign), the concluding chapter tracks India's performance so far in terms of its flagship policy initiative of "Make in India" and what role it has played in revitalising India's manufacturing sector. The book concludes by offering some insights into the economic policy vulnerabilities that policymakers should be cognisant of, which if neglected could threaten India's growth potential moving forward. The final section of the chapter sketches the importance of ACI's future research agenda pertaining to the impact of exchange rates on FDI inflows to India at the sub-national level.

References

Asian Development Outlook. 2016. "Asia's Potential Growth." Available from https://www.adb.org/sites/default/files/publication/182221/ado2016.pdf (last accessed on February 16, 2017).

Economic Times. 2016. "Secret Study Pegs Value of Fake Notes in Circulation at Rs. 400 Crore." Available from http://economictimes.indiatimes.com/news/defence/secret-study-pegs-value-of-fake-notes-in-circulation-at-rs-400-crore/articleshow/55424455.cms (last accessed on February 04, 2017).

Government of India. 2017. "2016–2017 Economic Survey." Ministry of Finance, Department of Economic Affairs, Economic Division January, 2017, New Delhi, available from, http://indiabudget.nic.in/es2016-17/echapter.pdf (last accessed on February 16, 2017).

Livemint. 2017. "IMF Cuts India's GDP Growth Forecast to 6.6% on Note Ban Woes." Available from http://www.livemint.com/Politics/RNFrr6eVDZpIyMDCRm5UdN/IMF-downgrades-Indias-201617-GDP-growth-forecast-to-66.html (last accessed on February 16, 2017).

Organisation for Economic Co-operation and Development. 2016. "OECD Economic Outlook." 2016 (2), available from http://www.oecd.org/eco/economicoutlook.htm (last accessed on February 22, 2017).

Sands, Peter and Lawrence H. Summers. 2016. "In Defense of Killing the $100 Bill." February 25, 2016, available from https://www.washingtonpost.com/news/wonk/wp/2016/02/25/in-defense-of-killing-the-100-bill/?utm_term=.17c4fb502174 (last accessed on February 04, 2017).

Schneider, Friedrich, Andreas Buehn and Claudio E. Montenegro. 2010. "New Estimates for the Shadow Economies all over the World." *International Economic Journal*, 24(2): 443–461. Also published as World Bank Policy Research Working Paper 5356, available from: http://www.gfintegrity.org/storage/gfip/documents/reports/world_bank_shadow_economies_all_over_the_world.pdf (last accessed February 04, 2017).

Swanson, Ana. 2016. "Maybe It's Time America Gets Rid of Most of Its Cash." Available from, https://www.washingtonpost.com/news/wonk/wp/2016/09/27/maybe-its-time-america-gets-rid-of-most-of-its-cash/?utm_term=.17dfca20b18f (last accessed on February 04, 2017).

Tan, Khee Giap, Nguyen Le Phuong Anh and Nguyen Trieu Duong Luu. 2017a. "*Annual Competitiveness Analysis and Growth Slowdown Analysis for ASEAN-10.*" Forthcoming.

Tan, Khee Giap, Mulya Amri, Nursyahida Binte Ahmad and Kong Yam Tan. 2017b. "*2016 Annual Competitiveness Studies of Indonesia's Sub-National Economies: Growth Slowdown Analysis and Ease of Doing Business Index.*" Forthcoming.

Tan, Khee Giap, Peng Wang and Teleixi Xie. 2017c. "*2016 Annual Update of Provincial and Regional Competitiveness Analysis for Greater China.*" Forthcoming.

The World Bank. 2016. "India Development Update." The World Bank Press Release, June 2016, available from http://documents.worldbank.org/curated/en/543111468194942579/pdf/106456-P156828-PUBLIC-MAKE-PUBLIC-8PM-DC-JUNE-19-IDU-Jun16-vweb.pdf (last accessed on February 16, 2017.

Chapter 2

2016 Annual Update on Competitiveness for 35 Sub-National Economies of India

2.1 Introduction

The notion of competitiveness has sought the attention of academic literature for a long time now but there is no consensus on how to define the term. Among the several studies that have explored the concept of competitiveness, the influential work of Porter (1980) brought the term competitiveness to prominence. Although Porter (1980)'s original definition of the notion of competitiveness was rooted in the perspective of a firm, the term has come to be used liberally in the broader macroeconomic literature applied especially to several regions as well as individual countries.[1]

At the national level, there are two prominent global competitiveness indices that are ubiquitous in all policy research pertaining to competitiveness. The first is the World Competitiveness Yearbook (WCY) published by International Institute for Management Development (IMD), World Competitiveness Centre and the second is the Global Competitiveness Index (GCI) produced by the World Economic Forum (WEF). These indices have been developed predominantly based on publicly available data sourced from international and national organisations and are sometimes supplemented with primary data through surveys. The WCY, for instance, defines competitiveness as a combination of four factors, namely (i) Economic Performance, (ii) Government Efficiency, (iii) Business Efficiency, and (iv) Infrastructure. Each factor is further divided into five sub-factors, with 20 sub-factors in total. It uses equal weights such that each sub-factor contributes 5 percent weight, and each factor contributes 25 percent weight to the Overall Competitiveness Index (IMD, 2015).

The GCI, on the other hand, describes competitiveness as the set of institutions, policies and factors that define the level of productivity of a country. The Global Competitiveness Index (World Economic Forum, 2015) is measured across 12 pillars which are divided into three sub-indices: (i) Basic Requirements, (ii) Efficiency Enhancers, and (iii) Innovation and Sophistication Factors. The weights for each of the sub-indices vary depending on a particular country's level of Gross Domestic Product (GDP) per capita. Thus, the higher a country's GDP per capita, more weight is assigned to the Innovation and Sophistication sub-index, and less weight is assigned to the Basic Requirements sub-index, and vice versa.

The GCI and WCY differ in their views of how they measure competitiveness. The GCI views the index as a measure of inputs to explain a particular output, which is prosperity (GDP per capita). As such, the GCI does not include GDP, population, or GDP per capita into its calculation. On the other hand, the WCY views the index as an aggregated snapshot of various factors that collectively shape competitiveness. The WCY thus uses all relevant criteria including those

[1] For a comprehensive discussion on the related literature, see for instance, Porter (1990), Begg (1999), Waheeduzzaman and Ryans (1996), Buckley *et al.* (2010) and Tan and Rao (2015).

Figure 2.1: IMD World Competitiveness Overall Ranking for Selected Emerging Market Economies (2012–2016)

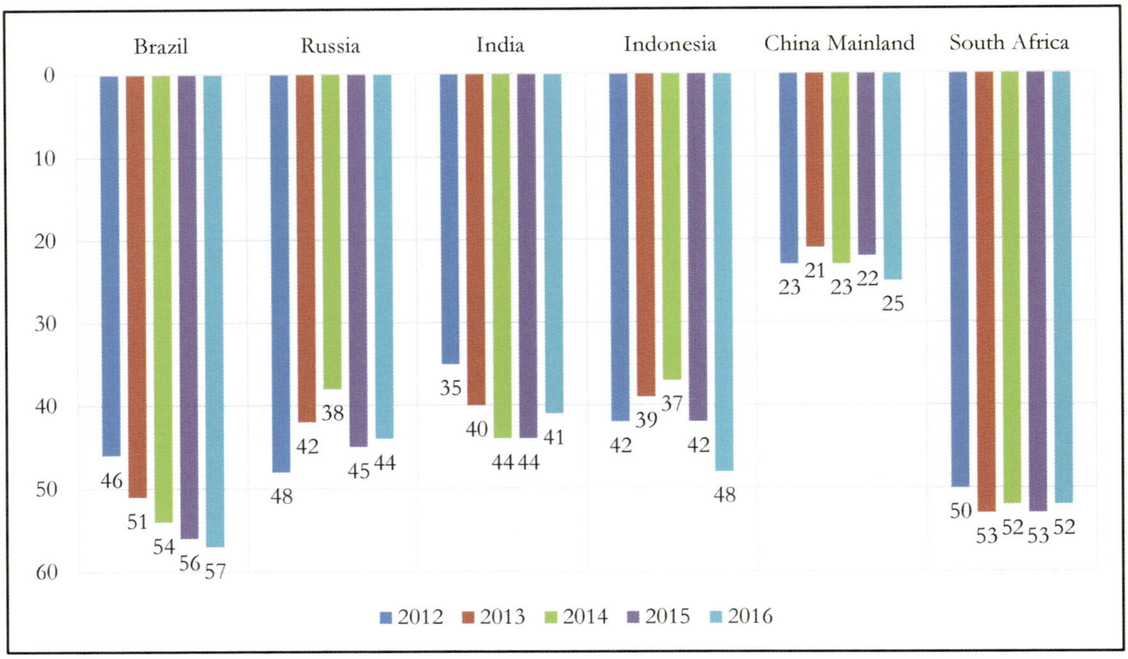

Note: *Y* Axis is reversed; lower rank indicates better performance.

Source: Asia Competitiveness Institute based on International Institute for Management Development Database.

that may be seen as "outcome indicators", such as GDP per capita. This difference illustrates the ongoing theoretical debate about competitiveness: whether it is a determinant of prosperity or revealed through prosperity, whether it determines productivity or vice versa, and whether competitiveness is a means to an end or an end in itself.

For illustration, an application of both these popular indices for a sample of emerging market economies involving Brazil, Russia, India, Indonesia, and China is shown in Figures 2.1–2.3. Figure 2.1 specifically contrasts India's competitiveness performance *vis-à-vis* selected emerging market peers across the world using the IMD's WCY from 2012 to 2016.

India appears to have lost some ground in terms of overall competitiveness relative to 2012 when it was placed 35th in the world. It slipped to the 40th position in 2013 and continued to slide to the 44th place in 2014. After stagnating at the 44th position in 2015, the turnaround appears to have come in 2016 with India managing to climb up three spots to be ranked 41st in 2016. A closer examination of the report appears to suggest that in 2016, India ranked 26th in terms of image, 11th in terms of openness and 32nd in managerial practices. While these improvements reflect to a large degree the policy emphasis of the current government towards attracting greater foreign investments, especially in the manufacturing sector and make India the future factory of the world, India still lags in terms of its competitiveness in education, health and environment.

Viewed from a comparative perspective, in 2016, with the exception of China which clearly lies far ahead of India and other emerging market economies, India appears to have outcompeted

Figure 2.2: IMD World Competitiveness Economic Performance Ranking for Selected Emerging Market Economies

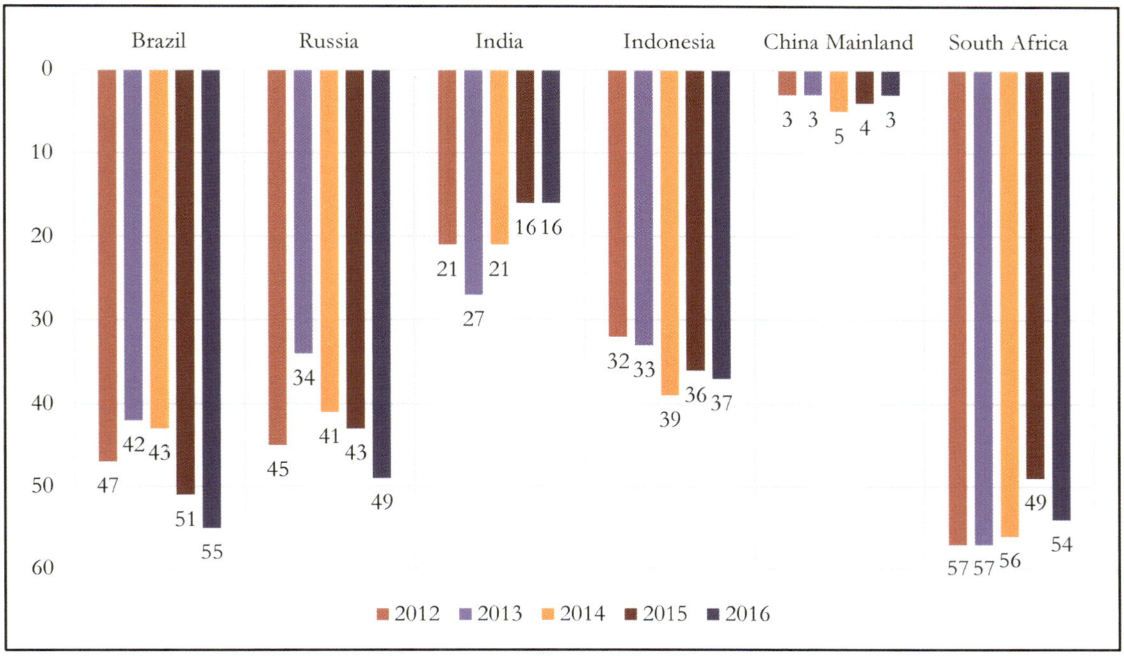

Note: *Y* Axis is reversed; lower rank indicates better performance.

Source: Asia Competitiveness Institute based on International Institute for Management Development Database.

the rest as shown in Figure 2.1. Specifically zooming in on "economic performance" which is one of the vital components of these rankings, India appears to be ranked much better than its overall ranking seen earlier. As Figure 2.2 reveals, since 2013, India has seen its economic performance improving and consistent with its overall trends, it does better relative to other emerging market peers with the exception of China.

The second most popularly used index is the GCI that comes from WEF. Figure 2.3 charts India's aggregate performance between 2012 and 2016 and we find that once again, India has seen tremendous improvements from 2014 and has risen dramatically from 71st position to 39th overall in 2016. In fact, the picture is much more favourable to India in GCI than IMD's ranking and India does quite well relative to its emerging market peers including China. Although China still remains ahead of India, the improvements over the years appear to be more significant for India than China over the years.

While these rankings seem to definitely give an idea about the notion of competitiveness, they still beg the question of how representative they actually are, especially seen in light of the significant degree of heterogeneity we observe in countries like India. To be sure, there are at the very least two notable inadequacies with these popular indices measuring competitiveness. First, these indicators do not tend to be holistic in the way they define competitiveness, viz. they do not appear to satisfactorily take into account the plethora of factors that collectively shape the ability of a nation or region to achieve substantial and inclusive economic development over a sustained

Figure 2.3: World Economic Forum Global Competitiveness Index Ranking

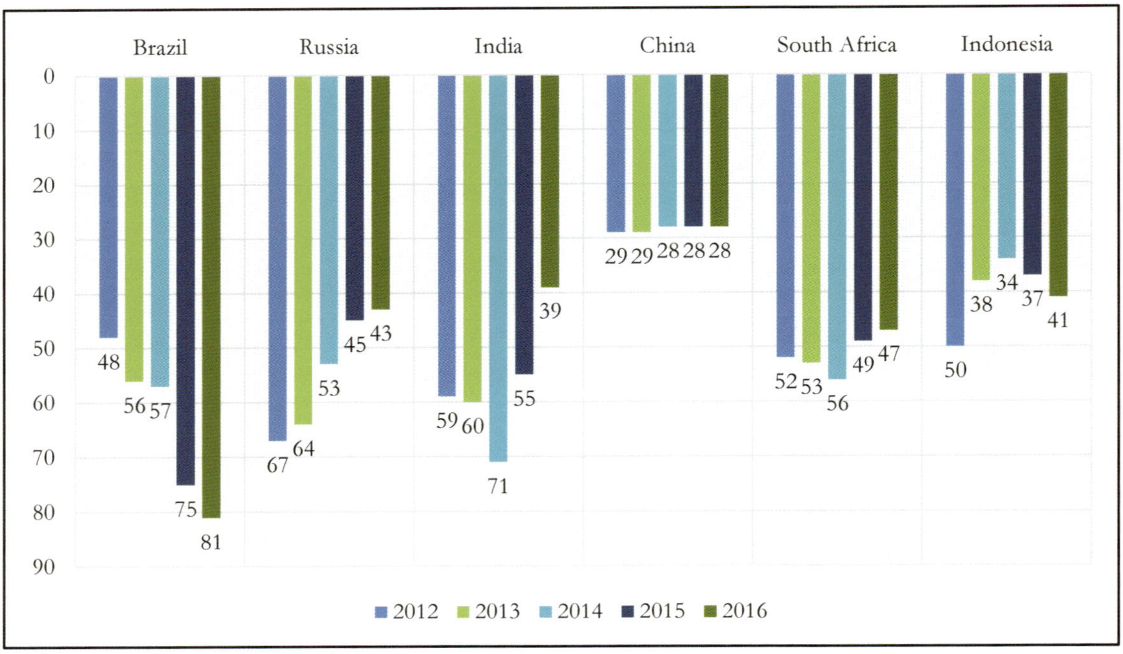

Notes: (i) *Y* Axis is reversed; lower rank indicates better performance.

(ii) Country coverage in GCI has varied every year. For 2012, the total number of countries in the sample was 144; for 2013 it was 148; for 2014 it was 144; for 2015 it was 140; and for 2016 it was 138.

Source: Asia Competitiveness Institute based on Global Competitiveness Report.

period of time. Second, more importantly, their very construction is aggregate in nature implying that there is no scope to factor in the heterogeneity at the sub-national level within countries.

This view also appears to have a reasonable degree of support in the relevant literature. For instance, while it has been acknowledged that measuring competitiveness at the sub-national or regional level is important for various reasons, several scholars argue that it cannot be reasonably defined by the role of export-oriented performance of regional clusters as defined by Porter (Kitson *et al*., 2004). They propose that regional competitiveness focusses more on the dynamics of a region's long-term prosperity to ultimately develop into places where companies and people want to locate and invest in. It can be said that regions are neither simple aggregation of firms, nor scaled down versions of nations (Cellini and Soci, 2002) and competitiveness takes on a different meaning as per the scale being referenced. However, despite the complexities and imperfections in measuring regional competitiveness, researchers have agreed that it is a key concept to better understand sources and dynamics of national and international competitiveness of a country (Čučković *et al.*, 2013).

The debate still continues and there is still a yawning gap in the related literature in terms of offering a better understanding of competitiveness capturing the various dimensions at the sub-national or regional level. It is in this context that Asia Competitiveness Institute's (ACI's) holistic competitiveness framework becomes an important contribution to this literature on measuring competitiveness. ACI's approach to competitiveness is not only holistic but also integrated and systematic that provides a window to be as all-encompassing as possible, effectively capturing the multi-dimensional attributes of competitiveness at the sub-national level. The framework will be elaborated in the sections below.

The remainder of the chapter is organised as follows: Section 2.2 first starts with explaining the research methodology that underpins ACI's competitiveness index at the sub-national level. Following this, Section 2.3 will present a comprehensive discussion of the results of our empirical analysis on competitiveness pertaining to India's 35 sub-national economies, using ACI's competitiveness framework. The section will also offer a detailed discussion of the *What-if* simulation analysis as a contribution to better understanding of policymaking and the various conclusions that can be drawn from the empirical results. Section 2.4 concludes with a summary of the key findings and the way forward.

2.2 Research Methodology

This section offers a discussion about the overarching competitiveness framework that forms the methodological basis for the research findings of our competitiveness analysis over the years. The focus is on the competitiveness framework applicable to the sub-national economies.

The competitiveness framework employed by ACI for sub-national competitiveness computes the rankings for the 35 sub-national economies of India by factoring in a plethora of socio-economic development indicators that determine competitiveness. Drilling data and analysis down to the level of sub-national economies, ACI's unique methodology provides the scope to recommend specific policies tailored to the specific sub-national economy. This approach also provides a platform for stimulating productive discussions between industrialists, administrators, and policy-makers at the sub-national level before engaging them at the national level.

2.2.1 Four Environments, 11 Sub-Environments and 75 Indicators

ACI's comprehensive approach to measuring competitiveness can be illustrated by Figure 2.4, where the overall competitiveness of an economy is captured through four different environments: (1) Macroeconomic Stability; (2) Government and Institutional Setting; (3) Financial, Businesses and Manpower Conditions; and (4) Quality of Life and Infrastructure Development. These four environments can be effectively visualised as quadrants, each contributing the same weight (25 percent) to the overall competitiveness ranking.

Further, ACI's competitiveness framework uses a nested approach, whereby each of the four environments is further divided into 11 sub-environments. In other words, each of the 11 sub-environments is nested within one of the four environments.

In aggregating sub-environments into environments, and the latter into an overall ranking, ACI assigns equal weights to the sub-environments and environments. While assigning weights according to the level of importance seems more appropriate, the practical difficulties are as

Figure 2.4: Asia Competitiveness Institute's (ACI) Competitiveness Framework

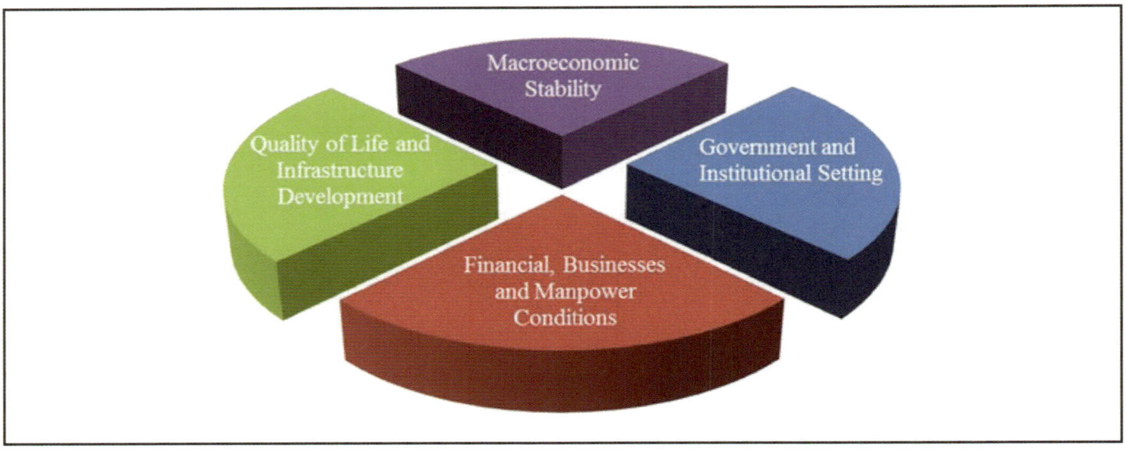

Source: Asia Competitiveness Institute.

controversial. Thus, a balanced view towards the different factors that make up the overall notion of competitiveness implies an assignment of equal weights. The four quadrants of ACI's competitiveness framework represent a holistic, integrated, and systemic view of competitiveness. The two environments of the ACI framework that are specifically dedicated to capturing the issues and concerns pertaining to the economy include: (1) Macroeconomic Stability, encompassing aggregate economic conditions and (3) Financial, Businesses and Manpower Conditions, representing issues related to the micro-economy, viz. revealing the performance of firms as well as the challenges they face in running their businesses.

The other two environments address political, institutional and social characteristics of an economy that determine competitiveness. The environment entitled (2) Government and Institutional Setting covers the efficacy of government institutions and includes analyses on expectations of progress while (4) Quality of Life and Infrastructure Development combines an analysis on infrastructure as well as basic services and an overall sense of "quality of life". For ease of reference, the four environments and their respective sub-environments are listed as follows:

1. Macroeconomic Stability

1.1. Regional Economic Vibrancy
1.2. Openness to Trade and Services
1.3. Attractiveness to Foreign Investors

2. Government and Institutional Setting

2.1. Government Policies and Fiscal Sustainability
2.2. Institutions, Governance and Leadership

3. Financial, Businesses and Manpower Conditions

3.1. Financial Deepening and Business Efficiency
3.2. Labour Market Flexibility
3.3. Productivity Performance

4. Quality of Life and Infrastructure Development

4.1. Physical Infrastructure
4.2. Technological Infrastructure
4.3. Standard of Living, Education and Social Stability

In this book, ACI's competitiveness analysis employs 75 different indicators (as listed in Appendix 1). Although the weights assigned to the four environments are equal (25 percent each), the weight for each indicator depends on the number of indicators present in each sub-environment. Depending on the availability of data, some environments and sub-environments have more indicators than others.

To a certain extent, having more number of indicators ensures a more robust interpretation of the aggregate sub-environment score. The uneven distribution of indicators across sub-environments due to data availability is, however, not an issue. Regardless of the number of indicators in a sub-environment, the indicators will simply average out. This enables the inclusion of a reasonable number of indicators that can comprehensively define the sub-environment while retaining equal weights for the four environments in the calculation of the overall competitiveness. Moreover, there is a certain degree of flexibility in adding or removing indicators when updating the index in ACI's annual exercises, as long as the overall structure of the 11 sub-environments and four environments does not change.

The 75 indicators used for the competitiveness study undertaken in this book include both determinant and outcome indicators. A comprehensive view encompassing both determinant and outcome indicators facilitates the answering of the question: "Which are the most and least competitive sub-national economies in the country?" Inclusion of both determinant and outcome indicators further highlights a sharp contrast between the high-performing and the low-performing sub-national economies.

2.2.2 The Standardised Score

The next pertinent issue that warrants an explanation at the outset, from a methodological standpoint, is how to aggregate the different types of data in one coherent and meaningful way that yields rich insights. Given that the 75 indicators have different units of measurements, such as Gross State Domestic Product (GSDP) in millions of Rupees (₹),[2] or length of paved roads expressed in kilometres, how can these differences be resolved?

To resolve this issue, ACI uses the "standardised score". The standardised score is a relative comparison of the performance of a certain sub-national economy to the average. Therefore, the

[2] We use rupees to define the generic units of the indicators. We use "₹" symbol to a particular value of any indicator for a specific economy or sub-national economy.

unit of measurement is no longer relevant. The standardised score has no unit of measurement because it measures relative performance among sub-national economies, regardless of the indicators used. In statistical terms, it measures the number of standard deviations each sub-national economy is from the average.

If a sub-national economy has a standardised score of zero, it is an average performer for that particular indicator. Having a negative score means the performance is below average. Having a positive score, on the other hand, means the performance is above average. The further away the score is from zero, the further away the performance of the sub-national economy is from the national average.

The standardised scores for each indicator are then aggregated at the sub-environment level, re-aggregated at the environment level, and finally aggregated at the overall level (as explained in Appendix 2). This allows a comparison of performance of the sub-national economies at different levels, from the specific indicators to overall competitiveness. With each aggregation, the scores are re-standardised as detailed earlier to calculate the "standardised score" at the sub-environment, environment, and overall levels.

2.2.3 *What-if* Competitiveness Simulation Analysis

As mentioned earlier, one of the unique features of this exercise that ACI undertakes is its significance to policy. A comprehensive ranking in itself is like a beauty contest if it merely identifies the sub-national economies which are doing well and those which are facing challenges without providing any constructive advice on how to improve the rankings.

Thus, ACI takes a step further by tackling the "so what?" question, moving beyond treating the ranking as an end in itself. Instead, the empirical exercise is extended to address the policy implications emanating from the competitiveness rankings generated for all the Indian sub-national economies. In other words, the analysis employs the available data to generate in-depth analysis of the performance of each sub-national economy according to the indicators, sub-environments, and environments. By exploring the said data, it identifies not just the overall competitiveness ranking, but also specific indicators for which the sub-national economy is doing well or otherwise. From such analysis, policy recommendations for each sub-national economy can be furnished.

As ACI's *What-if* competitiveness simulation analysis is based on an improvement of each sub-national economy's top 20 percent weakest indicators to the average, the re-calculation of the standardised score is also based on such an improvement. This is done by looking at sub-national economy, and sorting the different indicators from the highest to the lowest score. From this process, it identifies the 15 weakest indicators and groups them as the bottom 20 percent of the 75 indicators.

As the next step, through conducting policy simulations, the scores of these 15 weakest indicators are raised to match the average score. This means that if the score was previously negative, it would be raised to zero. If positive scores are already present among these sub-national economies, these scores are left unchanged. There is no discounting of scores under any circumstance.

Once these scores are raised, the ranking for the particular sub-national economy is re-calculated, assuming that the scores of other sub-national economies stay constant. This simulation is performed one by one for each of the sub-national economy. Each sub-national economy would then have a new and improved standardised score. This answers the question: "If a particular sub-national economy improves its 15 weakest indicators, while assuming the others remain constant, how would its competitiveness ranking improve?"

The next section provides a detailed discussion of the empirical results generated using the framework discussed above.

2.3 Competitiveness Analysis Results for 35 Sub-National Economies of India

2.3.1 Overall Competitiveness Ranking and Scores

Using the methodology described above, we compute and derive the competitiveness rankings by sorting the scores of each sub-national economy as shown in Table 2.1.[3]

The scores range from 3.4769 for top-ranked Maharashtra to –1.6979 for the last-placed Jharkhand. A score of 0, which indicates average performance, lies between Chandigarh at the 15th position (with a score of 0.0449) and Punjab at the 16th position (with a score of –0.2032). The 18th-ranked sub-national economy, Daman and Diu, is the median-performing state with a score of –0.2329. It is useful to note that the average score of 0 that falls between the 15th and 16th positions, is higher than the median score of –0.2329 at the 18th position, implying that the average score is skewed upwards as a result of Maharashtra's high score.

Some contrasting patterns emerge when we compare the ranking (first column) and scores (third column) in Table 2.1. We find that the scores of different sub-national economies are distributed unevenly, particularly for the top and bottom 10 sub-national economies. For instance, significant gaps are evident between the scores of the top two sub-national economies — Maharashtra (3.4769) and Delhi (1.9904); and bottom two sub-national economies Chhattisgarh (–1.2659) and Jharkhand (–1.6979). For the scores of sub-national economies that are ranked between 11 and 29, we can observe that the difference in the scores are not very large.

However, looking at the percentage difference in the scores, the largest gaps are between the middle-ranked sub-national economies, namely Madhya Pradesh (0.1021) and Chandigarh (0.0449) and Punjab (–0.2032). Although these sub-national economies are ranked sequentially based on their scores, the yawning gap between their relative scores indicate that their true lack of competitiveness is actually much larger than what their positions suggest.

Further, there are also certain sub-national economies with marginal score differences *vis-à-vis* their neighbouring counterparts. Examples include that of Sikkim (0.1179) and Rajasthan (0.1136), Manipur (–0.2927) and Arunachal Pradesh (–0.2979), Tripura (–0.9157), Assam (–0.9491) and Bihar (–0.9882). The sub-national economies ranked between 22 and 26, namely, Dadra and Nagar Haveli (–0.4302), Odisha (–0.4441), Himachal Pradesh (–0.4583), Jammu and Kashmir (–0.4609) and Mizoram (–0.4751) are consistent in terms of their competitiveness scores. Therefore, the scores provide a valuable piece of information beyond just rankings, when

[3] It is useful to recall that our analysis of competitiveness undertaken in Chapters 2 and 3 is based on 2013 data.

Table 2.1: 2016 Overall Competitiveness Ranking and Scores for 35 Sub-National Economies of India

Rank	Economy	Score
1	Maharashtra	3.4769
2	Delhi[#]	1.9904
3	Tamil Nadu	1.7269
4	Gujarat	1.2174
5	Karnataka	1.0698
6	Uttar Pradesh	1.0640
7	Andhra Pradesh	0.7361
8	West Bengal	0.3908
9	Kerala	0.3234
10	Haryana	0.2108
11	Goa	0.1653
12	Sikkim	0.1179
13	Rajasthan	0.1136
14	Madhya Pradesh	0.1021
15	Chandigarh[#]	0.0449
16	Punjab	–0.2032
17	Lakshadweep[#]	–0.2138
18	Daman and Diu[#]	–0.2329
19	Manipur	–0.2927
20	Arunachal Pradesh	–0.2979
21	Puducherry[#]	–0.3802
22	Dadra and Nagar Haveli[#]	–0.4302
23	Odisha	–0.4441
24	Himachal Pradesh	–0.4583
25	Jammu and Kashmir	–0.4609
26	Mizoram	–0.4751
27	Andaman and Nicobar Islands[#]	–0.4997
28	Nagaland	–0.5509
29	Meghalaya	–0.8149
30	Tripura	–0.9157
31	Assam	–0.9491
32	Bihar	–0.9882
33	Uttarakhand	–1.1785
34	Chhattisgarh	–1.2659
35	Jharkhand	–1.6979

Note: [#]Denotes federal territories.

Source: Asia Competitiveness Institute.

Figure 2.5: 2016 Map of Overall Competitiveness Ranking for 35 Sub-National Economies of India

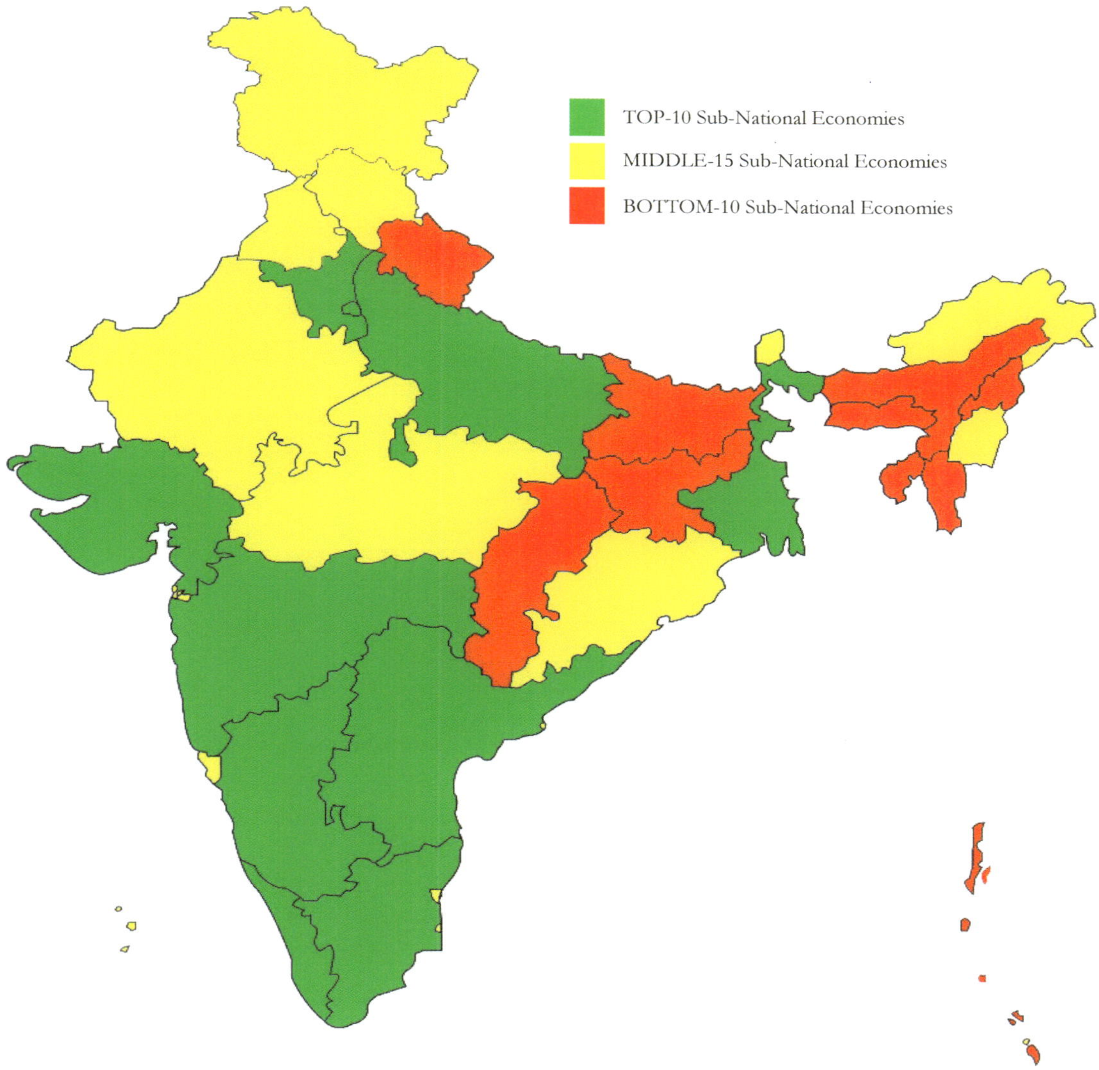

Source: Asia Competitiveness Institute.

analysing sub-national economies. This assumes a greater degree of importance when considering the fact that the scores can potentially help in the identification and consequent improvement in the performance of the respective sub-national economy under the various constituent environments, which may raise the overall economic standing of the sub-national economies.

We examine further the overall competitiveness ranking by projecting it on a map of India, as illustrated in Figure 2.5. The sub-national economies are colour-coded based on a traffic light scheme, viz. the top 10 positions are expressed in green, the middle 15 positions in yellow, and the bottom 10 positions in red. Based on the relationship between the overall competitiveness and geographical location of the sub-national economies, the following inferences can be made.

First, most of the highly competitive sub-national economies are concentrated in the Southern part of India. While a more detailed analysis of regions and their competitiveness rankings will be the subject of discussion in Chapter 3, suffice it to note here that the Southern states of Andhra Pradesh,[4] Karnataka, Kerala, and Tamil Nadu are ranked in the top 10 category in terms of overall competitiveness. However, the state that has consistently been in the top over the past four years, namely Maharashtra, is from the Western region.

Second, in stark contrast to the Southern states listed above, a majority of the Eastern states in India, namely Bihar, Chhattisgarh and Jharkhand, appear in the bottom 10 group. The performance of these low-ranked sub-national economies can be attributed to their relatively poor standing in the three environments — Macroeconomic Stability; Financial, Businesses and Manpower Conditions; and Quality of Life and Infrastructure Development. The only notable exception among the Eastern states is West Bengal, which is the only one to be ranked within the top 10.

Third, the bottom 10 group also features most of the sub-national economies in North Eastern India, also part of the so-called "seven-sister" states. These states include Assam, Meghalaya, Nagaland, and Tripura which are among the most underdeveloped states in the country. While the inadequate infrastructure in the hilly terrains that appear to characterise the region has predominantly hindered their growth, on a positive note, Sikkim, which defends its top 10 status despite possessing similar geographical conditions, can show the way forward for other sub-national economies in the region.

Fourth, it is important to keep in mind that geography is not the sole determining factor in shaping a sub-national economy's overall competitiveness. This can be observed in sub-national economies hailing from the Northern part of India where the levels of overall competitiveness are rather diverse. The nation's capital, Delhi, and the most populous state, Uttar Pradesh, are ranked within the top 10 group. However, the rankings of Himachal Pradesh and Uttarakhand (states having predominantly hilly terrains) fall within the bottom 10 group. As for Chandigarh, Punjab, and Rajasthan, they are placed in the middle 15 group.

Last but not the least, a strong private sector and a favourable environment for conducting business, which can be fostered by the efficient functioning of the sub-national governments, are indeed critical for achieving high overall competitiveness. In other words, having the political will and commitment to be pro-growth is the key. This is verified by the outstanding performance of Gujarat and Maharashtra, which are among the top five sub-national economies.

Table 2.2 provides a comparison of the trends in overall competitiveness ranking for the 35 sub-national economies between 2013 and 2016. Calculating the aggregate ranking movement of sub-national economies between 2013 and 2016, we find that those with the most improvement are Daman and Diu, Lakshadweep, Manipur and West Bengal. On the other

---

[4] The new state of Telangana was carved out of the state of Andhra Pradesh on 2nd June 2014. However, since a comprehensive set of bifurcated data is not available for the newly formed Andhra Pradesh and Telangana, we have used the available data for the former state of Andhra Pradesh.

Table 2.2: 2013–2016 Overall Competitiveness Ranking for 35 Sub-National Economies of India

Economy	Rank			
	2013	2014	2015	2016
Andaman and Nicobar Islands#	20	19	25	27
Andhra Pradesh	6	6	6	7
Arunachal Pradesh	8	15	24	20
Assam	30	35	32	31
Bihar	23	32	29	32
Chandigarh#	15	11	15	15
Chhattisgarh	33	30	34	34
Dadra and Nagar Haveli#	25	25	23	22
Daman and Diu#	29	21	17	18
Delhi#	2	2	2	2
Goa	9	13	14	11
Gujarat	4	4	5	4
Haryana	13	14	11	10
Himachal Pradesh	24	24	26	24
Jammu and Kashmir	22	28	27	25
Jharkhand	35	34	35	35
Karnataka	5	5	4	5
Kerala	11	8	8	9
Lakshadweep#	26	17	16	17
Madhya Pradesh	10	12	12	14
Maharashtra	1	1	1	1
Manipur	28	29	19	19
Meghalaya	32	31	30	29
Mizoram	21	20	20	26
Nagaland	31	27	28	28
Odisha	18	23	21	23
Puducherry#	19	22	22	21
Punjab	17	18	18	16
Rajasthan	12	16	13	13
Sikkim	16	10	10	12
Tamil Nadu	3	3	3	3
Tripura	34	33	31	30
Uttar Pradesh	7	7	7	6
Uttarakhand	27	26	33	33
West Bengal	14	9	9	8

Note: # Denotes federal territories.

Source: Asia Competitiveness Institute.

hand, we find that Daman and Diu jumped 11 places from 29th in 2013 to 18th in 2016; Lakshadweep moved up nine spots from 26th to 17th, Manipur climbed nine places from 28th to 19th while West Bengal climbed six places from 14th to 8th and entered the top 10 group during the same period.

On the other hand, those that experienced the largest declines in overall competitiveness ranking are Andaman and Nicobar Islands, Arunachal Pradesh, Bihar and Uttarakhand. Andaman and Nicobar Islands fell seven places from 20th to 27th, while Arunachal Pradesh fell 12 places from eighth to 20th between 2013 and 2016. Bihar and Uttarakhand both dropped nine and six spots from 23rd to 32th and 27th to 33rd, respectively, over the same period.

Finally, the top-ranked sub-national economies, such as Maharashtra (first), Delhi (second), Tamil Nadu (third), Gujarat (fourth), and Karnataka (fifth) have maintained the same ranking during the 2013–2016 period. Andhra Pradesh and Uttar Pradesh switched places in 2016.

2.3.2 Ranking and Scores by Four Environments

This section presents the results and analysis based on the competitiveness of the sub-national economies for the four constituent environments of overall competitiveness.

Table 2.3 presents the ranking and scores for the environment of Macroeconomic Stability for the 35 sub-national economies for 2016. Maharashtra is ranked first with a score of 3.4447 and significantly outperforms the other sub-national economies. The competition is much more intense between Tamil Nadu (second), Delhi (third), Haryana (fifth), and Gujarat (seventh) as their scores are in close proximity with each other.

In the middle 15 economies, the following pairs have very small score difference Dadra and Nagar Haveli (–0.3522) and Odisha (–0.3771); Kerala (–0.4572), Lakshadweep (–0.4788) and Bihar (–0.5048); Andaman and Nicobar Islands (–0.6129); and Assam (–0.6258).

Manipur is ranked last with a score of –1.1235 and is lagging all the other sub-national economies, particularly behind the 34th ranked Tripura by a difference of 0.1974. However, the other bottom 10 sub-national economies between the 27th ranked Chandigarh (–0.7173) to the 32nd ranked Uttarakhand (–0.8394) have scores that are relatively close, intensifying the competition at the lower tier of Table 2.3.

Figure 2.6 shows the performance of the sub-national economies for the environment of Macroeconomic Stability projected on a map of India.

Scanning the figure closely, we find that the top 10 sub-national economies are geographically spread across the whole country except for North Eastern region. The top 10 states include Delhi, Haryana, and Uttar Pradesh from the North; Andhra Pradesh, Karnataka, and Tamil Nadu from the South; West Bengal from the East; and Gujarat, Madhya Pradesh, and Maharashtra from the West.

The North Eastern sub-national economies of Arunachal Pradesh, Manipur, Mizoram, and Tripura fall in the bottom 10 group. Other sub-national economies that are part of the bottom 10 group are Chandigarh, Chhattisgarh, Jammu and Kashmir, Jharkhand, Puducherry, and Uttarakhand.

Table 2.4 compares the Macroeconomic Stability rankings for the 35 sub-national economies for 2013–2016. Calculating the sub-national economies' aggregate ranking movement from

Table 2.3: 2016 Macroeconomic Stability Ranking and Scores for 35 Sub-National Economies of India

Rank	Economy	Score
1	Maharashtra	3.4447
2	Tamil Nadu	1.9862
3	Delhi#	1.9640
4	Karnataka	1.2661
5	Haryana	1.1656
6	Gujarat	1.1574
7	Madhya Pradesh	0.8197
8	Uttar Pradesh	0.7952
9	Andhra Pradesh	0.5459
10	West Bengal	0.2426
11	Rajasthan	0.0550
12	Daman and Diu#	–0.0591
13	Goa	–0.0773
14	Punjab	–0.1247
15	Sikkim	–0.2292
16	Himachal Pradesh	–0.2911
17	Dadra and Nagar Haveli#	–0.3522
18	Odisha	–0.3771
19	Meghalaya	–0.4248
20	Kerala	–0.4572
21	Lakshadweep#	–0.4788
22	Bihar	–0.5048
23	Nagaland	–0.5738
24	Andaman and Nicobar Islands#	–0.6129
25	Assam	–0.6258
26	Mizoram	–0.6821
27	Chandigarh#	–0.7173
28	Arunachal Pradesh	–0.7274
29	Chhattisgarh	–0.7472
30	Jammu and Kashmir	–0.7666
31	Puducherry#	–0.8296
32	Uttarakhand	–0.8394
33	Jharkhand	–0.8944
34	Tripura	–0.9261
35	Manipur	–1.1235

Note: # Denotes federal territories.

Source: Asia Competitiveness Institute.

Figure 2.6: 2016 Map of Macroeconomic Stability Ranking for 35 Sub-National Economies of India

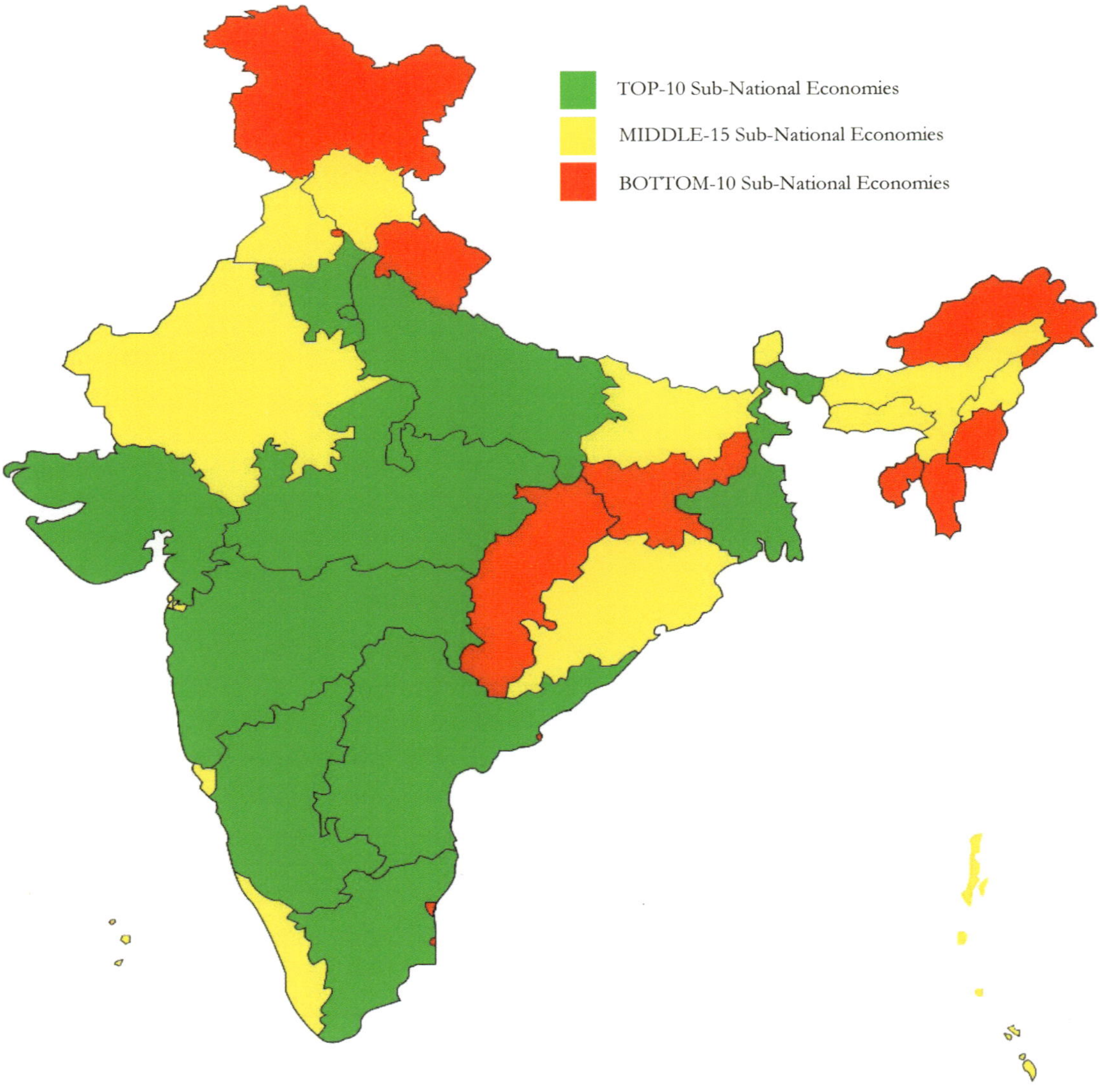

Source: Asia Competitiveness Institute.

2013 to 2016, the sub-national economies with the most progress are Daman and Diu, Sikkim, Lakshadweep and Mizoram. In particular, Daman and Diu jumped 22 places from 34th in 2013 to 12th in 2016. Sikkim climbed 13 spots from 28th in 2013 to 13th in 2016. Meanwhile, Lakshadweep and Mizoram both moved up 10 and seven places from 31st to 21st and 33rd to 26th, respectively, over the same period.

On the flip side, the sub-national economies that have deteriorated the most are Puducherry, Jharkhand, and Arunachal Pradesh. Puducherry fell 13 spots from 18th in 2013 to 31st in 2016,

Table 2.4: 2013–2016 Macroeconomic Stability Ranking for 35 Sub-National Economies of India

Economy	Rank			
	2013	2014	2015	2016
Andaman and Nicobar Islands#	30	29	33	24
Andhra Pradesh	7	9	7	9
Arunachal Pradesh	20	13	34	28
Assam	27	28	25	25
Bihar	17	17	14	22
Chandigarh#	29	22	28	27
Chhattisgarh	25	18	30	29
Dadra and Nagar Haveli#	19	33	22	17
Daman and Diu#	34	31	13	12
Delhi#	3	2	3	3
Goa	10	12	16	13
Gujarat	4	4	6	6
Haryana	6	6	5	5
Himachal Pradesh	15	20	20	16
Jammu and Kashmir	26	27	26	30
Jharkhand	22	30	19	33
Karnataka	5	5	4	4
Kerala	16	15	11	20
Lakshadweep#	31	24	29	21
Madhya Pradesh	8	8	9	7
Maharashtra	1	1	1	1
Manipur	35	35	27	35
Meghalaya	24	34	31	19
Mizoram	33	23	35	26
Nagaland	23	16	32	23
Odisha	14	14	15	18
Puducherry#	18	26	18	31
Punjab	13	19	21	14
Rajasthan	11	11	12	11
Sikkim	28	25	17	15
Tamil Nadu	2	3	2	2
Tripura	32	32	24	34
Uttar Pradesh	9	7	8	8
Uttarakhand	21	21	23	32
West Bengal	12	10	10	10

Note: # Denotes federal territories.

Source: Asia Competitiveness Institute.

while Jharkhand and Arunachal Pradesh slipped 10 and eight places from 22nd to 33rd and 20th to 28th, respectively, between 2013 and 2016.

Focusing on the top-performing sub-national economies, Maharashtra has been able to defend its first position from 2013 to 2016. Haryana (fifth), Karnataka (fourth), Madhya Pradesh (seventh), Uttar Pradesh (eighth), and West Bengal (10th) are able to improve their positions in 2016 as compared to 2013.

Table 2.5 shows the ranking and scores for the environment pertaining to Government and Institutional Setting for the 35 sub-national economies for 2016. Maharashtra is ranked first with a score of 2.9376. Delhi with a score of 2.5422 and Uttar Pradesh with a score of 2.2910 also perform strongly in this environment as they are ranked second and third, respectively. The top three sub-national economies are relatively secure at their respective positions, considering the large score difference of 0.8428 between the bloc and the fourth-ranked Tamil Nadu which had a score of 1.4482. Regardless, efforts should continue to be made by these sub-national economies to strengthen this environment.

At the lower tier of the ranking, Goa is ranked last with a score of −1.1855. Such negative scores can be observed in the other 22 sub-national economies, ranging from Rajasthan at 13th (−0.0197) to Himachal Pradesh at 34th (−1.1680). This result indicates that the average score is skewed upwards by the significantly high scores of the top-ranked sub-national economies. Nevertheless, there is a high probability of these below-average sub-national economies to climb up the ranking as the score differences between them are generally narrow.

In Figure 2.7, the ranking on Government and Institutional Setting shares a relatively similar pattern with that of Macroeconomic Stability, especially pertaining to the distribution of the top 10 sub-national economies. Specifically, the top 10 sub-national economies for this environment can be found to be dispersed across the entire country, like in the case of the ranking on Macroeconomic Stability. For instance, Delhi and Uttar Pradesh feature from the North; while Andhra Pradesh, Karnataka, and Tamil Nadu from the South; West Bengal from the East; and Gujarat, Madhya Pradesh, and Maharashtra representing the West. A minor difference between the two sets of ranking lies in the inclusion of one North Eastern sub-national economy, namely Manipur, in the top 10 group. This should inspire other North Eastern sub-national economies to reform their government capacity and emulate this achievement.

For the bottom 10 sub-national economies, they are concentrated in three geographical areas. The first area is Northern India which includes Himachal Pradesh and Uttarakhand. The second area lies in the East of the country where Chhattisgarh and Jharkhand are located. The third area refers to the North Eastern region which consists of Mizoram, Nagaland, and Tripura. The remaining sub-national economies in the bottom 10 group are Goa, Lakshadweep, and Puducherry.

Table 2.6 presents the trends in Government and Institutional Setting ranking for the 35 sub-national economies for the years 2013 to 2016. Tracking the sub-national economies' aggregate ranking movement from 2013 to 2016, we find that Sikkim has seen the most significant improvement in ranking, having climbed seven spots from 28th in 2013 to 21st in 2016. Similarly, another sub-national economy that has registered a significant jump from its ranking in 2013 is the 25th-ranked Meghalaya, which has jumped up by six places. It is of importance that these

Table 2.5: 2016 Government and Institutional Setting Ranking and Scores for 35 Sub-National Economies of India

Rank	Economy	Score
1	Maharashtra	2.9376
2	Delhi#	2.5422
3	Uttar Pradesh	2.2910
4	Tamil Nadu	1.4482
5	West Bengal	1.2101
6	Andhra Pradesh	0.8356
7	Karnataka	0.5971
8	Gujarat	0.5377
9	Manipur	0.3133
10	Madhya Pradesh	0.1804
11	Arunachal Pradesh	0.0855
12	Bihar	0.0784
13	Rajasthan	–0.0197
14	Kerala	–0.1680
15	Chandigarh#	–0.1745
16	Jammu and Kashmir	–0.2042
17	Odisha	–0.3618
18	Andaman and Nicobar Islands#	–0.3781
19	Daman and Diu#	–0.3904
20	Punjab	–0.4258
21	Sikkim	–0.4601
22	Dadra and Nagar Haveli#	–0.4812
23	Assam	–0.5083
24	Haryana	–0.5107
25	Meghalaya	–0.5200
26	Lakshadweep#	–0.5399
27	Tripura	–0.6627
28	Chhattisgarh	–0.6637
29	Jharkhand	–0.6950
30	Nagaland	–0.7261
31	Mizoram	–0.7448
32	Puducherry#	–0.9280
33	Uttarakhand	–1.1482
34	Himachal Pradesh	–1.1605
35	Goa	–1.1855

Note: # Denotes federal territories.

Source: Asia Competitiveness Institute.

Figure 2.7: 2016 Map of Government and Institutional Setting Ranking for 35 Sub-National Economies of India

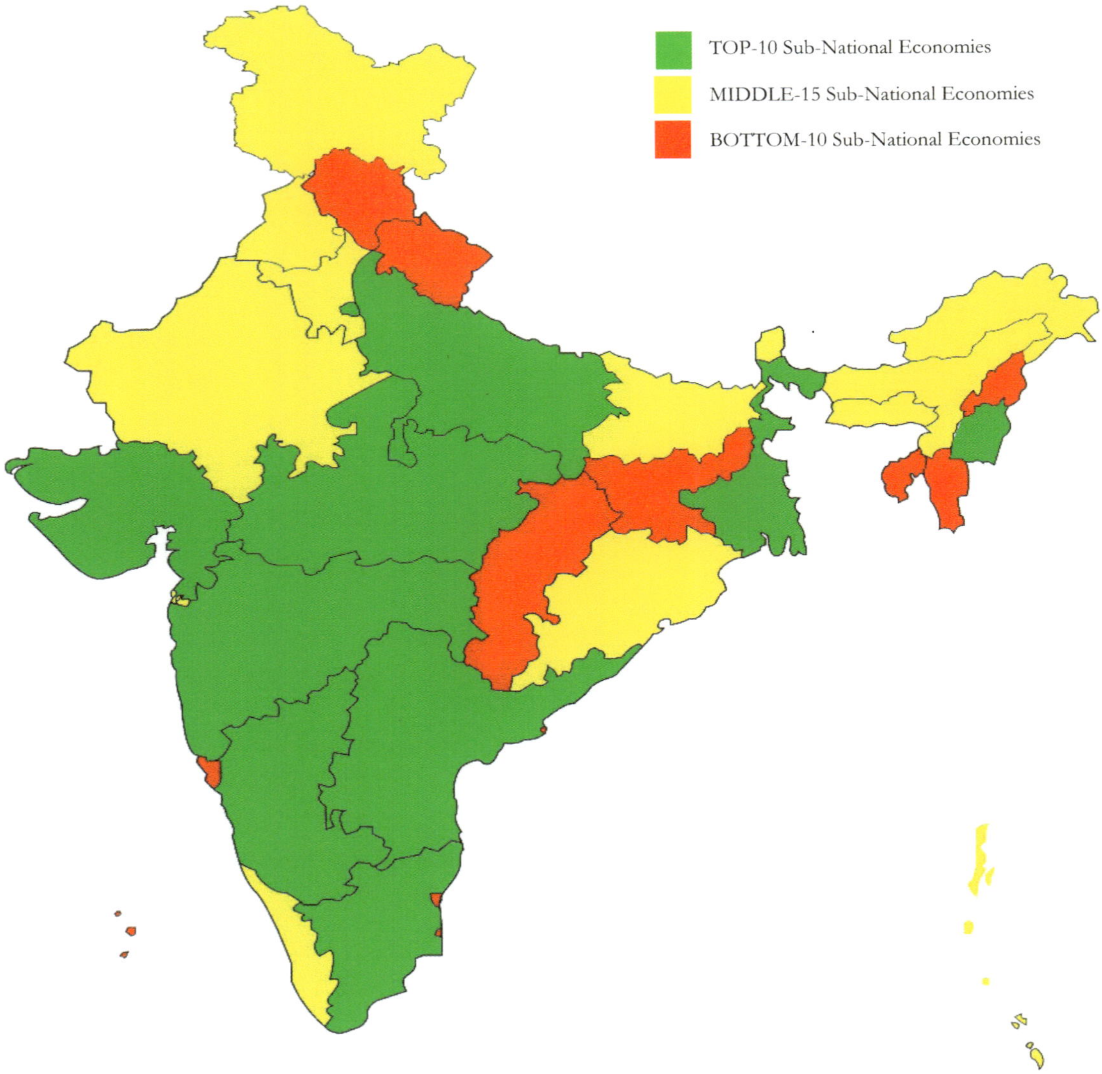

Source: Asia Competitiveness Institute.

smaller sub-national economies have been able to overcome their size constraints and exceed expectations in terms of their competitiveness performance over the last four years.

In contrast, the state with the largest drops in ranking between 2013 and 2016 is Mizoram, down by 13 places from 18th in 2013 to 31st in 2016. The sub-national economy has shown volatile jumps in this sub-environment implying unstable domestic governance. On the other end, among the high-ranked sub-national economies, Maharashtra remains at the top for four

Table 2.6: 2013–2016 Government and Institutional Setting Ranking for 35 Sub-National Economies of India

Economy	Rank			
	2013	2014	2015	2016
Andaman and Nicobar Islands#	22	18	16	18
Andhra Pradesh	5	5	6	6
Arunachal Pradesh	12	11	13	11
Assam	24	26	25	23
Bihar	10	10	12	12
Chandigarh#	17	16	19	15
Chhattisgarh	26	29	29	28
Dadra and Nagar Haveli#	21	20	17	22
Daman and Diu#	14	14	15	19
Delhi#	2	2	3	2
Goa	34	34	34	35
Gujarat	8	8	8	8
Haryana	23	27	26	24
Himachal Pradesh	33	32	32	34
Jammu and Kashmir	16	22	24	16
Jharkhand	30	31	31	29
Karnataka	6	7	7	7
Kerala	15	17	20	14
Lakshadweep#	25	24	18	26
Madhya Pradesh	11	9	11	10
Maharashtra	1	1	1	1
Manipur	9	19	10	9
Meghalaya	31	30	28	25
Mizoram	18	13	9	31
Nagaland	29	28	30	30
Odisha	19	21	23	17
Puducherry#	35	35	35	32
Punjab	20	23	22	20
Rajasthan	13	12	14	13
Sikkim	28	15	21	21
Tamil Nadu	4	4	4	4
Tripura	27	25	27	27
Uttar Pradesh	3	3	2	3
Uttarakhand	32	33	33	33
West Bengal	7	6	5	5

Note: # Denotes federal territories.

Source: Asia Competitiveness Institute.

consecutive years from 2013 to 2016. Strong-performing sub-national economies that rose in ranking from 2013 to 2016 include West Bengal at the fifth position in 2016, up from seventh in 2013.

Table 2.7 shows the ranking and scores for the environment relating to Financial, Businesses and Manpower Conditions for the 35 sub-national economies of India for 2016. Once again, we find that Maharashtra has consistently emerged as the top performer for this environment with a score of 3.0398. Delhi and Tamil Nadu are ranked second and third with standardised scores of 1.7342 and 1.3533, respectively.

It is worth noting the intense competition among the sub-national economies that fall within the lower tier of the top 10 group, considering the marginal score difference of 0.0637 between the fifth-ranked Karnataka (1.0741) and the sixth-ranked Uttar Pradesh (1.0104), and the almost similar score of 0.85 (approximately) of the seventh-ranked Chandigarh and eighth-ranked Gujarat. These sub-national economies have to constantly enhance their business environment to retain or improve their respective rankings.

At the opposite end of the spectrum, as captured by Table 2.7, Manipur is ranked last with a score of −1.6790. There is a significant difference in the competitiveness of the bottom 10 sub-national economies, with almost a three times decline between the 26th-ranked Mizoram (−0.6457) and 35th-ranked Manipur (−1.6790).

Figure 2.8 on Financial, Businesses and Manpower Conditions demonstrates the strong performance of the sub-national economies in the Southern and Western regions of India. For the Southern sub-national economies, Andhra Pradesh, Karnataka, Kerala, and Tamil Nadu are positioned among the top 10 group. As for the Western sub-national economies, Goa, Gujarat, and Maharashtra appear in the top 10 group. Chandigarh, Delhi, and Uttar Pradesh complete the top 10 list.

Sub-national economies which perform poorly in this environment are largely found in the Eastern and North Eastern parts of India. The Eastern sub-national economies include Andaman and Nicobar Islands, Bihar, and Chhattisgarh. The North Eastern sub-national economies comprise Arunachal Pradesh, Assam, Manipur, Mizoram, Meghalaya, Nagaland, and Tripura. Considering that these sub-national economies experience a destabilising political and economic environment due to international border disputes and/or domestic insurgencies, it is not surprising that these states tend to face difficulties in attracting adequate private investments.

Table 2.8 compares the Financial, Businesses and Manpower Conditions rankings for the 35 sub-national economies for the corresponding period of 2013 to 2016. Daman and Diu, its neighbouring federal territory Dadra and Nagar Haveli registered the biggest jumps in ranking over the study period. In particular, Daman and Diu climbed nine places from 29th to 20th between 2013 and 2016, while Dadra and Nagar Haveli moved up five spots from 30th to 25th over the same period.

In contrast, Sikkim and Meghalaya experienced the most substantial decline in their competitiveness performances in this environment between 2013 and 2016. Sikkim and Meghalaya slipped seven and six places from 4th to 11th and 28th to 34th, respectively, from 2013 to 2016.

Among the top 10 group, the Top-three sub-national economies, namely Maharashtra (first), Delhi (second), and Tamil Nadu (third) have been able to maintain their respective positions for

Table 2.7: 2016 Financial, Businesses and Manpower Conditions Ranking and Scores for 35 Sub-National Economies of India

Rank	Economy	Score
1	Maharashtra	3.0398
2	Delhi#	1.7342
3	Tamil Nadu	1.3533
4	Goa	1.2921
5	Karnataka	1.0741
6	Uttar Pradesh	1.0104
7	Chandigarh#	0.8510
8	Gujarat	0.8492
9	Kerala	0.7653
10	Andhra Pradesh	0.5900
11	Sikkim	0.5502
12	Haryana	0.5023
13	Punjab	0.2467
14	Himachal Pradesh	0.1725
15	Rajasthan	0.0369
16	Uttarakhand	−0.0458
17	West Bengal	−0.0579
18	Puducherry#	−0.0659
19	Lakshadweep#	−0.1801
20	Daman and Diu#	−0.3145
21	Madhya Pradesh	−0.3201
22	Odisha	−0.5210
23	Jammu and Kashmir	−0.5700
24	Jharkhand	−0.6047
25	Dadra and Nagar Haveli#	−0.6143
26	Mizoram	−0.6457
27	Chhattisgarh	−0.7967
28	Andaman and Nicobar Islands#	−0.8568
29	Arunachal Pradesh	−0.8630
30	Bihar	−0.9940
31	Assam	−1.1321
32	Tripura	−1.1852
33	Nagaland	−1.2468
34	Meghalaya	−1.3745
35	Manipur	−1.6790

Note: # Denotes federal territories.

Source: Asia Competitiveness Institute.

Figure 2.8: 2016 Map of Financial, Businesses and Manpower Conditions Ranking for 35 Sub-National Economies of India

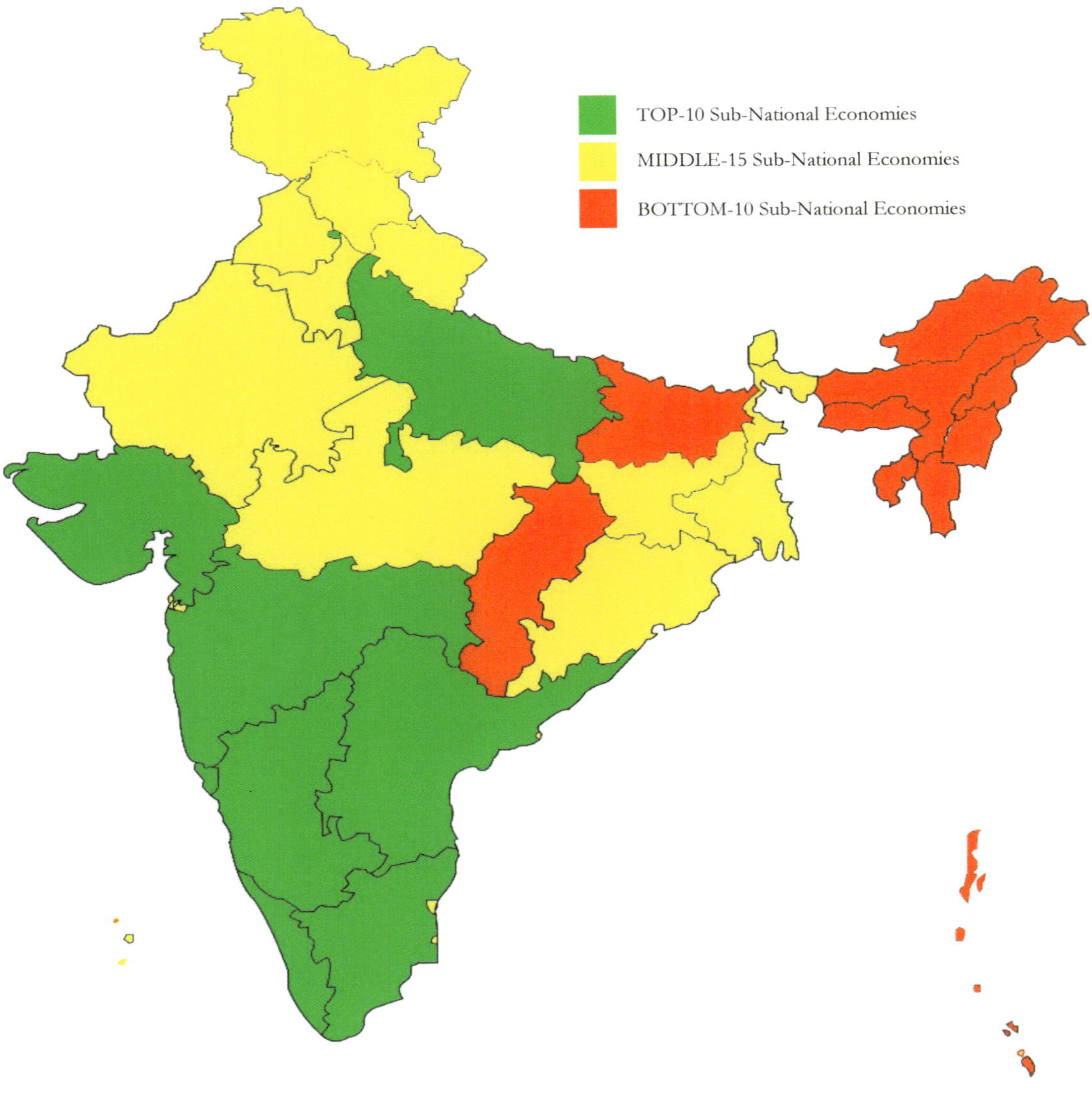

Source: Asia Competitiveness Institute.

four consecutive years from 2013 to 2016. In addition, Chandigarh has been on the steady rise since 2013, having jumped from 11th rank in 2013 and 2014 to 8th and then 7th rank in 2015 and 2016, respectively.

Table 2.9 presents the ranking and scores for the last environment of Quality of Life and Infrastructure Development for the 35 sub-national economies for 2016. Maharashtra, yet again, is ranked first with a score of 1.8561. The difference in scores narrows within the lower tier of

Table 2.8: 2013–2016 Financial, Businesses and Manpower Conditions Ranking for 35 Sub-National Economies of India

Economy	Rank			
	2013	2014	2015	2016
Andaman and Nicobar Islands#	26	24	22	28
Andhra Pradesh	8	9	7	10
Arunachal Pradesh	24	27	30	29
Assam	32	32	32	31
Bihar	31	30	28	30
Chandigarh#	11	11	8	7
Chhattisgarh	25	29	29	27
Dadra and Nagar Haveli#	30	25	24	25
Daman and Diu#	29	22	20	20
Delhi#	2	2	2	2
Goa	5	5	5	4
Gujarat	9	10	10	8
Haryana	12	13	14	12
Himachal Pradesh	18	16	13	14
Jammu and Kashmir	27	26	26	23
Jharkhand	23	23	27	24
Karnataka	6	7	4	5
Kerala	10	6	9	9
Lakshadweep#	21	19	19	19
Madhya Pradesh	20	21	21	21
Maharashtra	1	1	1	1
Manipur	33	34	34	35
Meghalaya	28	31	31	34
Mizoram	22	28	25	26
Nagaland	34	35	33	33
Odisha	19	20	23	22
Puducherry#	15	18	18	18
Punjab	13	12	12	13
Rajasthan	16	14	15	15
Sikkim	4	4	11	11
Tamil Nadu	3	3	3	3
Tripura	35	33	35	32
Uttar Pradesh	7	8	6	6
Uttarakhand	14	17	17	16
West Bengal	17	15	16	17

Note: # Denotes federal territories.

Source: Asia Competitiveness Institute.

Table 2.9: 2016 Quality of Life and Infrastructure Development Ranking and Scores for 35 Sub-National Economies of India

Rank	Economy	Score
1	Maharashtra	1.8561
2	Manipur	1.5398
3	Gujarat	1.4044
4	Kerala	0.9089
5	Tamil Nadu	0.8141
6	Nagaland	0.7598
7	Puducherry#	0.5902
8	Arunachal Pradesh	0.5386
9	Karnataka	0.5328
10	Mizoram	0.5315
11	Sikkim	0.5216
12	Goa	0.5070
13	Lakshadweep#	0.5052
14	Andhra Pradesh	0.4163
15	Rajasthan	0.2963
16	Andaman and Nicobar Islands#	0.2270
17	Delhi#	0.2158
18	Chandigarh#	0.1863
19	Dadra and Nagar Haveli#	0.0521
20	Jammu and Kashmir	0.0457
21	Daman and Diu#	0.0086
22	West Bengal	–0.1273
23	Odisha	–0.1807
24	Tripura	–0.1964
25	Himachal Pradesh	–0.2075
26	Meghalaya	–0.3241
27	Madhya Pradesh	–0.3488
28	Punjab	–0.3554
29	Haryana	–0.4735
30	Uttar Pradesh	–0.6452
31	Assam	–0.8126
32	Bihar	–1.7851
33	Uttarakhand	–1.7894
34	Chhattisgarh	–1.8986
35	Jharkhand	–3.3136

Note: # Denotes federal territories.

Source: Asia Competitiveness Institute.

the top 10 group and the top-tier of the middle 15 group. The score difference of 0.0850 separates the seventh-ranked Puducherry (0.5902) and the 13th-ranked Lakshadweep (0.5052). This spurs the top-ranked sub-national economies to provide high quality standards of living and infrastructure to retain or improve their positions.

Jharkhand is ranked last with a score of −3.3136, while Chhattisgarh (34th), Uttarakhand (33rd), and Bihar (32nd) register negative scores of −1.8986, −1.7894, and −1.7851, respectively. The large difference in scores between Jharkhand and rest of the low-ranked sub-national economies brings to light the diverse range of competitiveness in Quality of Life and Infrastructural Development. It is the need of the hour for Jharkhand to improve its lagging competitiveness in this particular environment.

The map of ranking based on Quality of Life and Infrastructure Development in Figure 2.9 unsurprisingly reveals that its strong performers are found in the Southern and Western parts of India.

The Southern sub-national economies include Karnataka, Kerala, Puducherry, and Tamil Nadu, while the Western sub-national economies consist of Gujarat and Maharashtra. Interestingly, this is the only sub-environment whereby four of the North Eastern sub-national economies, namely Arunachal Pradesh, Manipur, Mizoram, and Nagaland, feature in the top 10. This should motivate the remaining North Eastern sub-national economies to learn the best practices of developing social services and infrastructure and attain a top 10 spot.

The regional spread of the bottom 10 sub-national economies is quite wide. Except for the Southern region, sub-national economies from all the other regions are present in the bottom-10 group. In the North, Haryana, Punjab, Uttar Pradesh, and Uttarakhand enter with significantly low scores for this environment. This also applies to Eastern sub-national economies such as Bihar, Chhattisgarh, and Jharkhand. Assam and Meghalaya from the North Eastern region and Western sub-national economy of Madhya Pradesh complete the bottom 10 list.

Table 2.10 compares the performance of the 35 sub-national economies between 2013 and 2016 for the environment on Quality of Life and Infrastructure Development. The comparison once again appears to suggest that sub-national economies such as Manipur and Nagaland have experienced substantial improvements in terms of their rankings relative to where they were in 2013. Manipur is ranked second in 2016, having jumped 21 places since 2013, while the sixth-ranked Nagaland climbed 13 spots from 19th in 2013 to sixth in 2016. Further, the 13th-ranked Lakshadweep and the 24th-ranked Tripura both show promising improvement with a jump of 11 and nine places, respectively, between 2013 and 2016.

Conversely, the sub-national economies with the biggest decline in ranking are Uttar Pradesh, Madhya Pradesh, and Andaman and Nicobar Islands. In particular, both Uttar Pradesh and Madhya Pradesh fell 13 places from 17th in 2013 to 30th in 2016, and 14th in 2013 to 27th in 2016, respectively. Andaman and Nicobar Islands dropped 10 places from sixth to 16th between 2013 and 2016.

Focusing on the top 10 group, Maharashtra retained the top spot after reaching the first place in 2015. As for the remaining nine top-ranked sub-national economies, eight of them have maintained their top 10 positions *vis-à-vis* their 2015 rankings. Only Mizoram is the new entrant to the top 10 group in 2016, indicating the difficulty for outsiders to break into this elite band.

Figure 2.9: 2016 Map of Quality of Life and Infrastructure Development Ranking for 35 Sub-National Economies of India

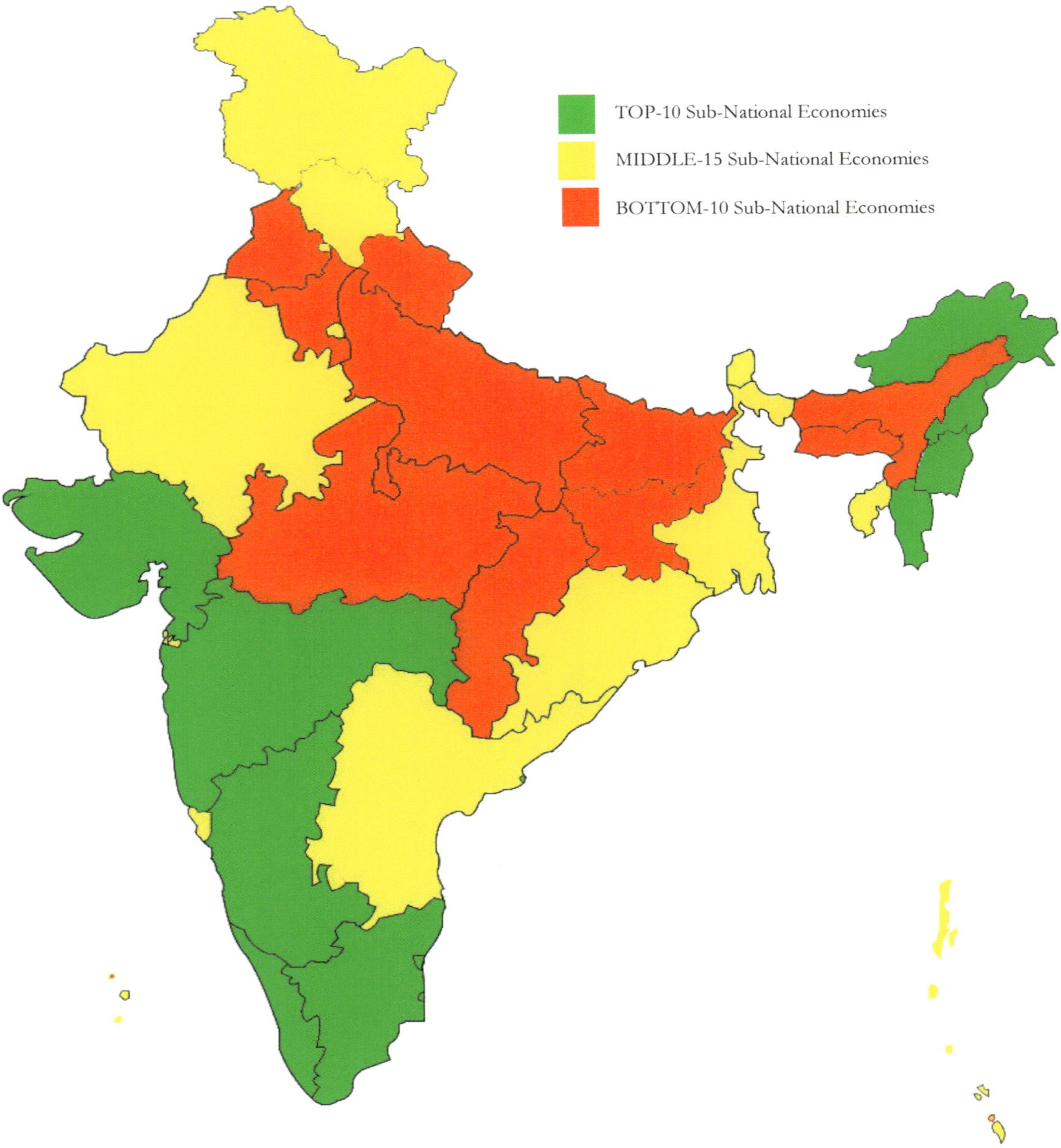

Source: Asia Competitiveness Institute.

Table 2.10: 2013–2016 Quality of Life and Infrastructure Development Ranking for 35 Sub-National Economies of India

Economy	Rank			
	2013	2014	2015	2016
Andaman and Nicobar Islands#	6	7	16	16
Andhra Pradesh	9	10	10	14
Arunachal Pradesh	1	9	6	8
Assam	27	33	31	31
Bihar	30	35	34	32
Chandigarh#	10	14	20	18
Chhattisgarh	34	32	33	34
Dadra and Nagar Haveli#	21	23	19	19
Daman and Diu#	28	17	23	21
Delhi#	15	12	15	17
Goa	5	11	14	12
Gujarat	3	2	2	3
Haryana	26	25	29	29
Himachal Pradesh	25	20	24	25
Jammu and Kashmir	20	31	21	20
Jharkhand	35	34	35	35
Karnataka	4	5	7	9
Kerala	12	1	4	4
Lakshadweep#	24	4	13	13
Madhya Pradesh	14	24	25	27
Maharashtra	2	3	1	1
Manipur	23	13	3	2
Meghalaya	32	30	26	26
Mizoram	11	15	11	10
Nagaland	19	18	5	6
Odisha	18	27	22	23
Puducherry#	7	6	9	7
Punjab	22	19	28	28
Rajasthan	13	22	17	15
Sikkim	16	16	12	11
Tamil Nadu	8	8	8	5
Tripura	33	29	27	24
Uttar Pradesh	17	28	30	30
Uttarakhand	31	26	32	33
West Bengal	29	21	18	22

Note: # Denotes federal territories.

Source: Asia Competitiveness Institute.

2.3.3 *What-if* Competitiveness Simulation Analysis on Overall Competitiveness

This section examines the results of the *What-if* competitiveness simulation analysis for the 35 sub-national economies of India for 2016. To quickly recall the discussion from Section 2.2.3, *What-if* competitiveness simulation analysis assists sub-national economies in directing their limited resources into areas which can increase their competitiveness significantly. The primary objective is to effectively identify the top 20 percent weakest indicators for a particular sub-national economy and show through policy simulations how its overall ranking can possibly change when its weakest indicators are improved. Such an exercise helps a more focussed policy discussion and assists policymakers in the respective sub-national economies to specifically target the low-hanging fruits to spur sustained economic growth and development.

Table 2.11 shows the ranking and scores for each sub-national economy before and after simulation. The improvement in the results after policy simulation shows how the ACI's analysis helps sub-national economies in India to improve through constructive policy intervention.

The simulated results (Table 2.11) show that different sub-national economies have different potential to improve their ranking and scores. With the simulation that improves their top 20 percent weakest indicators (assuming other sub-national economies remain unchanged), some sub-national economies experience significant jumps in their respective positions while others improve by only a few notches.

Sub-national economies which demonstrate the maximum potential for improving their competitiveness after the *What-if* competitiveness simulation analysis include Andaman and Nicobar Islands, Mizoram, and Bihar. In particular, Andaman and Nicobar Islands and Mizoram see the most significant jump of 17 places from 27th to tenth and 26th to ninth, respectively, after having the scores of its top 20 percent weaknesses raised to 0 which is the average score. It is followed by Bihar with an improvement of 16 places from 32nd to 16th.

Within the top 10 group, Uttar Pradesh registers the most significant rise in ranking from sixth to third after the policy simulation. It is clear that the competition at the top gets more intense, requiring these sub-national economies to work harder to retain their respective positions.

Meanwhile, the bottom 10 sub-national economies demonstrate a jump of at least six places after the simulation. All the three sub-national economies — Andaman and Nicobar Islands, Mizoram, and Bihar — that register the highest jump are from the bottom 10 group. In addition, addressing the top 20 percent weaknesses allows Andaman and Nicobar Islands, Mizoram and Nagaland to turn their negative scores to positive ones, indicating an incentive for poorly-performing sub-national economies to improve their competitiveness.

In this regard, it is important to note that the potential to move up the ranking by multiple places depends on two critical factors: (1) the spread of scores among the different indicators for each sub-national economy, and (2) the difference in aggregate scores between a particular sub-national economy and the one that is in a higher position. It is intuitive to understand that if two consecutively ranked sub-national economies have a wide gap between their scores, viz. have a greater dispersion, then the sub-national economy with the lower score will experience difficulties in overtaking the one with the higher score.

Table 2.11: 2016 *What-if* Competitiveness Simulation Analysis on Overall Competitiveness for 35 Sub-National Economies of India

Economy	Rank		Score	
	Before	After	Before	After
Andaman and Nicobar Islands#	27	10	−0.4997	0.2779
Andhra Pradesh	7	5	0.7361	1.1445
Arunachal Pradesh	20	10	−0.2979	0.2732
Assam	31	21	−0.9491	−0.3793
Bihar	32	16	−0.9882	−0.0191
Chandigarh#	15	8	0.0449	0.5952
Chhattisgarh	34	28	−1.2659	−0.5343
Dadra and Nagar Haveli#	22	9	−0.4302	0.3196
Daman and Diu#	18	8	−0.2329	0.5445
Delhi#	2	2	1.9904	2.4486
Goa	11	8	0.1653	0.6852
Gujarat	4	4	1.2174	1.5510
Haryana	10	8	0.2108	0.5757
Himachal Pradesh	24	16	−0.4583	−0.0202
Jammu and Kashmir	25	16	−0.4609	−0.0639
Jharkhand	35	27	−1.6979	−0.5461
Karnataka	5	4	1.0698	1.4409
Kerala	9	7	0.3234	0.8260
Lakshadweep#	17	8	−0.2138	0.4062
Madhya Pradesh	14	8	0.1021	0.6146
Maharashtra	1	1	3.4769	3.7276
Manipur	19	8	−0.2927	0.4989
Meghalaya	29	16	−0.8149	−0.1852
Mizoram	26	9	−0.4751	0.3437
Nagaland	28	15	−0.5509	0.0645
Odisha	23	16	−0.4441	−0.0143
Puducherry#	21	11	−0.3802	0.1863
Punjab	16	10	−0.2032	0.2665
Rajasthan	13	8	0.1136	0.5748
Sikkim	12	7	0.1179	0.8037
Tamil Nadu	3	2	1.7269	2.0774
Tripura	30	21	−0.9157	−0.3486
Uttar Pradesh	6	3	1.0640	1.6819
Uttarakhand	33	22	−1.1785	−0.4636
West Bengal	8	7	0.3908	0.8630

Note: # Denotes federal territories.

Source: Asia Competitiveness Institute.

2.3.4 *What-if* Competitiveness Simulation Analysis on Four Environments

What-if competitiveness simulation analysis is also performed on each of the four environments using the same methodology as discussed in Section 2.2.3.

Table 2.12 shows the results of the *What-if* competitiveness simulation analysis on the first environment which is Macroeconomic Stability. Among the sub-national economies, those with the potential to experience a marked jump in their respective rankings include Puducherry, Jharkhand, and Uttarakhand.

In particular, Puducherry registers the most significant rise in ranking from 31st to 17th after the simulation, followed by Jharkhand which moves up by 11 places from 33rd to 22nd. Uttarakhand experiences a jump of 10 spots from 32nd to 22nd after having the scores of their top 20 percent weaknesses raised to the average score.

Focusing on the top 10 group, seven sub-national economies retain the same ranking after simulation, highlighting the difficulty of scaling up the ladder within a highly competitive group.

As for the bottom 10 sub-national economies, they are unable to turn their negative scores into positive ones, despite being able to jump by four to 14 places in the ranking after the simulation. Understandably, this is a result of top-ranked sub-national economies performing rather strongly in terms of macroeconomic stability. Nonetheless, the bottom 10 sub-national economies should improve on this environment to improve their competitiveness, as demonstrated by ACI's *What-if* simulation analysis exercise.

Table 2.13 shows the results of the *What-if* competitiveness simulation analysis on the Government and Institutional Setting environment. Among them, those with the potential to make large leaps (15 places or above) in ranking include Dadra and Nagar Haveli, Goa, Lakshadweep, Meghalaya, Mizoram, Nagaland, and Puducherry.

Specifically, Mizoram and Nagaland demonstrate the most impressive jump of 25 and 20 places from 31st to sixth and 30th to 10th, respectively, after the simulation. Lakshadweep registers a rise of 19 places from 26th to seventh while Goa moves up 18 spots from 35th to 17th. Meghalaya jumps 16 places from 25th to ninth. Dadra and Nagar Haveli and Puducherry both experience a rise of 15 places from 22nd to seventh and 32nd to 17th, respectively.

Among the top 10 sub-national economies, six of them are able to elevate their rankings by at least one place in the post-simulation scenario, with Manipur increasing the most from ninth to sixth. This opens the possibility for top-ranked sub-national economies to raise their competitiveness standing if efforts are focussed on bureaucratic reforms.

As for the bottom 10 group, it is encouraging to see four low-ranked sub-national economies improving their scores from negative to positive. The possibility of achieving above average performance could incentivise these sub-national economies to address their top 20 percent weaknesses.

Table 2.14 shows the results of the *What-if* competitiveness simulation analysis on the Financial, Businesses and Manpower Conditions environment. Among the sub-national economies, those with the most significant rise in ranking after the simulation include Andaman and Nicobar Islands and Manipur.

Table 2.12: 2016 *What-if* Competitiveness Simulation Analysis on Macroeconomic Stability for 35 Sub-National Economies of India

Economy	Rank		Score	
	Before	After	Before	After
Andaman and Nicobar Islands[#]	24	18	–0.6129	–0.3661
Andhra Pradesh	9	9	0.5459	0.5994
Arunachal Pradesh	28	24	–0.7274	–0.5941
Assam	25	20	–0.6258	–0.4626
Bihar	22	19	–0.5048	–0.4017
Chandigarh[#]	27	22	–0.7173	–0.4922
Chhattisgarh	29	24	–0.7472	–0.5899
Dadra and Nagar Haveli[#]	17	12	–0.3522	0.0190
Daman and Diu[#]	12	11	–0.0591	0.1494
Delhi[#]	3	2	1.9640	2.1493
Goa	13	12	–0.0773	–0.0092
Gujarat	6	4	1.1574	1.3024
Haryana	5	5	1.1656	1.1656
Himachal Pradesh	16	15	–0.2911	–0.1388
Jammu and Kashmir	30	23	–0.7666	–0.5345
Jharkhand	33	22	–0.8944	–0.5037
Karnataka	4	4	1.2661	1.3569
Kerala	20	14	–0.4572	–0.0977
Lakshadweep[#]	21	16	–0.4788	–0.2705
Madhya Pradesh	7	7	0.8197	0.8870
Maharashtra	1	1	3.4447	3.4927
Manipur	35	31	–1.1235	–0.7972
Meghalaya	19	19	–0.4248	–0.4248
Mizoram	26	19	–0.6821	–0.4139
Nagaland	23	16	–0.5738	–0.2724
Odisha	18	15	–0.3771	–0.1687
Puducherry[#]	31	17	–0.8296	–0.3787
Punjab	14	14	–0.1247	–0.1247
Rajasthan	11	11	0.0550	0.1720
Sikkim	15	12	–0.2292	–0.0341
Tamil Nadu	2	2	1.9862	2.1258
Tripura	34	25	–0.9261	–0.6357
Uttar Pradesh	8	7	0.7952	0.9595
Uttarakhand	32	22	–0.8394	–0.5010
West Bengal	10	10	0.2426	0.3684

Note: [#] Denotes federal territories.

Source: Asia Competitiveness Institute.

Table 2.13: 2016 *What-if* Competitiveness Simulation Analysis on Government and Institutional Setting for 35 Sub-National Economies of India

Economy	Rank		Score	
	Before	After	Before	After
Andaman and Nicobar Islands[#]	18	7	–0.3781	0.7544
Andhra Pradesh	6	4	0.8356	1.4089
Arunachal Pradesh	11	6	0.0855	1.0216
Assam	23	23	–0.5083	–0.5083
Bihar	12	9	0.0784	0.4480
Chandigarh[#]	15	14	–0.1745	–0.0685
Chhattisgarh	28	28	–0.6637	–0.6637
Dadra and Nagar Haveli[#]	22	7	–0.4812	0.6173
Daman and Diu[#]	19	7	–0.3904	0.5889
Delhi[#]	2	1	2.5422	2.8674
Goa	35	17	–1.1855	–0.2635
Gujarat	8	6	0.5377	0.9949
Haryana	24	11	–0.5107	0.1257
Himachal Pradesh	34	29	–1.1605	–0.7083
Jammu and Kashmir	16	10	–0.2042	0.2116
Jharkhand	29	29	–0.6950	–0.6950
Karnataka	7	6	0.5971	0.9988
Kerala	14	9	–0.1680	0.3946
Lakshadweep[#]	26	7	–0.5399	0.6362
Madhya Pradesh	10	10	0.1804	0.2830
Maharashtra	1	1	2.9376	3.3681
Manipur	9	6	0.3133	1.0813
Meghalaya	25	9	–0.5200	0.3811
Mizoram	31	6	–0.7448	1.0651
Nagaland	30	10	–0.7261	0.1693
Odisha	17	17	–0.3618	–0.2629
Puducherry[#]	32	17	–0.9280	–0.3123
Punjab	20	9	–0.4258	0.3031
Rajasthan	13	8	–0.0197	0.5607
Sikkim	21	9	–0.4601	0.4908
Tamil Nadu	4	4	1.4482	1.8600
Tripura	27	13	–0.6627	0.0043
Uttar Pradesh	3	3	2.2910	2.2910
Uttarakhand	33	23	–1.1482	–0.5231
West Bengal	5	4	1.2101	1.7272

Note: [#] Denotes federal territories.

Source: Asia Competitiveness Institute.

Table 2.14: 2016 *What-if* Competitiveness Simulation Analysis on Financial, Businesses and Manpower Conditions for 35 Sub-National Economies of India

Economy	Rank		Score	
	Before	After	Before	After
Andaman and Nicobar Islands#	28	16	–0.8568	–0.0547
Andhra Pradesh	10	10	0.5900	0.5900
Arunachal Pradesh	29	25	–0.8630	–0.6182
Assam	31	22	–1.1321	–0.4356
Bihar	30	22	–0.9940	–0.4968
Chandigarh#	7	5	0.8510	1.0805
Chhattisgarh	27	20	–0.7967	–0.2296
Dadra and Nagar Haveli#	25	19	–0.6143	–0.1389
Daman and Diu#	20	14	–0.3145	0.1767
Delhi#	2	2	1.7342	1.7342
Goa	4	3	1.2921	1.3986
Gujarat	8	6	0.8492	1.0319
Haryana	12	12	0.5023	0.5023
Himachal Pradesh	14	13	0.1725	0.4350
Jammu and Kashmir	23	20	–0.5700	–0.3160
Jharkhand	24	19	–0.6047	–0.1005
Karnataka	5	5	1.0741	1.2714
Kerala	9	5	0.7653	1.0720
Lakshadweep#	19	15	–0.1801	0.0763
Madhya Pradesh	21	13	–0.3201	0.3356
Maharashtra	1	1	3.0398	3.1034
Manipur	35	24	–1.6790	–0.6335
Meghalaya	34	27	–1.3745	–0.7339
Mizoram	26	22	–0.6457	–0.3990
Nagaland	33	27	–1.2468	–0.7256
Odisha	22	16	–0.5210	–0.0437
Puducherry#	18	14	–0.0659	0.1787
Punjab	13	13	0.2467	0.4118
Rajasthan	15	13	0.0369	0.4252
Sikkim	11	4	0.5502	1.2515
Tamil Nadu	3	3	1.3533	1.4607
Tripura	32	27	–1.1852	–0.7190
Uttar Pradesh	6	5	1.0104	1.1630
Uttarakhand	16	15	–0.0458	0.0387
West Bengal	17	13	–0.0579	0.2500

Note: # Denotes federal territories.

Source: Asia Competitiveness Institute.

In particular, Andaman and Nicobar Islands registers a jump of 12 places from 28th to 16th after having the scores of their top 20 percent weaknesses raised to the average score. Manipur moves up by 11 positions from 35th to 24th, after the simulation.

Among the top 10 sub-national economies, five of them, namely Chandigarh, Goa, Gujarat, Kerala, and Uttar Pradesh, experience a noteworthy rise in ranking between one to four places after the policy simulation. Despite the inability of the aforementioned sub-national economies to attain top two positions, their upward movement in terms of both ranking and scores justifies the need to create a more conducive business environment. This also applies to Maharashtra and Delhi even though they are secured in their respective first and second positions in the ranking.

As for the bottom 10 group, none of the sub-national economies has managed to attain a positive score after the simulation. Nonetheless, it is encouraging to note that seven of the bottom 10 sub-national economies are able to graduate into the middle 15 group by improving on their top 20 percent weaknesses.

Table 2.15 shows the results of the *What-if* competitiveness simulation analysis on the Quality of Life and Infrastructure Development environment. Among them, those with the largest improvement in ranking include Bihar, Chandigarh, Daman and Diu, Madhya Pradesh, and Uttar Pradesh.

Specifically, Uttar Pradesh sees the most impressive jump of 26 places from 30th to fourth following the simulation. Bihar and Daman and Diu move up 18 and 16 spots from 32nd to 14th, 21st to fifth, respectively, while Chandigarh and Madhya Pradesh both climb 15 places from 18th to third and 27th to 12th, respectively, after the simulation.

Zooming in on the top 10 group, the post-simulation results reveal that Manipur possesses the opportunity to grab the top spot after addressing issues pertaining to Quality of Life and Infrastructure Development. In addition, Gujarat is able to seize the runner-up position after improving on its top weaknesses in this environment. The tussle for the top positions indicates that Quality of Life and Infrastructure Development is an underperforming environment that top-ranking sub-national economies should focus on.

Among the bottom 10 group, introducing policy simulation results in Assam, Bihar, Haryana, Madhya Pradesh, Meghalaya, Punjab and Uttarakhand graduating into the middle 15 group with notable jumps between seven to 18 places in ranking. Better still, Uttar Pradesh is able to leapfrog into the top 10 group upon simulating this environment. Moreover, except for Chhattisgarh, Jharkhand, and Uttarakhand, rest of the seven sub-national economies were able to attain above average scores after the simulation. Thus, these simulations provide huge incentives for low-ranked sub-national economies to enhance their standard of living and develop supportive physical and technological infrastructure.

2.3.5 Median and Maximum Competitiveness Web Analysis

In the final analysis, we present the median and maximum competitiveness web analyses. These are tools that provide a succinct visual snapshot of the performances of the 35 sub-national economies at the sub-national level, as well as the strengths and weaknesses of these sub-national

Table 2.15: 2016 *What-if* Competitiveness Simulation Analysis on Quality of Life and Infrastructure Development for 35 Sub-National Economies of India

Economy	Rank		Score	
	Before	After	Before	After
Andaman and Nicobar Islands#	16	8	0.2270	0.5682
Andhra Pradesh	14	4	0.4163	1.1233
Arunachal Pradesh	8	4	0.5386	1.0750
Assam	31	18	−0.8126	0.1816
Bihar	32	14	−1.7851	0.3891
Chandigarh#	18	3	0.1863	1.4099
Chhattisgarh	34	26	−1.8986	−0.2377
Dadra and Nagar Haveli#	19	8	0.0521	0.5392
Daman and Diu#	21	5	0.0086	0.8538
Delhi#	17	4	0.2158	1.3478
Goa	12	4	0.5070	1.1154
Gujarat	3	2	1.4044	1.7265
Haryana	29	19	−0.4735	0.0836
Himachal Pradesh	25	15	−0.2075	0.3465
Jammu and Kashmir	20	14	0.0457	0.4316
Jharkhand	35	28	−3.3136	−0.4704
Karnataka	9	4	0.5328	1.0743
Kerala	4	4	0.9089	1.3215
Lakshadweep#	13	5	0.5052	0.8776
Madhya Pradesh	27	12	−0.3488	0.4935
Maharashtra	1	1	1.8561	2.3316
Manipur	2	1	1.5398	1.9785
Meghalaya	26	18	−0.3241	0.1774
Mizoram	10	5	0.5315	0.8592
Nagaland	6	4	0.7598	1.0385
Odisha	23	14	−0.1807	0.4291
Puducherry#	7	4	0.5902	1.1180
Punjab	28	15	−0.3554	0.2740
Rajasthan	15	7	0.2963	0.7085
Sikkim	11	4	0.5216	0.9099
Tamil Nadu	5	4	0.8141	1.3532
Tripura	24	16	−0.1964	0.2231
Uttar Pradesh	30	4	−0.6452	1.1376
Uttarakhand	33	29	−1.7894	−0.5134
West Bengal	22	14	−0.1273	0.4538

Note: # Denotes federal territories.

Source: Asia Competitiveness Institute.

Figure 2.10: 2016 Median Competitiveness Web Analysis: Maharashtra and Jharkhand

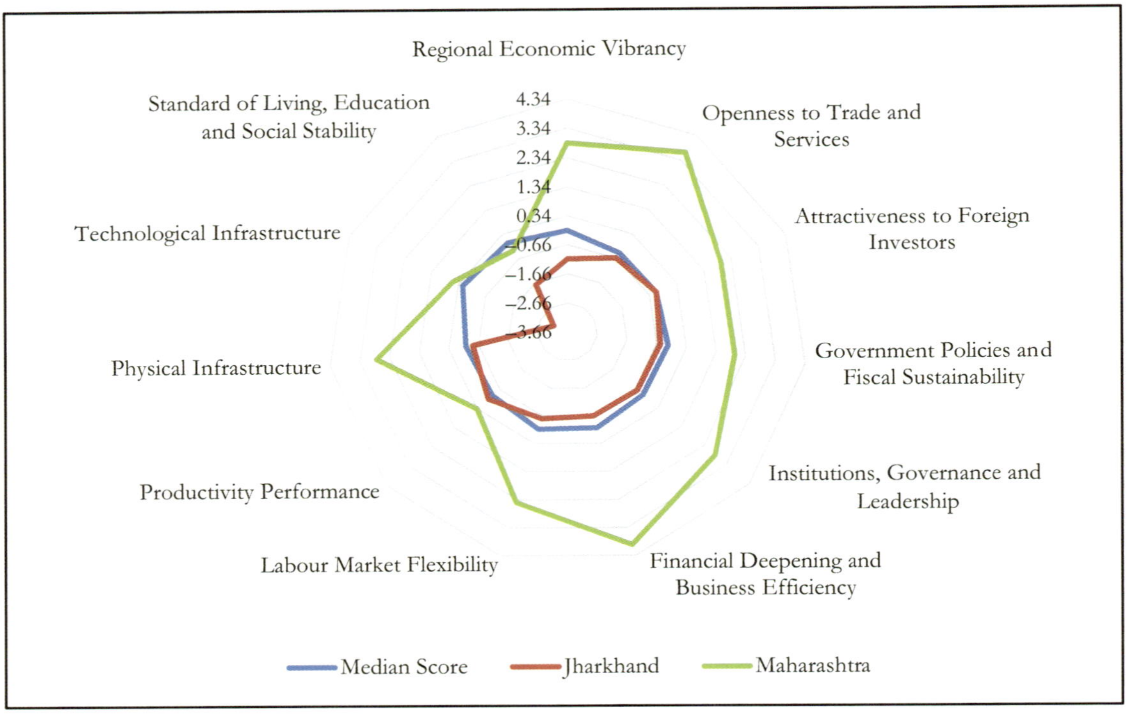

Source: Asia Competitiveness Institute.

economies. Also more generally, the web analysis can assist the sub-national governments to channel their limited resources into specific areas where the introduction of improved policies can result in generating positive spillover effects to the rest of the sub-national economies.

To better understand the relative strengths and weaknesses of a particular sub-national economy, it is useful to compare and contrast its performance against a benchmark. The benchmark can be either the median or the maximum scores obtained by the 35 sub-national economies for the 11 sub-environments which make up the four environments.

The median competitiveness web analysis in Figure 2.10 plots the attained scores across the 11 sub-environments for Maharashtra (ranked first) and Jharkhand (ranked last), along with the median scores for the 35 sub-national economies of India. The contrast between the performances of the two sub-national economies at the opposite ends of the spectrum is evident from Figure 2.10.

Top-ranked Maharashtra scores above the median score for all the sub-environments, except standard of living, education and social stability. On the other hand, Jharkhand, which is positioned last, scores lower than the median for all sub-environments, except for attractiveness to foreign investors and productivity performance.

The maximum competitiveness web analysis in Figure 2.11 plots the obtained scores across the 11 sub-environments for Maharashtra (ranked first) and Jharkhand (ranked last), along with the maximum scores for the 35 sub-national economies of India.

Figure 2.11: 2016 Maximum Competitiveness Web Analysis: Maharashtra and Jharkhand

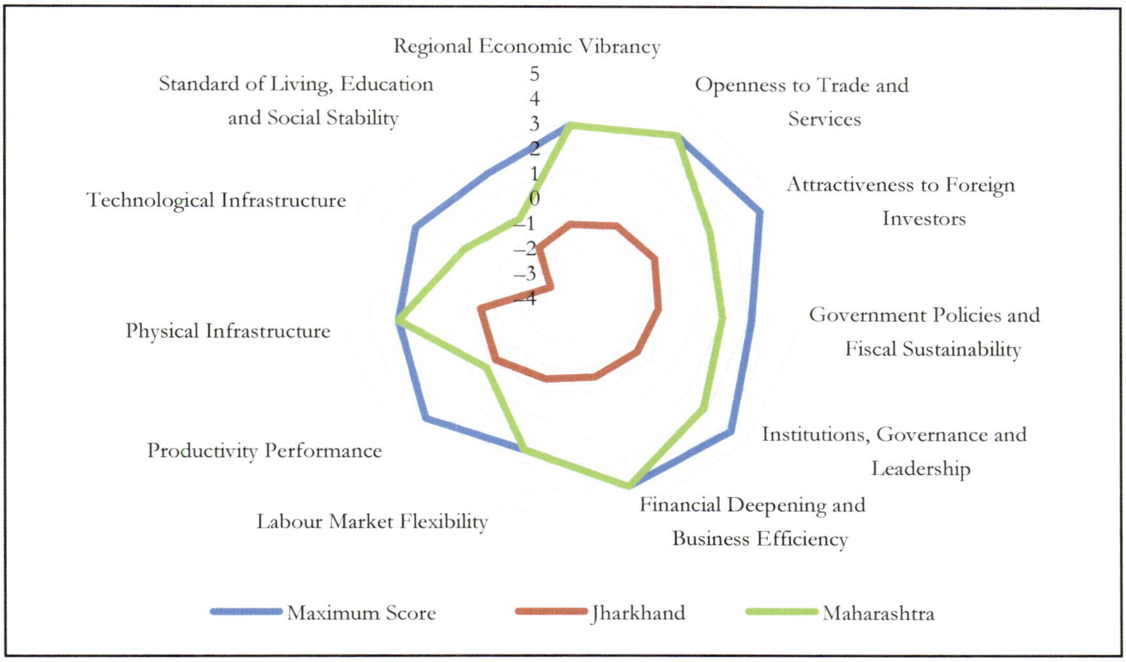

Source: Asia Competitiveness Institute.

Top-ranked Maharashtra sets the maximum score for six sub-environments, namely regional economic vibrancy, openness to trade and services, attractiveness to foreign investors, financial deepening and business efficiency, labour market flexibility and physical infrastructure. On the other hand, the scores for Jharkhand across all 11 sub-environments seem very distant from the maximum scores. The wide gaps highlight the difference between Jharkhand and other top-performing sub-national economies.

2.4 Concluding Notes

To sum up the foregoing discussion, this chapter has undertaken a comprehensive competitiveness analysis for the 35 sub-national economies of India using ACI's competitiveness framework explained earlier in the chapter.

To summarise, our findings in this chapter reveal that the Western state of Maharashtra has consistently emerged as the most competitive sub-national economy in India over the last four years. However, with the exception of Maharashtra, the clusters of highly competitive sub-national economies based on our ACI competitiveness index are all concentrated in the Southern region of India. Notably, the four major Southern states of Andhra Pradesh, Karnataka, Kerala, and Tamil Nadu have been ranked in the top 10 category in terms of overall competitiveness.

Further, our empirical results also suggest that contrary to the distinct performance of Southern states, a significant majority of the Eastern sub-national economies such as Bihar, Chhattisgarh, and Jharkhand find a place in the Bottom-10 group in terms of overall competitiveness, largely driven by their poor performance in three environments, namely Macroeconomic Stability, Financial, Businesses and Manpower Conditions, and Quality of Life and Infrastructure Development.

Given this context, a greater understanding of the dynamics of regional competitiveness in the country would be helpful to ascertain the way forward for India to address the growing regional imbalances. This will be the subject of discussion in our next chapter.

Finally, an analysis of competitiveness since 2013 clearly suggests that sub-national economies including Daman and Diu, Lakshadweep, Manipur and West Bengal have shown the most promise in terms of their jump in performance and ranking. On the other hand, sub-national economies such as Andaman and Nicobar Islands, Arunachal Pradesh, Bihar, and Uttarakhand have registered the largest drops in ranking during the corresponding period. However, two of these four sub-national economies, namely Andaman and Nicobar Islands as well as Bihar demonstrate the maximum potential in terms of improving their competitiveness if they improve their weakest 20 percent of their indicators, as suggested by our *What-if* simulation analysis.

References

Begg, Iain. 1999. "Cities and Competitiveness." *Urban Studies*, 36(5–6): 795–809.

Buckley, Peter Je, Christopher Le Pass and Kate Prescott. 2010. "Measures of International Competitiveness: A Critical Survey." *Journal of Marketing Management*, 4(2): 175–200.

Cellini, Roberto and Anna Soci. 2002. "Pop Compétitivités." *Banca Nazionale del Lavoro Quarterly Review*, 55: 71–101.

Čučković, Nevenka, Kresimir Jurlin and Valentina Vučković. 2013. "Measuring Regional Competitiveness: The Case of Croatia." *Southeast European and Black Sea Studies*, 13: 503–523.

Kitson, Michael, Ron Martin and Peter Tyler. 2004. "Regional Competitiveness: An Elusive yet Key Concept?" *Regional Studies*, 38: 991–999.

Porter, Michael E. 1980. *Competitive Strategy*. New York: Free Press.

Porter, Michael E. 1990. *The Competitive Advantage of Nations*. New York: Free Press.

Tan, Khee Giap and Kartik Rao. 2015. "Sub-national Competitiveness Analysis and Simulation Studies for 35 States and Union Territories of India." *International Journal of Indian Culture and Business Management*, 10(4): 476–493.

Waheeduzzaman, ANM and John K. Ryans Jr. 1999. "Definition, Perspectives, and Understanding of International Competitiveness: A Quest for a Common Ground." *Competitiveness Review: An International Business Journal*, 6(2): 7–26.

World Economic Forum. 2015. "The Global Competitiveness Report 2015–16". Available from http://reports.weforum.org/global-competitiveness-report-2015–2016/ (last accessed on February 22, 2017).

World Competitiveness Centre, IMD. 2015. *IMD World Competitiveness Yearbook*. Lausanne: IMD.

Chapter 3
2016 Annual Update on Competitiveness for Five Regions of India

3.1 Introduction

Regional imbalances in economic development have been part of India's policy discourse since independence. Since the erstwhile days of the five-year plans under the auspices of the now-defunct national planning commission, several papers have discussed the importance of achieving a balanced regional economic development (Nath, 1970; Sarker, 1994; Minocha, 1983; Kurian, 2000). The issue of regional inequality in India's development path shot to greater prominence when India embarked on its liberalisation agenda in 1991. Nearly 25 years since it embraced economic liberalisation, the issue of asymmetric regional development still remains a matter of debate.

There is a long strand of literature examining this subject, and several empirical studies try to understand the dynamics of regional growth through income convergence analysis. The fundamental question that still remains unanswered is whether poorer states and regions catch up with their richer counterparts within the country, i.e. is there evidence of convergence or divergence?[1]

Despite this growing strand of empirical papers on this issue, there is no consensus as to whether income levels are converging or diverging. For instance, in one of the widely quoted papers done by Singh *et al.* (2010, p. 1), the authors argue that, "...using region and district level data, we find no evidence for divergence, but evidence for conditional convergence in some cases. At the region level, while partial measures of economic activity do not indicate any strong evidence for conditional convergence or divergence, there is clear evidence of conditional convergence in per capita consumption levels." A contrarian view is provided by Sanga and Shaban (2017), who find that there is strong divergence of the aggregate economy between 1970–1971 and 2013–2014 and that their empirical findings are not consistent with the neoclassical convergence hypothesis wherein poorer regions tend to catch up with the richer regions in the long-run, paving the way for regional convergence.

In the context of such an academic debate, a question that is intrinsically tied to the broader issue of income growth convergence is whether competitiveness at the regional level is heterogeneous. In Chapter 2, we dedicated ample space to understand competitiveness at the sub-national level. Tied to this closely is the issue of regional development considering the spatial proximity of the sub-national economies. The land area covered by India is almost 75 percent of the total area covered by the 10 economies of Association of Southeast Asian Nations (ASEAN). In addition to

[1] Some comprehensive empirical studies on the income convergence–divergence debate among Indian sub-national economies and regions can be found in Singh *et al.* (2003, 2010, 2013), Sanga and Shaban (2017), Bakshi *et al.* (2015), Stewart and Moslares (2014), Rao *et al.* (1999), and Kar *et al.* (2011).

Figure 3.1: 2016 Map of the Five Regions of India

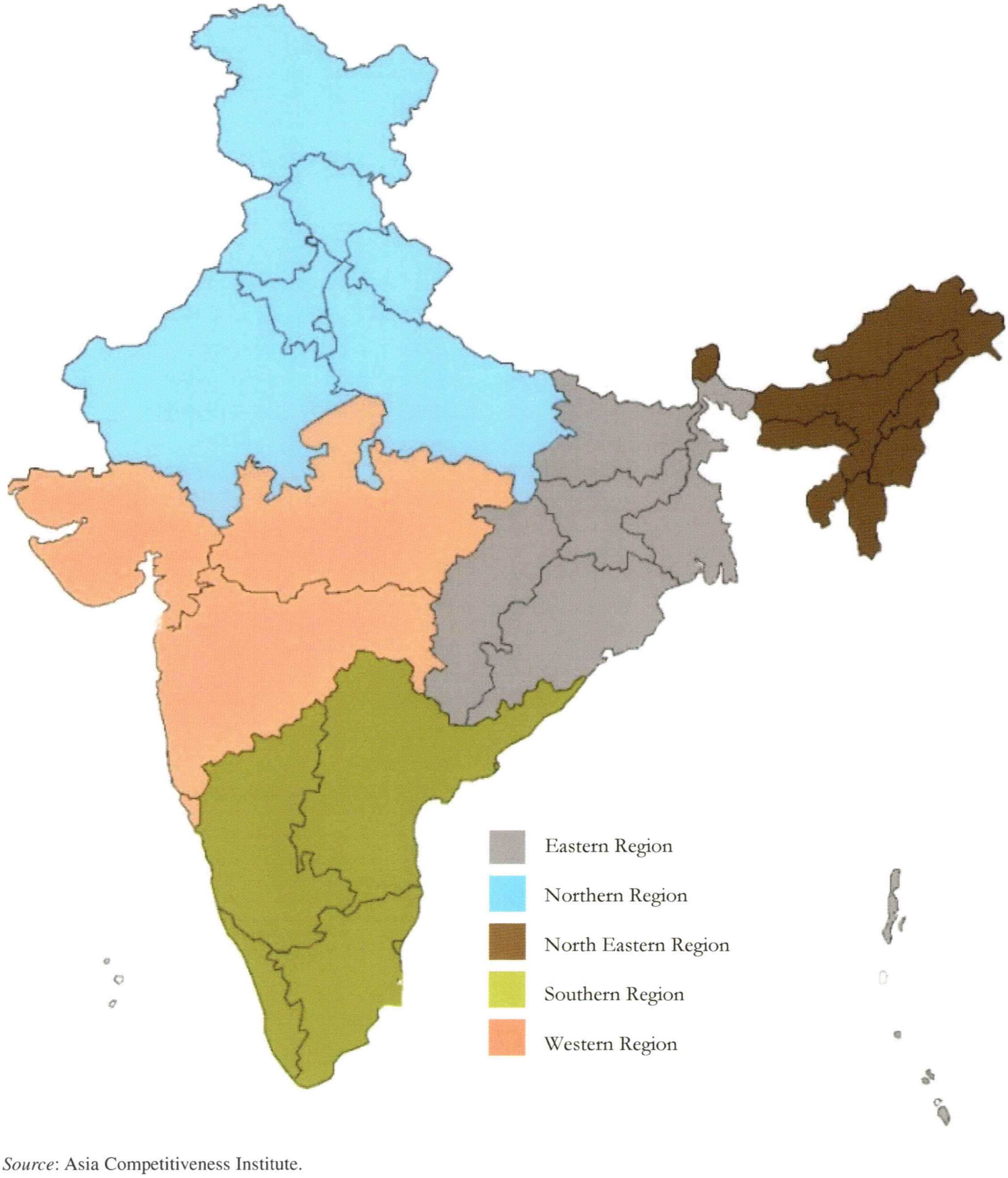

Source: Asia Competitiveness Institute.

the land area, the spatial characteristics of Indian sub-national economies are quite diverse. The cultural and linguistic barriers supplement this heterogeneity. So, based on our competitiveness framework developed and discussed in Chapter 2, Asia Competitiveness Institute (ACI) has extended the analysis to understand the dynamics of regional competitiveness.

Regional competitiveness measures the overall development level of regions. In our analysis, we have divided the sub-national economies according to their spatial arrangements into five regions. Similar to the concentration of high-scale development in small pockets across India, as seen in the previous chapter, regional analysis could also showcase this concentration.

To begin with some preliminaries, ACI employs the regional classification as identified by the Confederation of Indian Industry (CII) to define the five regions within India, as shown in Figure 3.1. The five CII categories are Eastern region, Northern region, North Eastern region, Southern region, and Western region. These are close to the official Zonal Councils set up by Part III of the States Reorganisation Act, 1956, but without a central region so that the states in that region are divided among other regions. As a result of the absence of a central region in the CII classification, the states in the Central Zonal Council are grouped with the other regions to which they are geographically more similar (Tan *et al.*, 2015a).

The remainder of the chapter will proceed as follows. In Section 3.2, we will provide the framework for analysis which will tackle the question of data aggregation from the sub-national level to the regional level. Following this discussion, in Section 3.3, we focus on the empirical findings of competitiveness analysis for the five regions of India. We also offer a detailed analysis on the strongest and the weakest indicators which will provide the basis for targeted policy recommendations. The *raison d'être* of having such a competitiveness ranking at the regional level is not just to pit the regions against each other, but instead to understand the standardised scores at the environment and sub-environment levels which will allow us to draw inferences regarding the potential of each region for holistic development. Section 3.4 concludes with a summary of the findings of the chapter, highlighting some policy implications.

3.2 Regional Competitiveness Framework

The competitiveness ranking by region follows the same methodology as the one used to analyse competitiveness for the sub-national economies, as shown in Chapter 2. However, since each region in India consists of a few states and/or federal territories, the main problem with such an exercise remains to be one of data aggregation. When extending the ranking analysis from the sub-national level to regional level, how should we tackle data aggregation?

To be sure, several of the indicators used for the sub-national level ranking can be directly aggregated to get the indicator values for a region by summing the values for all constituent economies in that region, conditional on those indicators being based on absolute quantities, such as Gross Regional Domestic Product (GRDP) and population. Indicators that are defined as ratios can be computed according to their definitions upon aggregating the absolute quantities in the numerator and denominator.

As an illustration, we outline below three different methods for data aggregation to derive the regional indicator values. The first example is for the indicator on GRDP. Since it is an absolute value, the regional value can be obtained by summing across all sub-national economies within a particular region.

The second example is for the indicator on gross capital formation (percent). According to its definition, it is calculated as the ratio between the gross capital formation of the region and the GRDP of that region. Since both numerator and denominator are in absolute quantities, they are aggregated across all sub-national economies within the region to obtain regional values, from which the ratio is computed, hence arriving at the regional value for gross capital formation (percent).

The third example shows that the calculation is average-weighted at the regional level by population (or Gross Domestic Product (GDP) or land area) of the sub-national economies in the region, such as the indicator on student–teacher ratio (primary).

Method 1: Indicator 1.1.01 GSDP; Unit: 10 million Rupees[2] (₹), real GRDP (base year 2000)
For region A with n economies at time t,

$$GRDP_{A,t} = \sum_{i=1}^{n} Real\,GSDP_{i,t}.$$

Method 2: Indicator 1.1.07 gross capital formation (percent); unit: percent of GRDP
For region A with n economies at time t,

$$Gross\,Capital\,Formation_{A,t} = \frac{\sum_{i=1}^{n} Real\,Gross\,Capital\,Formation_{i,t}}{\sum_{i=1}^{n} Real\,GSDP_{i,t}}.$$

Method 3: Indicator 4.3.05 student–teacher ratio (primary); unit: ratio
For region A with n economies at time t,

$$Student - Teacher\,Ratio(Primary)_{A,t} = \sum_{i=1}^{n}\left(Student - Teacher\,Ratio(Primary)_{i,t} \times \frac{Population_{i,t}}{\sum_{i=1}^{n} Population_{i,t}}\right).$$

The method of aggregation used for each indicator is listed in Appendix 3.

[2] We use rupees to define the generic units of the indicators. We use "≠" symbol to a particular value of any indicator for a particular sub-national economy.

3.3 Empirical Findings: An Analysis of Regional Competitiveness

3.3.1 Overall Competitiveness Ranking and Scores

The five regions of India have been ranked based on their overall competitiveness as well as on the basis of their performances in different environments. As shown in Table 3.1, the Western region ranks first with a standardised score of 0.8917. The Northern region follows closely behind at second with a standardised score of 0.8285.

The overall standardised score provides a detailed comparison between the five regions. The standardised scores of the Western and Northern regions are very similar for the year 2016 (0.8917 and 0.8285, respectively), indicating comparable competitiveness between the top two regions. Similarly, the Southern region also has a comparable standardised score with the first two regions. A large disparity can be observed in the first three and the bottom two regions of India. There is a significant difference between the third and the fourth ranked regions and the disproportionate gap in the overall competitiveness ranking across the five regions highlights the stark contrast in the regional development patterns of the country.

The overall competitiveness ranking has been projected on a map of India as shown in Figure 3.2. The five regions are colour-coded in a multi-coloured scheme whereby the darkest refers to the top-ranked region and the lightest refers to the bottom-ranked region.

Based on Table 3.1 and Figure 3.2, it can be inferred that geographical proximity is a determining factor for a region's overall development. The Western region consists of all the top ranking sub-national economies, namely Maharashtra, Gujarat and Madhya Pradesh, and two federal territories of Daman and Diu, and Dadra and Nagar Haveli. Moreover, the Eastern region and North Eastern region include the sub-national economies with the lowest overall competitiveness ranking. Thus, the aggregated indicators at the regional level show a similar picture.

Table 3.1: 2016 Overall Competitiveness Ranking and Scores for Five Regions of India

Region	Rank	Score
Eastern	4	−1.1629
Northern	2	0.8285
North Eastern	5	−1.2814
Southern	3	0.7240
Western	1	0.8917

Source: Asia Competitiveness Institute.

Figure 3.2: 2016 Map of Overall Competitiveness Ranking for Five Regions of India

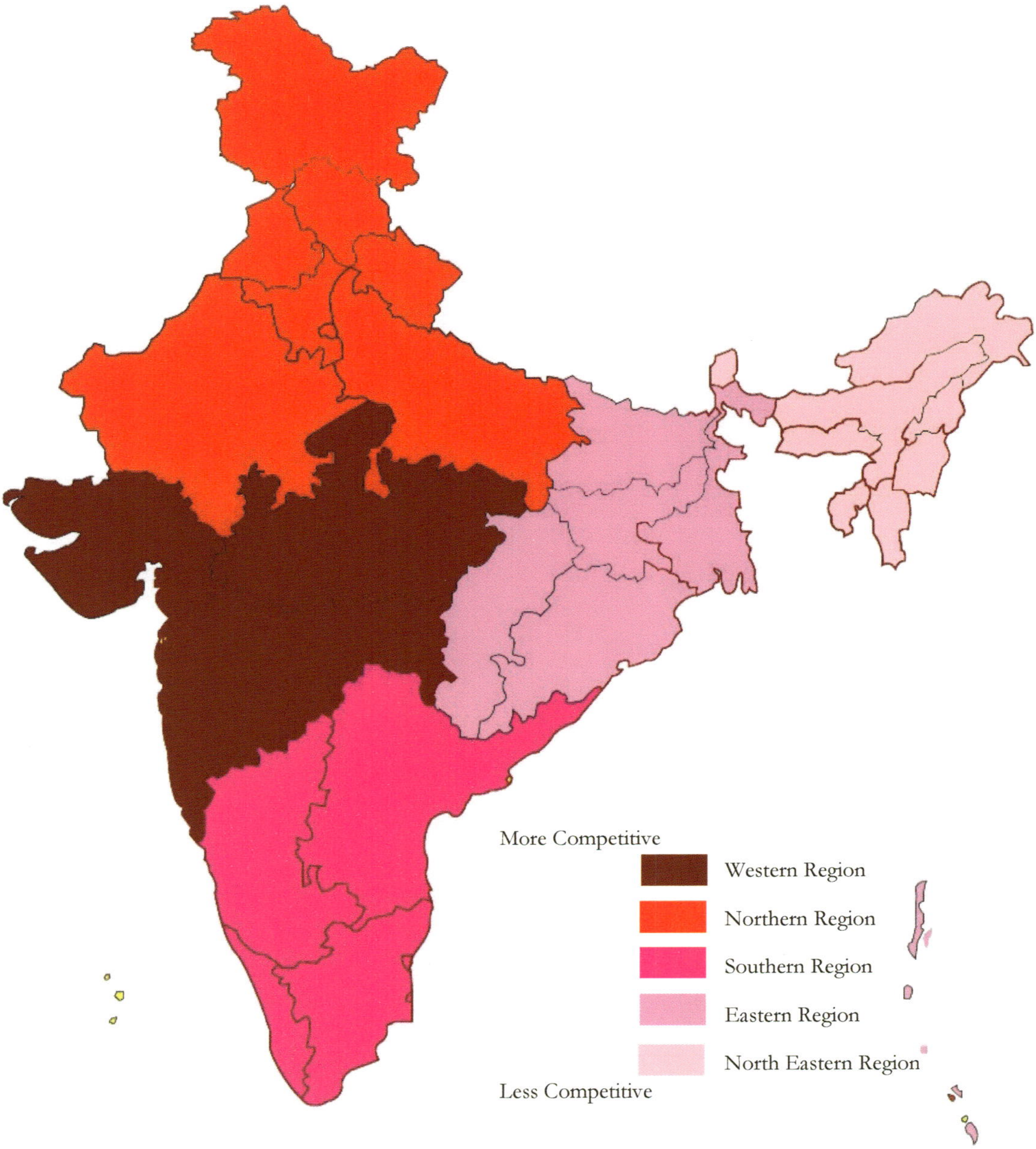

Source: Asia Competitiveness Institute.

3.3.2 Ranking and Scores by Four Environments

This section presents the ranking and scores for the four environments at the regional level. To recall, the four environments constitute variables that represent (1) Macroeconomic Stability, (2) Government and Institutional Setting, (3) Financial, Businesses and Manpower Conditions, and finally (4) Quality of Life and Infrastructure Development. These environments, constructed by ACI, provide a holistic view of the competitiveness positions of each region in India.

Table 3.2 presents the ranking and scores relating to the Macroeconomic Stability environment for the five regions of India. The results clearly indicate that the Western region ranks first with a high standardised score of 1.1026. The Northern region ranks second with a score of 0.8235. From Table 3.2, it is also evident that the regions are uneven in terms of their performances under Macroeconomic Stability. While the Western region leads, the Northern and Southern regions follow and the Eastern region is ranked fourth. Further down the ranking sits the North Eastern region that is ranked fifth and is separated from the Eastern region by a score of 0.3511.

These trends bring out the huge contrast between the most economically developed Western region and the least developed North Eastern region. Such contrast can be attributed to the macroeconomic conditions of the sub-parts of these regions. It is useful to recall that the results shown in Table 2.3 in Chapter 2 revealed that Maharashtra emerged as the top state with the highest standardised score of 3.4447, followed by Tamil Nadu and Delhi at the second and third places with a score of 1.9862 and 1.9640, respectively. Moreover, in the top 10 states, three states are from Western, three are from the Northern region, while three are from the Southern region and one hails from the Eastern region. On comparing the aggregate scores, we can see the correlation between the regional and sub-national rankings. On the other hand, parts of the North Eastern region rank low in Macroeconomic Stability, which is consistent with the results presented in the previous chapter where four states from this region including Mizoram, Arunachal Pradesh, Tripura, and Manipur were part of the bottom 10 group.

Figure 3.3 shows the visual plots of standardised scores for the sub-environments of Macroeconomic Stability. The sub-environments include economic vibrancy, openness to trade and services, and attractiveness to foreign investors. It also depicts the strengths and weaknesses of each region and explains the large inequality between the regions' scores.

Table 3.2: 2016 Macroeconomic Stability Competitiveness Ranking and Scores for Five Regions of India

Region	Rank	Score
Eastern	4	−1.0154
Northern	2	0.8235
North Eastern	5	−1.3665
Southern	3	0.4558
Western	1	1.1026

Source: Asia Competitiveness Institute.

Figure 3.3: Regional Sub-Environment Scores

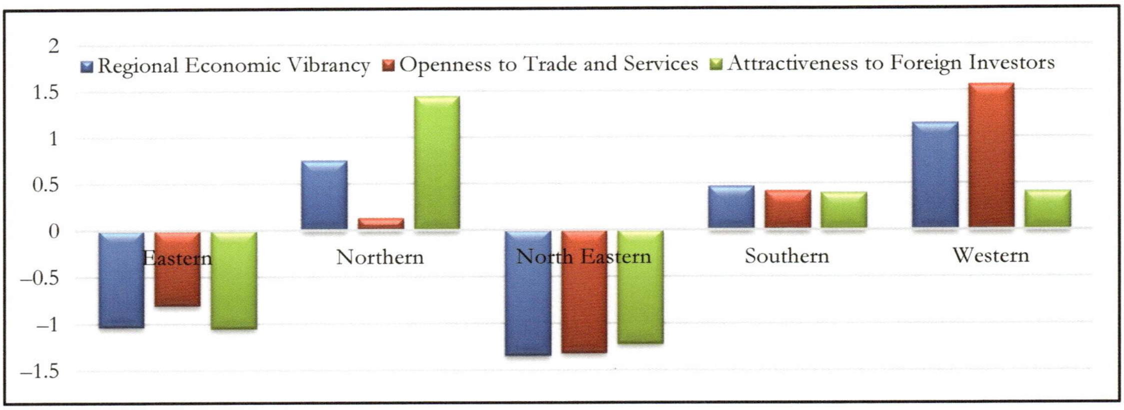

Source: Asia Competitiveness Institute.

From Figure 3.3, we can also infer that the Western region emerges as the most competitive in all the three sub-environments. The main strength of the Western region is its regional economic vibrancy and openness to trade and services.

Another observation to note here is that there is a sharp contrast in the scores for attractiveness to foreign investors between the North Eastern and Eastern regions and the rest. Apart from these two, the rest of the regions score above average. In addition, the North Eastern region also fares the poorest in all the three sub-environments, relative to the other regions.

In Figure 3.4, the regions are shown in a multi-coloured scheme whereby the darkest refers to the top-ranked region and the lightest refers to the bottom-ranked region. The figure presents a clear picture of how the geographical location of each region affects their performance under Macroeconomic Stability. The regions which enjoy long coastlines are ranked higher than the regions that are landlocked or share borders with other nations like China, Myanmar, Pakistan, Nepal, Bhutan, and Bangladesh.

Table 3.3 presents the ranking and scores for the Government and Institutional Setting environment for the five regions of India. In this particular environment, the Northern region ranks first, followed by the Southern and Western regions at second and third places, respectively. Again, the score differences between the five regions are quite large, with only the top two regions obtaining above average scores.

The Government and Institutional Setting environment captures key indicators like government revenue, tax revenue, tax revenue/government revenue, government consumption expenditure, police expenditure, public and private limited companies, etc.

From the 13 indicators that make up the Government and Institutional Setting environment, the Northern region scores particularly high for seven of them. On a detailed analysis, it can be seen that the Northern region has a competitive advantage in numbers due to its large land size.

However, the tax revenues (as a percent of government revenues) are the highest for the Southern region (80 percent) and lowest for the North Eastern region (38 percent). The North

Figure 3.4: 2016 Map of Macroeconomic Stability Ranking for Five Regions of India

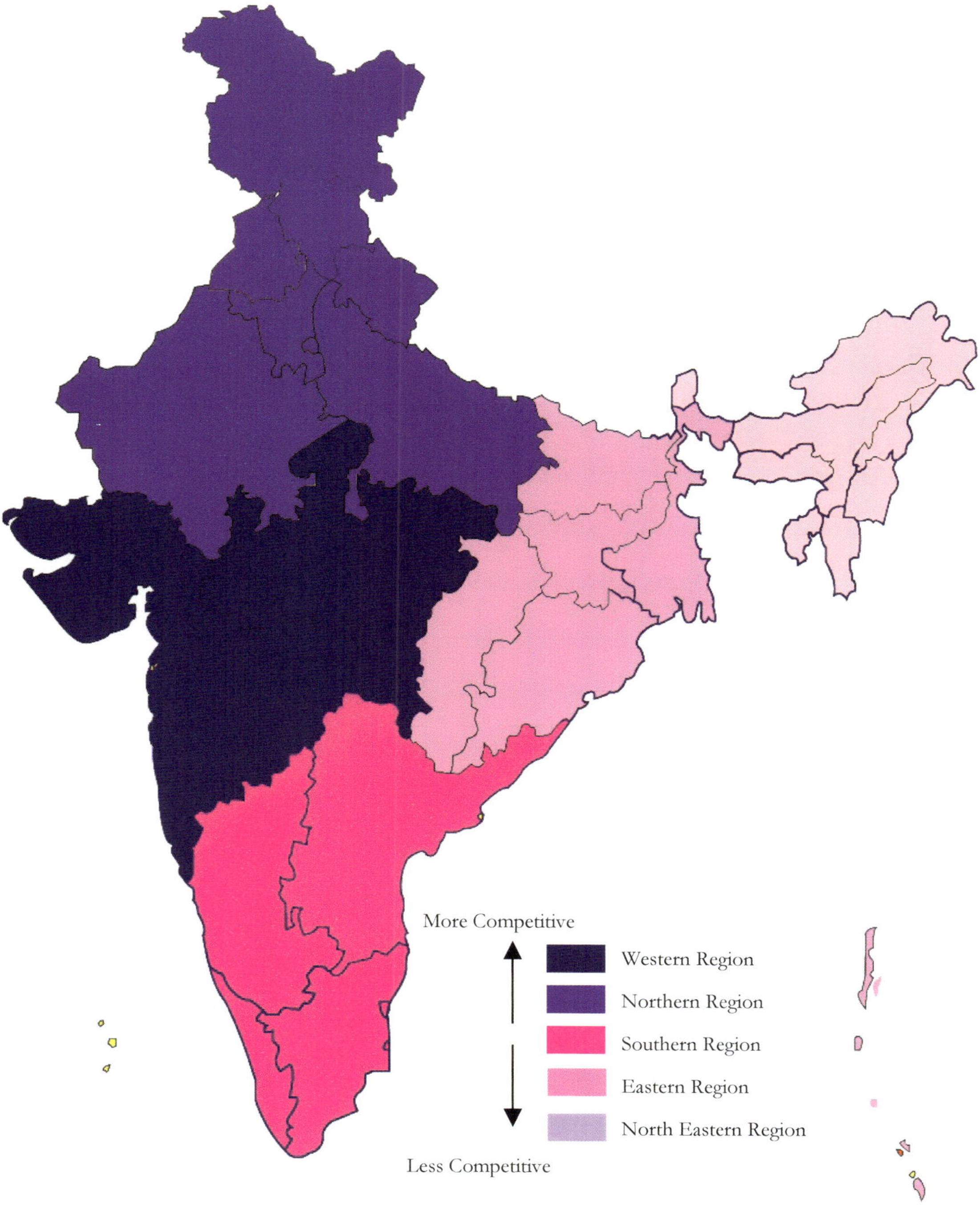

Source: Asia Competitiveness Institute.

Table 3.3: 2016 Government and Institutional Setting Competitiveness Ranking and Scores for Five Regions of India

Region	Rank	Score
Eastern	4	−0.6744
Northern	1	1.7778
North Eastern	5	−1.1554
Southern	2	0.1812
Western	3	−0.1292

Source: Asia Competitiveness Institute.

Figure 3.5: Regional Sub-Environment Scores

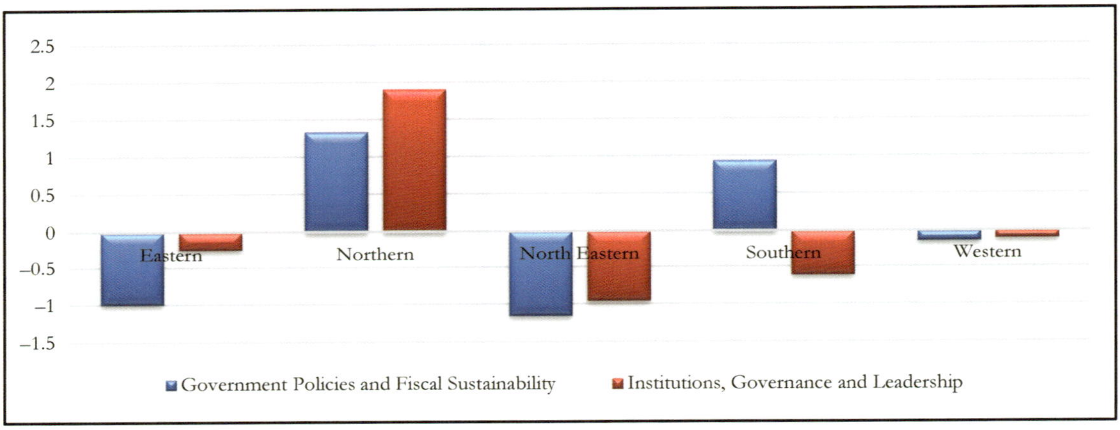

Source: Asia Competitiveness Institute.

Eastern region has been the recipient of numerous government subsidies for its economic development. It enjoys the highest government consumption expenditure (31 percent) among all the other regions of India. The lowest contribution comes from the Western region (12 percent).

Although, it can be viewed that less developed regions enjoy higher government attention, in the case of developing countries, higher government expenditures are considered vital for economic development of a region. Thus, even though the Western region stands second in the overall ranking, strengthening state intervention might lead to faster growth, provided the expenditures are productive and leakages are minimised. Over time, as private sector grows and matures, some shrinkage in the size of the government sector could probably spur growth and development.

Figure 3.5 presents the standardised scores for the two sub-environments under the Government and Institutional Setting, namely fiscal sustainability and institutions, governance and leadership.

Figure 3.6: 2016 Map of Government and Institutional Setting Ranking for Five Regions of India

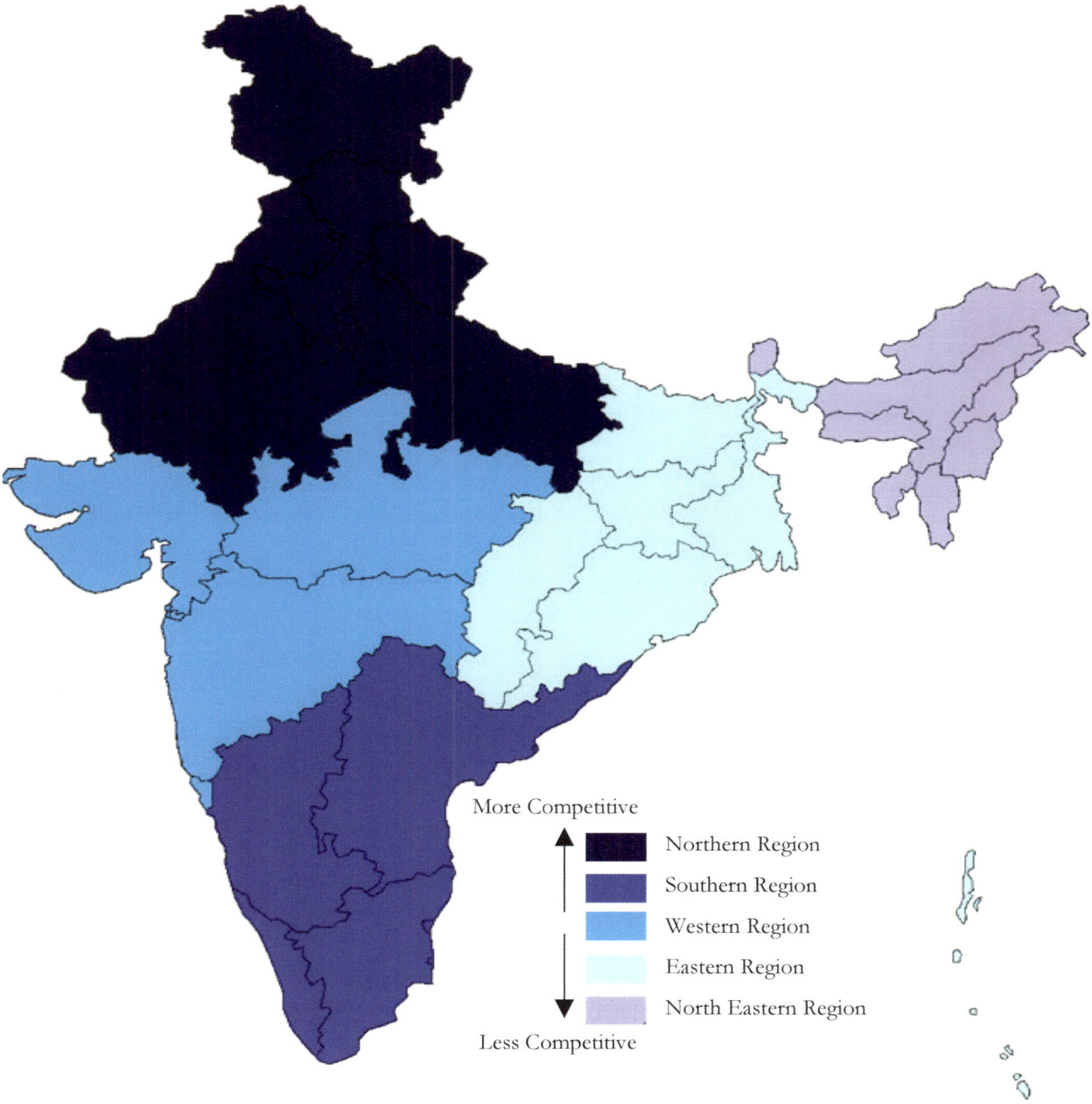

Source: Asia Competitiveness Institute.

The Northern region has significantly high standardised scores for both sub-environments. High tax revenues and government revenues, along with significantly large number of public and private limited companies, add to its advantage.

Figure 3.6 presents a snapshot of how land size is a competitiveness advantage when it comes to the Government and Institutional Setting environment. The figure also shows that the largest region, namely the Northern region, ranks first and is followed by the Southern, Western, Eastern, and North Eastern regions, respectively.

Table 3.4 presents the rank and score for the environment of Financial, Businesses and Manpower Conditions for the five regions of India. The Western region ranks the highest with the standardised score of 1.0724 and is followed by the Southern region (0.7864). Even the Northern region fares well in this environment, with a score of 0.5216. However, the Eastern and North Eastern regions have very low standardised scores at –0.9391 and –1.4413, respectively. They are considerably below the regional average.

Figure 3.7 presents the sub-environment standardised scores for all five regions. The sub-environments that constitute the environment on Financial, Businesses and Manpower Conditions are financial deepening and business efficiency, labour market flexibility and productivity performance. The top three regions, namely the Western, Southern, and Northern regions, do comparably well in the financial deepening and business efficiency environment.

Table 3.4: 2016 Financial, Businesses and Manpower Conditions Competitiveness Ranking and Scores for Five Regions of India

Region	Rank	Score
Eastern	4	–0.9391
Northern	3	0.5216
North Eastern	5	–1.4413
Southern	2	0.7864
Western	1	1.0724

Source: Asia Competitiveness Institute.

Figure 3.7: Regional Sub-Environment Scores

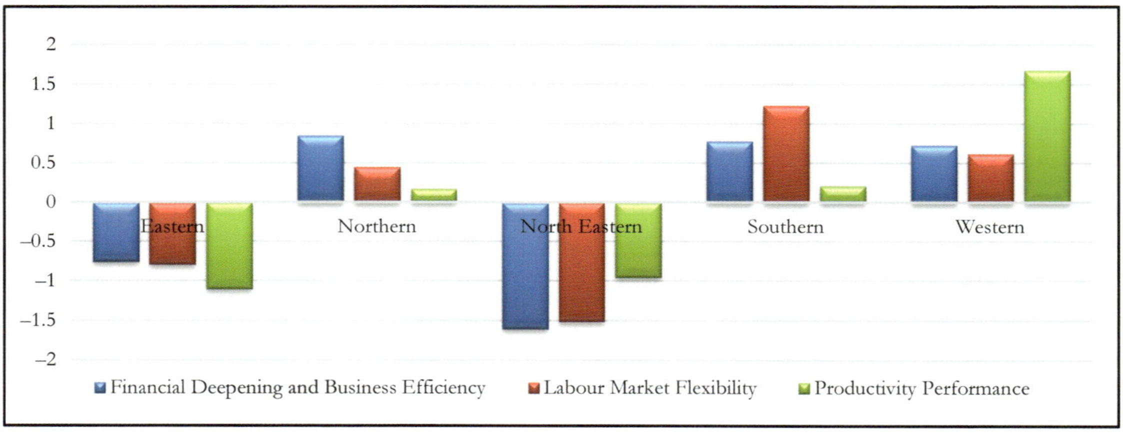

Source: Asia Competitiveness Institute.

In the labour market flexibility sub-environment, the North Eastern region has the lowest score. This may be attributed to its lowest number of total workers (0.018 million), significantly lower wages and salaries in the region (aggregate amounting to just ₹178.4 million at constant 2000 prices as compared to the regional average of ₹2007.3 million) and lowest number of industrial training institutes (79). The Western region has the lowest monthly agricultural wages (₹64.09 at constant 2000 prices), but this appears to be in line with its highly industrialised image.

For the productivity performance sub-environment, the Western region secures the highest score due to its high overall labour productivity (₹97,297 per person-year at constant 2000 prices) with high value added per worker in secondary industry (₹482,043 per person-year at constant 2000 prices). A unique insight from the analysis of this sub-environment yields that the eastern region's overall labour productivity (₹58,199 per person-year at constant 2000 prices) is the lowest among all five regions. Fortunately, this does not cause the Eastern region to perform the worst in Financial, Businesses and Manpower Conditions. In fact, the lowest position is held by the North Eastern region which can be attributed to its low value added per worker in secondary industry (₹212,413 per person-year at constant 2000 prices). An interesting insight in the productivity performance sub-environment comes from concentrating on the Northern region. The region has the second highest value added per worker in secondary industry, but significantly lags behind the Western and Southern regions in overall labour productivity. This is consistent with the inference we drew from the Government and Institutional Setting environment earlier that the Northern region due to its size has the benefit in numbers, but is unable to efficiently utilise this advantage.

Figure 3.8 presents a colour-coded map of India. As above, the region with the highest standardised score is coded with the brightest colour and the worst-performing region is coded with the lightest colour. The Western region ranks the highest due to its advanced Financial, Business and Manpower Conditions and is closely followed by the Southern region.

Table 3.5 presents the ranking and scores for the environment of Quality of Life and Infrastructure Development for the five regions of India. In this particular environment, apart from the Southern and Western regions, all other regions perform below average. This environment is also the only one in which the Eastern region ranks last.

Figure 3.9 presents the three sub-environments under the Quality of Life and Infrastructure Development environment, namely physical infrastructure, technological infrastructure, and standard of living, education and social stability. The North Eastern region ranks the lowest in the first sub-environment which relates to physical infrastructure.

For the second sub-environment on technological infrastructure, the Western region leads while the Southern region occupies the first runner-up position. A unique highlight in this sub-environment is the indicator measuring the expenditure on science, technology and environment. In this particular indicator, the North Eastern region ranks first (0.041 percent) and is followed by the Eastern region (0.033 percent). This may be due to the high expenditures spent by the government to improve human resource development in these regions.

This links us to the next sub-environment of standard of living, education and social stability. One of the indicators is the illiteracy rate. The Eastern region has the highest illiteracy rate (28 percent) followed closely by the Northern region (27 percent) and the North Eastern region

Figure 3.8: 2016 Map of Financial, Businesses and Manpower Conditions Ranking for Five Regions of India

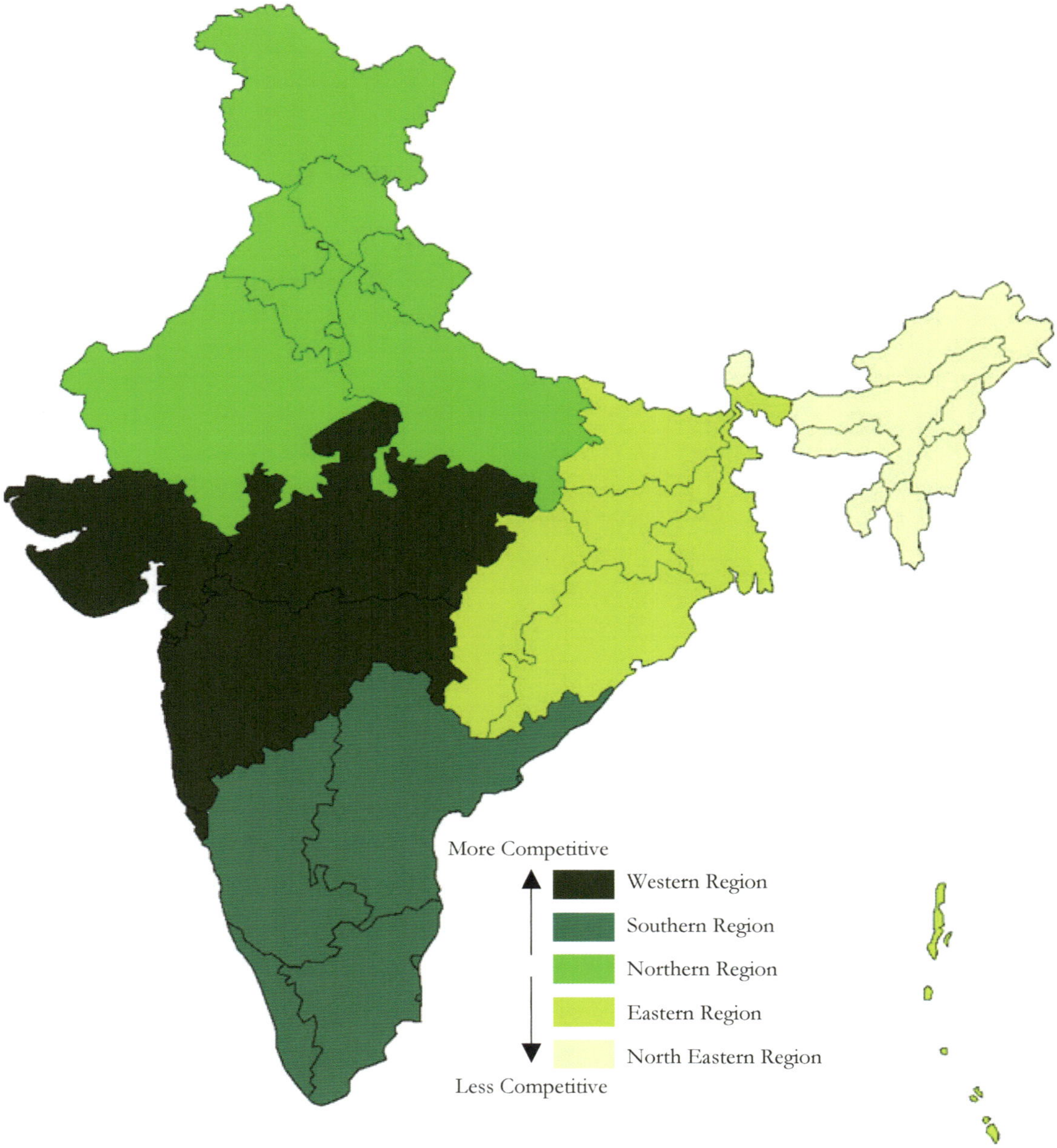

Source: Asia Competitiveness Institute.

Table 3.5: 2016 Quality of Life and Infrastructure Development Competitiveness Ranking and Scores for Five Regions of India

Region	Rank	Score
Eastern	5	–1.4720
Northern	3	–0.2012
North Eastern	4	–0.5555
Southern	1	1.1298
Western	2	1.0989

Source: Asia Competitiveness Institute.

Figure 3.9: Regional Sub-Environment Scores

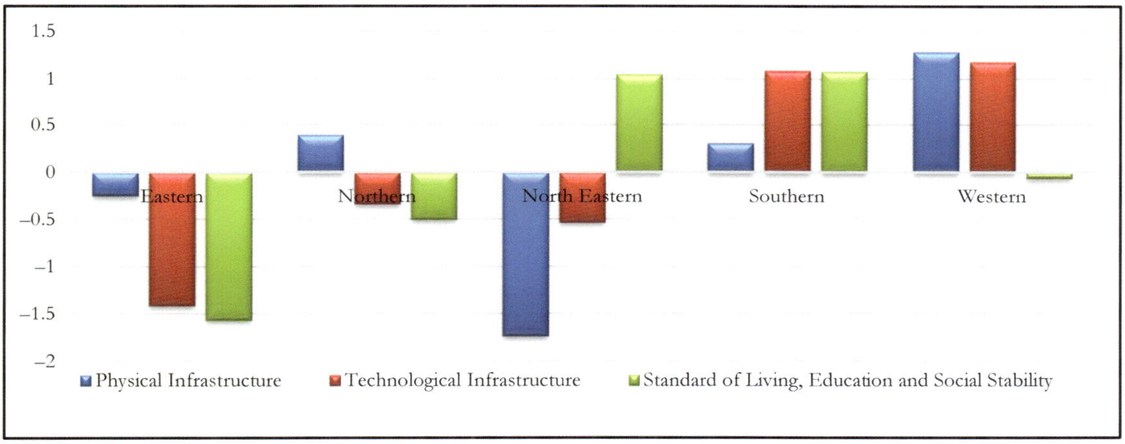

Source: Asia Competitiveness Institute.

(23 percent), respectively. The Eastern region also has the poorest student–teacher ratio (for primary, secondary and tertiary institutions, approximately 30), and per capita public health expenditure (₹334.67 at constant 2000 prices compared to the regional average of ₹560.41). Consequently, the contribution of the Eastern region to human resource development remains low. Thus, in the last sub-environment, Eastern region ranks the lowest. The Western region also attains a below-average score for this third sub-environment. The North Eastern region ranks the highest in the urban population growth (3.4 percent), expenditure on education (6.5 percent of GRDP) and per capita public health expenditure (₹745.76 at constant 2000 prices compared to the regional average of ₹560.41).

Figure 3.10 presents the multi-coloured map of the regions. The Southern region is marked the darkest followed by the Western, Northern, North Eastern, and Eastern regions.

Figure 3.10: 2016 Map of Quality of Life and Infrastructure Development Ranking for Five Regions of India

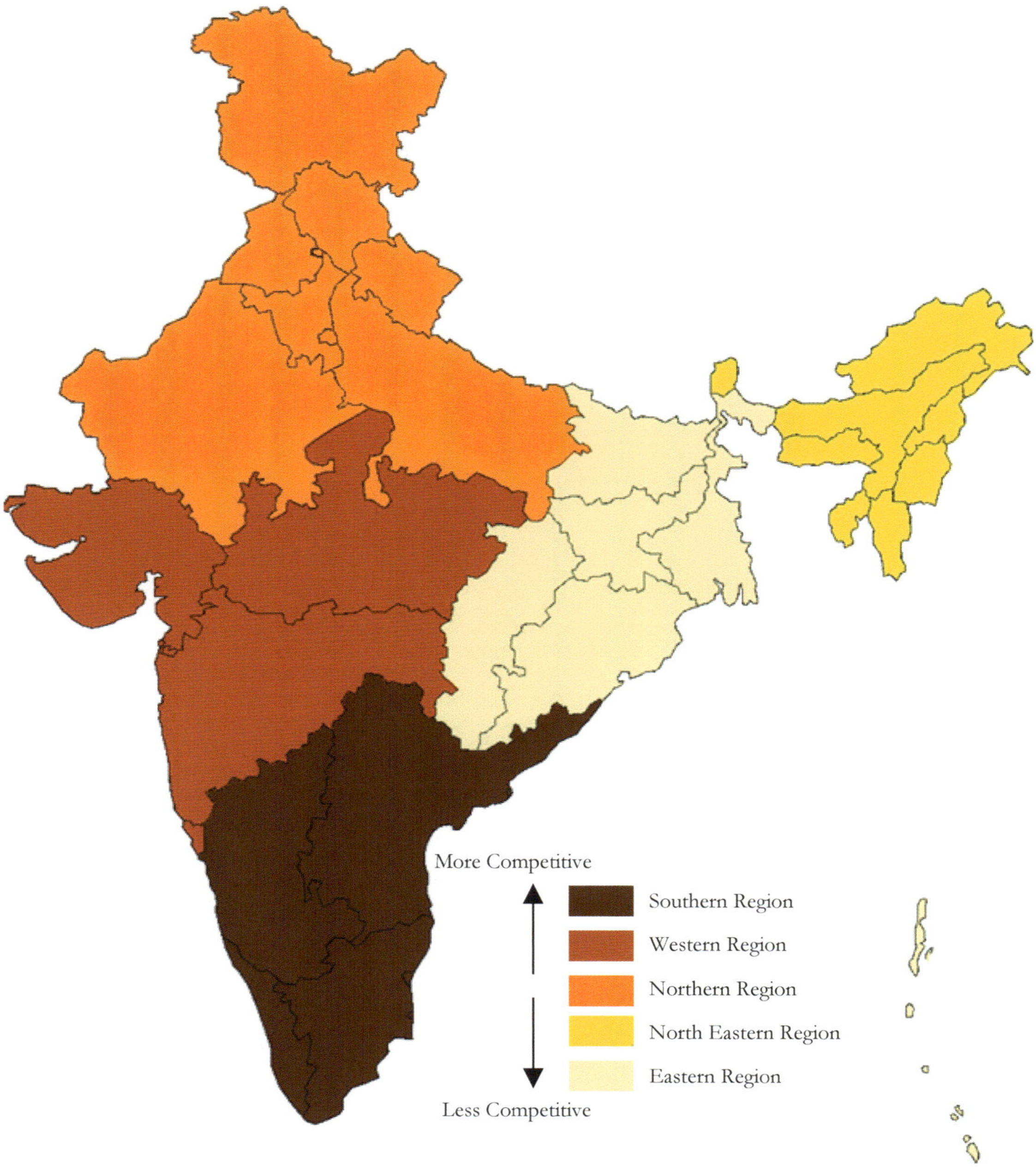

Source: Asia Competitiveness Institute.

3.3.3 Median and Maximum Competitiveness Web Analysis

The median and maximum competitiveness web analysis is a tool that provides a snapshot of the performance of the regions at the sub-environment level. The charts can be analysed to better understand the strengths and weaknesses of a particular region, enabling them to channel their limited resources into areas which might have the maximum impact.

To better understand the North Eastern region's relative strengths and weaknesses, it is useful to compare and contrast its scores against the median and maximum scores of India's five regions for the 11 sub-environments that constitute the four environments.

The median competitiveness web analysis in Figure 3.11 plots the attained scores across the 11 sub-environments for the Western region (ranked first) and the North Eastern region (ranked last), along with the median scores for the five regions of India. The contrast in performance from the two regions at the opposite ends of the spectrum can be clearly seen in Figure 3.11. The top-ranked Western region scores equivalent to or higher than the median for all sub-environments.

On the other hand, the last-ranked North Eastern region scores below the median for all sub-environments, except for standard of living, education and social stability, where its score matches the maximum score. North Eastern region's performance is especially poor for regional economic vibrancy, physical infrastructure and financial deepening and business efficiency where it scores significantly lower than the respective median score.

The maximum competitiveness web analysis in Figure 3.12 plots the attained scores across the 11 sub-environments for the Western region (ranked first) and the North Eastern region (ranked last), along with the maximum scores for the five regions of India. The top-ranked

Figure 3.11: 2016 Median Competitiveness Web Analysis: Western and North Eastern Region

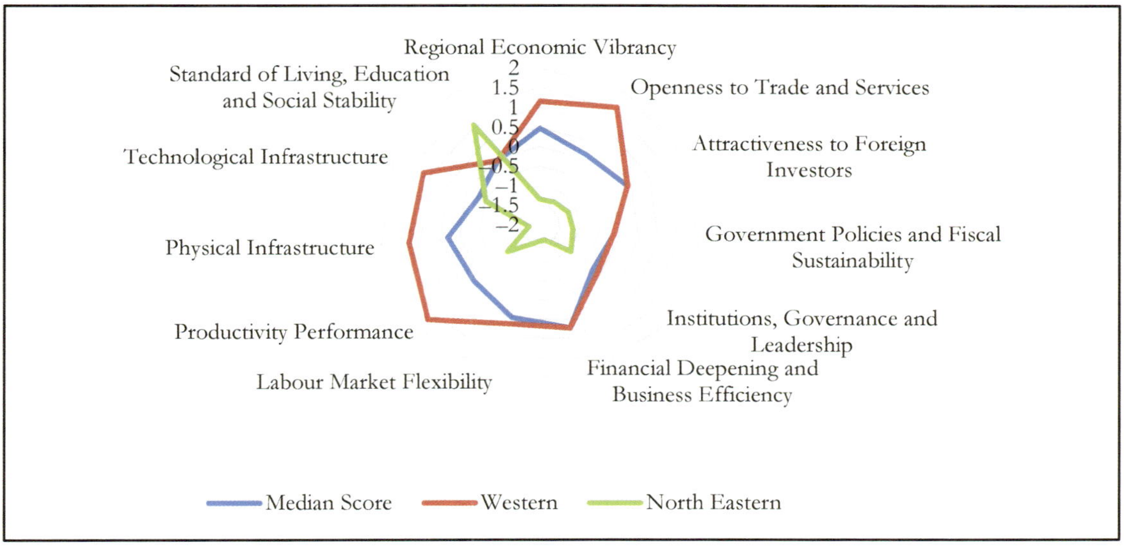

Source: Asia Competitiveness Institute.

Figure 3.12: 2016 Maximum Competitiveness Web Analysis: Western and North Eastern Region

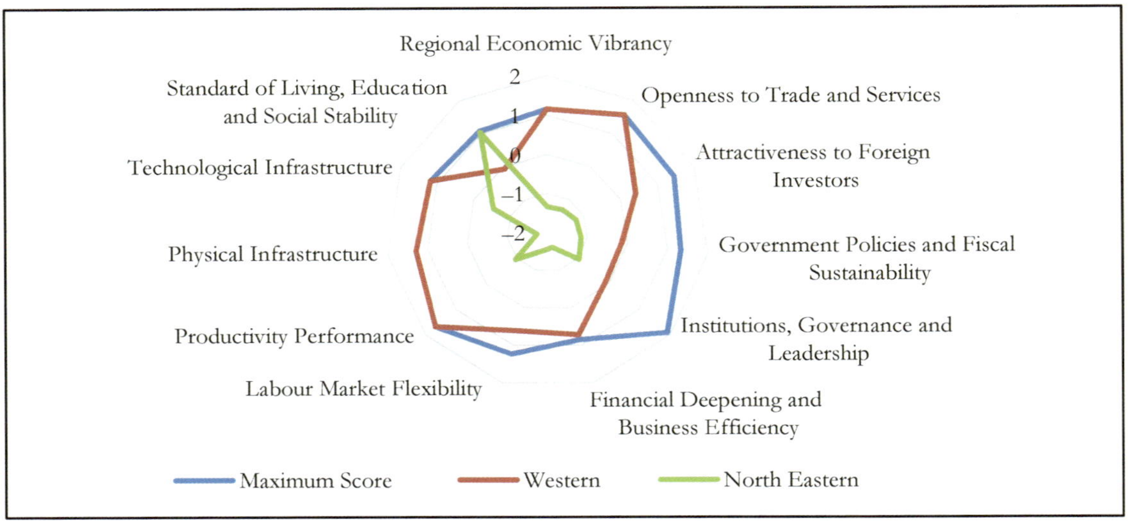

Source: Asia Competitiveness Institute.

Western region sets the maximum score for five sub-environments, namely regional economic vibrancy, openness to trade and services, productivity performance, physical infrastructure, and technological infrastructure. On the other hand, the scores for the North Eastern region across all 11 sub-environments seem very distant from the maximum scores except for the standard of living, education and social stability sub-environment. The gap between the regions' score and the maximum score highlights the potential that each region has to improve their competitiveness even if they remain within the same frontier.

3.3.4 Analysis of Top 20 Percent Strongest and Weakest Indicators

We further extend our regional analysis by taking a peek into the top 20 percent strongest and weakest indicators for the different regions in order to provide in-depth knowledge of the strengths and weaknesses of each region. Following the analysis at the environment and sub-environment level, this section focusses on understanding regional competitiveness at a more disaggregated level. The indicators are the foundation of the competitiveness framework, and understanding them is the key to develop a sound development plan. The following sub-sections present the strongest and weakest indicators for individual regions.

3.3.4.1 *Eastern Region*

The Eastern region ranks fourth in the overall competitiveness ranking with a below-average standardised score. Despite that, the region has its own strengths and weaknesses. Tables 3.6 and 3.7 present the top and the bottom 15 indicators for the region.

Table 3.6: 2016 Top 20 Percent Strongest Indicators of Eastern Region

Rank	20 Percent Strongest Indicator	Score	Environment
1	Policemen per 100 km^2	1.0905	GIS
2	Expenditure on Science, Technology and Environment	0.8982	QLID
3	Motor Vehicles per km of Road	0.8427	QLID
4	Air Pollution	0.5708	QLID
5	Adequacy of Hospitals	0.5361	QLID
6	Population	0.5086	QLID
7	Gross Capital Formation (%)	0.4613	MS
8	Total Workers	0.4152	FBMC
9	Cultivated Land	0.3605	QLID
10	Death Rate	0.3221	QLID
11	Tax Revenue/Government Revenue	0.2862	GIS
12	Number of Educational Institutions	0.2360	QLID
13	Ageing Profile	0.2233	QLID
14	Length of Roads	0.2112	QLID
15	Public Limited Companies	0.1524	GIS

Note: MS denotes Macroeconomic Stability; GIS denotes Government and Institutional Setting; FBMC denotes Financial, Businesses and Manpower Conditions; and QLID denotes Quality of Life and Infrastructure Development.

Source: Asia Competitiveness Institute.

Table 3.7: 2016 Top 20 Percent Weakest Indicators of Eastern Region

Rank	20 Percent Weakest Indicator	Score	Environment
61	Population Served per Bank Office	−1.1165	FBMC
62	Persons per Mobile Telephone Subscriber	−1.1167	QLID
63	Motor Vehicles per Person	−1.2116	QLID
64	GRDP per Capita	−1.2243	MS
65	Unemployment Rate (Urban Area)	−1.2279	FBMC
66	Budget Balance	−1.2680	GIS
67	Disparity between Primary and Secondary Institutions	−1.3164	QLID
68	Illiteracy Rate	−1.3348	QLID
69	Overall Labour Productivity	−1.3478	FBMC
70	Persons per Internet Subscriber	−1.4469	QLID
71	Population Density	−1.5136	QLID
72	Per Capita Public Health Expenditure	−1.5749	QLID
73	Health Expenditure	−1.6533	QLID
74	Student–Teacher Ratio (Tertiary)	−1.6989	QLID
75	Population per Medical Personnel	−1.9448	QLID

Note: MS denotes Macroeconomic Stability; GIS denotes Government and Institutional Setting; FBMC denotes Financial, Businesses and Manpower Conditions; and QLID denotes Quality of Life and Infrastructure Development.

Source: Asia Competitiveness Institute.

This region enjoys the highest policemen per 100 km^2, second highest expenditure on science, technology and environment as a percentage of Gross State Domestic Product (GSDP) as well as gross capital formation. It has the second lowest number of motor vehicles per km of roads and low levels of air pollution. The region has a higher number of total workers as compared to the more developed Southern region and higher tax revenues as a percentage of government revenues than the Northern region. Interestingly, the region has a more favourable ageing profile than the Southern and Western regions.

However, the bottom 15 indicators give more insights into the benefits that the Eastern region can derive from its strengths. The region's GRDP per capita is the lowest amongst all the regions. Additionally, high illiteracy rate, high student–teacher ratio (tertiary), disparity between primary and secondary institutions, population per medical personnel, and low overall labour productivity provide explanation for the inability of the region's strengths to translate into higher competitiveness (Table 3.7).

The region suffers from non-realisation of its own strengths due to unequal distribution of GRDP, inadequate teachers at the tertiary educational institutes, especially when one of its strongest indicator is total workers. The region needs appropriate investments in enhancing employability of its present and future workers to ensure that it benefits from its demographic dividend. Additionally, inadequate health expenditure for the growing population is also a concern. The above tables summarise that the region enjoys adequacy of hospitals but suffers from its underutilisation due to lack of funds.

3.3.4.2 *Northern Region*

The Northern region is the most populous region with the highest population as well as the number of total workers, closely followed by the Eastern region. Unlike the Eastern region, the Northern region has a much larger land area that can be utilised to take advantage of the growing working population. The output produced by the primary industry in the Northern region is the largest among all the other regions. The expenditure on police force by the region is almost double that of the Eastern region, which is second in its police expenditure. The high number of foreign companies and public limited companies in the region depict the pro-business sentiment despite it being landlocked, mainly due to its efficient railway connectivity. Additionally, the region enjoys high government revenues, health expenditures and number of educational institutions (Table 3.8).

The list of the bottommost indicators is given in Table 3.9 and underlines the need to improve the developmental indicators. In particular, the region has to focus on improving its illiteracy rate, infant mortality rate, air pollution and the capacity of the existing health infrastructure.

The large land size and population pose a challenge for the region. Despite having high primary industry output, the region still suffers from high unemployment rate. The region's GRDP growth is almost half of that of the Western region and about a fourth of that registered by the North Eastern region. Additionally, the high health expenditure falls short when it comes to the population per hospital bed. The high illiteracy rate also calls into question the adequacy of

Table 3.8: 2016 Top 20 Percent Strongest Indicators of Northern Region

Rank	20 Percent Strongest Indicator	Score	Environment
1	Police Expenditure	1.8631	GIS
2	Foreign Companies	1.7071	GIS
3	Number of Foreign Companies (%)	1.5544	MS
4	Number of Educational Institutions	1.5252	QLID
5	Health Expenditure	1.4810	QLID
6	Total Land Area	1.4052	QLID
7	Foreign Direct Investment	1.3275	MS
8	Primary Industry	1.3262	MS
9	Length of Railways in Operation	1.2286	QLID
10	Government Revenue	1.1905	GIS
11	Population	1.1866	QLID
12	Industrial Training Institutes	1.1773	FBMC
13	Bank Offices	1.1708	FBMC
14	International Tourists	1.1404	MS
15	Private Limited Companies	1.0936	GIS

Note: MS denotes Macroeconomic Stability; GIS denotes Government and Institutional Setting; FBMC denotes Financial, Businesses and Manpower Conditions; and QLID denotes Quality of Life and Infrastructure Development.

Source: Asia Competitiveness Institute.

Table 3.9: 2016 Top 20 Percent Weakest Indicators of Northern Region

Rank	20 Percent Weakest Indicator	Score	Environment
61	Openness to Trade	–0.4309	MS
62	Population per Hospital Bed	–0.5645	QLID
63	Public Limited Companies (%)	–0.5845	GIS
64	Unemployment Rate (Urban Area)	–0.5873	FBMC
65	GRDP Growth	–0.7699	MS
66	Urban Population Growth	–0.7706	QLID
67	Motor Vehicles per km of Road	–0.8823	QLID
68	Infant Mortality Rate	–0.9178	QLID
69	Total Cargo Handled	–0.9268	QLID
70	Illiteracy Rate	–1.0034	QLID
71	Expenditure on Science, Technology and Environment	–1.0458	QLID
72	Number of Ports	–1.0552	QLID
73	Student–Teacher Ratio (Secondary)	–1.2856	QLID
74	Student–Teacher Ratio (Primary)	–1.3049	QLID
75	Air Pollution	–1.8487	QLID

Note: MS denotes Macroeconomic Stability; GIS denotes Government and Institutional Setting; FBMC denotes Financial, Businesses and Manpower Conditions; and QLID denotes Quality of Life and Infrastructure Development.

Source: Asia Competitiveness Institute.

the large number of educational institutes in the region. The region thus needs to focus on increasing government attention towards the educational and health sector by empowering their primary sector further.

3.3.4.3 *North Eastern Region*

The North Eastern region is known for its strong development indicators (Table 3.10). As can be seen from Table 3.10, it has the highest policemen per 100,000 population and expenditure on education and expenditure on science, technology and environment. The region also has the highest GRDP growth rate of 8.01 percent, but this might be a result of its low GSDP base. The region also boasts of the highest per capita public health expenditure and lowest population density amongst all regions.

The North Eastern region is connected to the rest of the India through a single corridor called the Siliguri Corridor in West Bengal. The tribal conflicts and inaccessible terrain makes it unattractive for industrialisation. It is primarily agrarian, but has low power generation and poor connectivity (as can been seen from Table 3.11), which make it difficult to achieve high GRDP.

The region has benefitted from excise duty holiday scheme for 10 years after setting up of the manufacturing unit, but the scheme is due to end by April 2017. Without help from the central government, the region has to strengthen its primary sector to sustain itself.

Furthermore, the region has direct access to China, Bhutan, Bangladesh, Myanmar and Nepal. The policy of 'Look East', which is now set to be morphed into 'Act East' to bolster

Table 3.10: 2016 Top 20 Percent Strongest Indicators of North Eastern Region

Rank	20 Percent Strongest Indicator	Score	Environment
1	Policemen per 100,000 Population	1.9692	GIS
2	Expenditure on Education	1.9391	QLID
3	Government Consumption Expenditure	1.9185	GIS
4	Public Limited Companies (%)	1.8909	GIS
5	Budget Balance	1.7795	GIS
6	Gross Regional Domestic Product Growth	1.6921	MS
7	Old Age Dependency Ratio	1.6619	QLID
8	Inflation (Consumer Price Index — Industrial Labourers)	1.6213	MS
9	Population Density	1.5458	QLID
10	Motor Vehicles per km of Road	1.5316	QLID
11	Ageing Profile	1.4777	QLID
12	Expenditure on Science, Technology and Environment	1.4676	QLID
13	Per Capita Public Health Expenditure	1.3769	QLID
14	Student–Teacher Ratio (Secondary)	1.2977	QLID
15	Inflation (Consumer Price Index — Rural Labourers)	1.2939	MS

Note: MS denotes Macroeconomic Stability; GIS denotes Government and Institutional Setting; FBMC denotes Financial, Businesses and Manpower Conditions; and QLID denotes Quality of Life and Infrastructure Development.

Source: Asia Competitiveness Institute.

Table 3.11: 2016 Top 20 Percent Weakest Indicators of North Eastern Region

Rank	20 Percent Weakest Indicator	Score	Environment
61	Primary Industry	−1.7654	MS
62	Secondary Industry	−1.7659	MS
63	Tertiary Industry	−1.7683	MS
64	Length of Railways in Operation	−1.7700	QLID
65	Gross Capital Formation (%)	−1.7980	MS
66	Public Limited Companies	−1.7991	GIS
67	Private Limited Companies	−1.8031	GIS
68	Limited Companies	−1.8051	GIS
69	Tax Revenue	−1.8054	GIS
70	Gross Regional Domestic Product	−1.8154	MS
71	Population	−1.8234	QLID
72	Power Generation	−1.9064	QLID
73	Tax Revenue/Government Revenue	−1.9500	GIS
74	Total Workers	−1.9515	FBMC
75	Length of Roads	−1.9784	QLID

Note: MS denotes Macroeconomic Stability; GIS denotes Government and Institutional Setting; FBMC denotes Financial, Businesses and Manpower Conditions; and QLID denotes Quality of Life and Infrastructure Development.

Source: Asia Competitiveness Institute.

relations with the ASEAN, can pave the way for improved connectivity and market access of the North Eastern region of India with that of the ASEAN region. This will not only improve the primary industry by providing it access to new markets but will also make it more competitive. However, it is imperative for the respective state governments of the region to create awareness among the farmers through removing middle men as well as providing better access to knowledge regarding new markets. It is also equally important to provide adequate infrastructure to promote and develop the already existing plantation industry, especially tea and bamboo. Handicrafts and silk industry should also be promoted as they offer promising returns.

3.3.4.4 *Southern Region*

The Southern region is ranked third in terms of regional competitiveness, relative to the rest of the country. The region has the second highest GRDP per capita, after Western region among all regions. In addition, the region also boasts of performing the best among all the five regions in the top 11 of its strongest indicators (Table 3.12).

As has been seen with most developed nations, higher development appears to be followed by improved human development indicators and slower economic growth. A similar trend can be seen in the Southern region. GRDP growth rate, ageing profile and old age dependency ratio are some of the weakest indicators in the region (Table 3.13). Unlike developed nations, the Southern

Table 3.12: 2016 Top 20 Percent Strongest Indicators of Southern Region

Rank	20 Percent Strongest Indicator	Score	Environment
1	Disparity between Primary and Secondary Institutions	1.7720	QLID
2	Agricultural Wages	1.7525	FBMC
3	Tertiary Institutions	1.6873	QLID
4	Infant Mortality Rate	1.6570	QLID
5	Domestic Tourists	1.5431	MS
6	Population per Hospital Bed	1.5264	QLID
7	Population Served per Bank Office	1.4038	FBMC
8	Student–Teacher Ratio (Tertiary)	1.3523	QLID
9	Urban Workers	1.2968	FBMC
10	Urban Population	1.2840	QLID
11	Motor Vehicles per Person	1.2598	QLID
12	Gross Regional Domestic Product per Capita	1.1620	MS
13	Urban Population Growth	1.1543	QLID
14	Student–Teacher Ratio (Primary)	1.1519	QLID
15	Persons per Internet Subscriber	1.1117	QLID

Note: MS denotes Macroeconomic Stability; GIS denotes Government and Institutional Setting; FBMC denotes Financial, Businesses and Manpower Conditions; and QLID denotes Quality of Life and Infrastructure Development.

Source: Asia Competitiveness Institute.

Table 3.13: 2016 Top 20 Percent Weakest Indicators of Southern Region

Rank	20 Percent Weakest Indicator	Score	Environment
61	Budget Balance	–0.4241	GIS
62	Cultivated Land	–0.4735	QLID
63	Government Consumption Expenditure	–0.4920	GIS
64	Policemen per 100,000 Population	–0.51749	GIS
65	Secondary Industry, Value Added per Worker	–0.5540	FBMC
66	Expenditure on Education	–0.6948	QLID
67	Inflation (Consumer Price Index — Industrial Labourers)	–0.7622	MS
68	Expenditure on Science, Technology and Environment	–0.8528	QLID
69	GRDP Growth	–0.8832	MS
70	Motor Vehicles per km of Road	–0.9082	QLID
71	Public Limited Companies (%)	–0.9703	GIS
72	Inflation (Consumer Price Index — Rural Labourers)	–1.3664	MS
73	Old Age Dependency Ratio	–1.4255	QLID
74	Ageing Profile	–1.5872	QLID
75	Death Rate	–1.7363	QLID

Note: MS denotes Macroeconomic Stability; GIS denotes Government and Institutional Setting; FBMC denotes Financial, Businesses and Manpower Conditions; and QLID denotes Quality of Life and Infrastructure Development.

Source: Asia Competitiveness Institute.

region still has high death rate, high inflation, and low expenditure on science, technology and environment. The region has almost half of the value added per worker in the secondary sector as that of the Western region.

The region has developed a strong base for utilising its resources; however, to improve its GRDP growth, it has to take advantage of its coastal location and compete with the Western, Northern and Eastern regions in terms of boosting investment, both domestic and foreign. Expenditure on innovation should also be given priority to promote high value-addition manufacturing and trade.

3.3.4.5 *Western Region*

The Western region ranks first in the regional competitiveness ranking. It performs the best in all its top 15 strongest indicators among the five regions. Specifically, the region's merchandise export and total cargo handled are almost double of that of Southern region. It has the highest GRDP per capita, openness to trade (exports as ratio of GRDP) and gross capital formation. This might be due to the strong trade supporting framework that is in place in the region (Table 3.14), for example, it has the highest value added per worker (in secondary sector) and the highest overall labour productivity as well. Additionally, the region has the lowest illiteracy rate and unemployment rate. As a result, we can see that the region enjoys the highest wages and salaries (almost 20 times of that in North Eastern region).

Table 3.14: 2016 Top 20 Percent Strongest Indicators of Western Region

Rank	20 Percent Strongest Indicator	Score	Environment
1	Secondary Industry, Value Added per Worker	1.8956	FBMC
2	Openness To Trade	1.8536	MS
3	Exports of Merchandise Goods	1.8316	MS
4	Unemployment Rate (Urban Area)	1.7468	FBMC
5	Total Cargo Handled	1.7190	QLID
6	Number of Ports	1.5567	QLID
7	Death Rate	1.3306	QLID
8	Wages and Salaries	1.2701	FBMC
9	Illiteracy Rate	1.2658	QLID
10	Gross Capital Formation (%)	1.2407	MS
11	Cultivated Land	1.2367	QLID
12	Gross State Domestic Product per Capita	1.1909	MS
13	Bank Credit	1.1879	FBMC
14	Bank Deposits	1.1839	FBMC
15	Consumption of Electricity per Capita	1.1799	QLID

Note: MS denotes Macroeconomic Stability; GIS denotes Government and Institutional Setting; FBMC denotes Financial, Businesses and Manpower Conditions; and QLID denotes Quality of Life and Infrastructure Development.

Source: Asia Competitiveness Institute.

Table 3.15: 2016 Top 20 Percent Weakest Indicators of Western Region

Rank	20 Percent Weakest Indicator	Score	Environment
61	Policemen per 100,000 Population	–0.3482	GIS
62	Public Limited Companies (%)	–0.3744	GIS
63	Police Expenditure	–0.4034	GIS
64	Ageing Profile	–0.4040	QLID
65	Old Age Dependency Ratio	–0.4256	QLID
66	Expenditure on Science, Technology and Environment	–0.4672	QLID
67	Motor Vehicles per km of Road	–0.5837	QLID
68	Population per Hospital Bed	–0.7134	QLID
69	Expenditure on Education	–0.7668	QLID
70	Inflation (Consumer Price Index — Industrial Labourers)	–0.7973	MS
71	Government Consumption Expenditure	–0.9647	GIS
72	Urban Population Growth	–1.2239	QLID
73	Agricultural Wages	–1.2442	FBMC
74	Adequacy of Hospitals	–1.7947	QLID
75	Policemen per 100 km^2	–1.8151	GIS

Note: MS denotes Macroeconomic Stability; GIS denotes Government and Institutional Setting; FBMC denotes Financial, Businesses and Manpower Conditions; and QLID denotes Quality of Life and Infrastructure Development.

Source: Asia Competitiveness Institute.

Table 3.15 depicts that the region has high inflation, high old age dependency ratio, and a an underdeveloped health and education sector. It also has the lowest agricultural wages among all the other regions. The security profile as can be seen from indicators like policemen per 100,000 population and policemen per 100 km^2 can also be improved to enjoy a higher standard of living.

The region's average GRDP Growth Rate from 2000 to 2013 is second only to the Southern region, which has been experiencing an average growth rate of 6.8 percent (ACI, 2013), slightly higher than the 6.6 percent growth rate of the Western region. The three geographically large states with population of more than 10 million are Gujarat, Maharashtra and Madhya Pradesh. Gujarat and Maharashtra remain unequivocally the champions in the Western region, with 83 product clusters, 257 industrial estates and 32 notified special economic zones (SEZs) (Tan *et al.*, 2016).

The region has to focus on achieving higher GRDP growth; however, it should not come at the cost of its already existing primary sector. The region has ample land area to improve the production frontier for all the three sectors. Maharashtra has achieved high production in all the three sectors, and Gujarat has been hailed as the state with the highest total factor productivity in the agricultural sector (Tan *et al.*, 2015b). Madhya Pradesh is also focussing on attracting investment in the agro-based industries. Nonetheless, the region can improve further by revamping its existing infrastructure as well as developing their health and education sector to narrow down the income inequality and to promote its urban population growth.

3.4 Concluding Notes

To sum up, this chapter has undertaken a comprehensive analysis of competitiveness of India's five regions. Our empirical analysis reveals that the Western region ranks first in terms of competitiveness performance, followed by the Northern region which follows closely behind at second and then the Southern region which ranks third in overall competitiveness. It is interesting that despite the prevalence of so many Southern states in top 10 indicators of competitiveness in Chapter 2, as a region, the Southern region slipped to the third place this year from being at the top in 2015. The primary reason for this to happen is its relatively unsatisfactory performance in terms of macroeconomic stability which pulled its ranking down in 2016. However, it must be reiterated that despite the fall in rankings, the competitiveness scores of the Southern region are comparable to the top two regions which underlines that the disparities are not very huge between these three regions.

That being said, there is evidence of wide gaps that can be observed between the top three regions and the bottom two regions of India. A significant difference between the third and the fourth-ranked regions and the disproportionate gap in the overall competitiveness ranking across the five regions highlights the stark contrast in the regional development patterns of the country.

The analysis has brought to forefront the stark regional inequality prevalent among the five regions in India. While the issue of regional inequality is not a new phenomenon in India, the renewed policy emphasis of the new government to correct for such imbalanced regional development makes it important to gain a greater degree of understanding of what ails the different regions and how to overcome the aggravation of those problems. To that end, the competitiveness analysis done in this chapter assumes significance as it sheds light on the specific policy areas within each region that require immediate policy intervention.

The current policy of competitive federalism promoted by the central government has tried to shake off the policy lethargy that haunted the previous regime. While it is important to promote state-level competition to promote competitiveness, a healthy competition must take into account the respective comparative advantages of the states. Keeping this in mind, a state-level competition with inter-regional cooperation might prove to be a sustainable strategy in the long-run for India.

References

Asia Competitiveness Institute (ACI). 2013. *Technical Data Description Notes.* Singapore: ACI.

Bakshi, Sanchita, Arunish Chawla and Mihir Shah. 2015. "Regional Disparities in India: A Moving Frontier." *Economic and Political Weekly,* 1: 44–52.

Kar, Sabyasachi, Debajit Jha and Alpana Kateja. 2011. "Club-convergence and Polarization of States: A Nonparametric Analysis of Post-reform India." *Indian Growth and Development Review*, 4(1): 53–72.

Kurian, NJ. 2000. "Regional Disparities in India." Planning Commission Report, Government of India, available from planningcommission.nic.in/reports/sereport/ser/vision2025/regdsprty.doc (last accessed on February 17, 2017).

Minocha, AC. 1983. "Regional Disparities in India: Some Basic Issues", *Social Scientist*, 11(5): 51–57.

Nath, V. 1970. "Regional Development in Indian Planning." *Economic and Political Weekly*, 17(5): 242–260.

Rao, M. Govinda, Richard T. Shand and Kaliappa P. Kalirajan 1999. "Convergence of Incomes across Indian States: A Divergent View." *Economic and Political Weekly*, 34(12): 769–778.

Sanga, Prerna and Abdul Shaban. 2017. "Regional Divergence and Inequalities in India." *Economic and Political Weekly*, 52(1): 102–110.

Sarker, PC. 1994. "Regional Imbalances in Indian Economy over Plan Periods." *Economic and Political Weekly*, 29(11): 621–633.

Singh, Nirvikar, Laveesh Bhandari, Aoyu Chen and Aarti Khare. 2003. "Regional Inequality in India: A Fresh Look." *Economic and Political Weekly,* 28(11): 15–21, 1069–1073.

Singh, Nirvikar, Jake Kendall, RK Jain and, Jai Chander. 2010. "Regional Inequality in India in the 1990s: Trends and Policy Implications." Department of Economic Analysis and Policy, Reserve Bank of India, Mumbai, available from https://rbidocs.rbi.org.in/rdocs/Publications/PDFs/NSSD170510F.pdf (last accessed on February 17, 2017).

Singh, Nirvikar, Jake Kendall, RK Jain and Jai Chander. 2013. "Regional Inequality in India in the 1990s: A District-Level View." Working Paper Reserve Bank of India, available from https://pdfs.semanticscholar.org/71dc/9dfdf78cdc1bcb2fc90c5f1e5b5082dd652f.pdf (last accessed on February 17, 2017).

Stewart, Ross and Carlos Moslares. 2014. "Regional Disparities Across Indian States: Are the Trends Reversing?", *Journal of Economics and Development Studies,* 2(3): 95–111, available from http://jedsnet.com/journals/jeds/Vol_2_No_3_September_2014/7.pdf (last accessed on February 17, 2017).

Tan, Khee Giap, Linda Low, Kartik Rao and Kong Yam Tan. 2015a. *2014 Regional Competitiveness Analysis and a Master Plan on Regional Development Strategies for India: Annual Competitiveness Update and Evidence on Economic Development Model for Selected States of India.* Singapore: World Scientific.

Tan, Khee Giap, Kartik Rao and Ramkishen S. Rajan. 2015b. "How Productive is the Agricultural Sector across Indian States?" *International Journal of Development*, 14(3): 231–248.

Tan, Khee Giap, Kartik Rao and Sasidaran Gopalan. 2016. "Assessing Regional Competitiveness in the Five Regions of India." *International Journal of Business Competition and Growth*, 4(3/4): 1–28.

Discussant Note 3.1

Comments on "Competitiveness Ranking for Sub-National Economies and Five Regions of India"

Professor Pulapre Balakrishnan
Ashoka University, India

This is a timely study as the current ministry in India has been elected on the basis of the promises of faster economic growth and greater development all round. Two comments may be offered at the very beginning. First, the authors start by presenting their methodology for measuring competitiveness. The methodology is clearly laid out. However, I believe they take far too many indicators into account, 75 in all. This makes it difficult to draw focussed public policy conclusions from the study. Secondly, the use of a little more theory in approaching competitiveness would have helped. Consider for instance Michael Porter's work on what determines the competitive advantage of nations. Such an approach would be directly relevant for a study of regions as is this one.

Methodology

The 'what if' simulation by the authors is interesting but I remain unconvinced of its practical value. It relies on the assumption that other states do not respond to one of the group's trying to raise its lowest indicators to the group average. Moreover, I would have thought that members of a group would aim higher than the average in order to establish a competitive advantage.

A central part of the study is the Overall Competitiveness ranking of 35 sub-national economies of India. I am surprised by Uttar Pradesh emerging 6th in Overall Competitiveness in the study for it is among India's poorest states. I am particularly surprised by its emerging in 2nd place under the category 'Government and Institutional Setting', as in the public mind in India it is associated with poor governance. Unsurprisingly, however, Uttar Pradesh ranks among the lowest on 'Infrastructural Development'. In light of the above considerations, I believe it would be worthwhile for the authors to evaluate their methodology which yielded the result that UP finishes so high in the rankings for competitiveness when it has such poor infrastructure.

Competitiveness Webs

Maximum and minimum 'competitiveness webs' are presented for Maharashtra and Jharkhand, the top and bottommost states, respectively, on the overall competitiveness ranking. This is a useful exercise as it gives the backward region an idea of what is holding it back. For instance, the web shows Jharkhand to be very close to the median on almost all indicators. So, it has been dragged to the bottom for being handicapped on only a few indicators.

Quality of Life and Infrastructural Development

It would have been helpful to know how the scoring has been done with respect to the indicators 'Illiteracy rate' and 'Death rate' when scoring for the 'quality of life' environment. Next, two variables that I would like to have seen included when determining the scores for 'Macroeconomic stability' and 'Business conditions', respectively, are the 'public debt to G(S)DP' ratio and the ease of doing business. The first determines the capacity for public spending on infrastructure while the importance of the second for private investment should be obvious. The present government in India places considerable importance to the ease of doing business.

Ranking as an Exercise

The ranking of regions within a country is an important exercise but it may be more important for the evolution of public policy in India to know how its economy falls short of global benchmarks. So, you see, I am making the best of my time at Singapore figuring out how it works so efficiently!

Finally, the authors may want to check if investment flows in India are in accordance with the predictions of their ranking of the regions. It would act as a check on the validity of their methodology.

Chapter 4
Growth Slowdown Analysis by Income Thresholds for India's Sub-National Economies

4.1 Introduction

4.1.1 Background

Since the inception of economic liberalisation and reforms in 1991, India has experienced rapid economic growth. The average annual growth rate of India's Gross Domestic Product (GDP) over the 1991–2014 period was 6.6 percent.[1] Meanwhile, India's GDP per capita has increased from US$398 to US$1,234 in constant 2005 US dollars (US$) over the same period.[2] In 2014, India had the ninth largest nominal GDP in the world recorded at US$2.07 trillion. In purchasing power parity terms, India's GDP was US$7.39 trillion and the country was ranked third in the world (see Table 4.1). This remarkable growth performance has enabled India to graduate from the low-income group to the lower-middle-income in 2007 (Shrinivasan, 2010).

Although the proportion of people living below the poverty line has fallen over the past two decades, from 46.1 percent in 1993 to 21.3 percent in 2011,[3] there is still much work to be done to raise the standard of living of the people. One key challenge for the Indian government is therefore to sustain the positive growth momentums and at the same time allow more people to reap the benefits of economic development. Continuous efforts in pushing through reforms are therefore vital going forward as India's economic growth prospect is challenged both by external risks and domestic macroeconomic conditions.

Prime Minister Narendra Modi's new administration has raised expectations of a quantum growth in economic engagement as India liberalises its investment regime, improves ease of doing business and attracts foreign direct investment (FDI) in the pursuit of growth and development including the commitment to build 100 smart cities across India. The umbrella project of "Make in India" which aims to make India the "Factory of the World" and create 100 million jobs needs a strong foundation.[4]

[1] The average annual growth rate of GDP for India for the period 1991–2014 is calculated based on data from the World Bank's World Development Indicators.

[2] The GDP per capita denoted in 2005 US$ for the period 1991–2014 is obtained from the World Bank's World Development Indicators.

[3] Figures quoted are obtained from the World Bank's World Development Indicators and it measures the percentage of population living on less than US$1.90 a day at 2011 Purchasing Power Parity dollar.

[4] See Chapter 5 for more discussion on "Make in India" and the opportunities and policy challenges of this initiative, moving forward.

Table 4.1: Ranking for Top 10 Economies by Total GDP and GDP per Capita, 2014

Economy	Nominal GDP (in US$)		Nominal GDP (in Purchasing Power Parity Dollar)	
	Total (Rank)	per Capita (Rank)	Total (Rank)	per Capita (Rank)
United States	17.42 trillion (1st)	54,629 (8th)	17.42 trillion (2nd)	54,629 (8th)
China	10.36 trillion (2nd)	7,594 (73rd)	18.03 trillion (1st)	13,216 (75th)
Japan	4.60 trillion (3rd)	36,194 (23rd)	4.63 trillion (4th)	36,426 (24th)
Germany	3.85 trillion (4th)	47,627 (15th)	3.69 trillion (6th)	45,615 (14th)
United Kingdom	2.94 trillion (5th)	45,603 (17th)	2.52 trillion (10th)	39,136 (22nd)
France	2.83 trillion (6th)	42,736 (18th)	2.57 trillion (9th)	38,850 (23rd)
Brazil	2.35 trillion (7th)	11,613 (56th)	3.26 trillion (7th)	16,155 (64th)
Italy	2.14 trillion (8th)	34,960 (24th)	2.13 trillion (11th)	34,757 (25th)
India	2.07 trillion (9th)	1,631 (131st)	7.39 trillion (3rd)	5,833 (113th)
Russian Federation	1.86 trillion (10th)	12,736 (52nd)	3.75 trillion (5th)	25,635 (39th)
Singapore	307.87 billion (35th)	56,287 (7th)	452.69 billion (37th)	82,763 (3rd)

Source: Asia Competitiveness Institute's compilation based on data from the World Bank's World Development Indicators.

The major challenge for the Modi government is pertaining to its determination to reform the Land Acquisition Act, which is supposed to improve the livelihood of farmers. The reform, if successful, will facilitate the ambitious mission to build industrial parks and construct infrastructure projects including highways and railway tracks across the Indian subcontinent to reduce imbalanced regional development. Furthermore, employment creation is critical for the next stage of India's development as the country has to grapple with widespread underemployment and low woman labour force participation rate. Employment creation is especially important given that the country is tipped to become the world's most populated nation by 2025, over taking China's population of close to 1.4 billion people.[5]

Also, the Indian government needs more revenues and resources to improve the provision of important public services including affordable healthcare, education, housing and public transportation. Thus, having prolonged periods of consistent, good quality and sustainable investment-driven economic growth is paramount, especially as Prime Minister Modi is also pushing for improving ease of doing business across the sub-national economies of India. Nevertheless, the Indian government remains optimistic of the growth prospect of India and are ambitious to perform better. Mr. Arun Jaitley, Minister for Finance of India, expressed during the World Economic Forum in Davos, Switzerland that India's annual growth rate could reach as high as 9 percent under certain favourable conditions (Petroff, 2016).

Up till now, much work on growth trajectories of India as well as whether India is or will be experiencing growth slowdown and hence derailed from the national economic development for successful transition into upper-middle-income group has focussed on the country as a whole

[5] Data obtained from the World Bank's World Development Indicators.

(Rodrik and Subramanian, 2004; Ranjan *et al.*, 2005; Tsounta, 2014; Pritchett and Summers, 2014). Given India's regional diversity and variation in terms of Gross Regional Domestic Product (GRDP) per capita,[6] it is more appropriate if one analyses growth slowdown at the sub-national level. Our research therefore attempts to fill this gap by studying growth slowdown based on data of the sub-national economies of India.

This chapter provides a comprehensive analysis of growth slowdown for the India's sub-national economies against the backdrop of other developing Asian economies including the Association of Southeast Asian Nations (ASEAN) economies, the Greater China economies and the Indonesian sub-national economies[7] to inform policy directions. In other words, we investigate episodes where growth had hitherto been fast but has then slowed substantially. Our analysis covers economies at all levels of development, including low-income, lower-middle-income, upper-middle-income and high-income economies. For each income group, we construct a specific logistic model in order to identify the relevant determinants of growth slowdown. In doing so, we aim to answer two research questions. First, do determinants of economic slowdown likely to differ across income groups? Second, what are the probabilities that India's sub-national economies will experience a growth slowdown in the near future?

4.1.2 Understanding Growth Slowdowns and "Income Traps"

Economists have expended great efforts to understand the challenges to continued economic growth at different levels of development. Many have conceptualised the problems to growth through the idea of income traps. "Poverty trap" and, more recently, "middle-income trap" are common parlances in the development policy community. This section provides a brief review on the existing research on poverty trap and middle-income trap and seeks to distinguish our study on growth slowdown from these literature.

Much have been written about poverty trap. The literature on poverty trap is motivated by the observation that the very rich and very poor countries do not seem to converge in GDP per capita over time. Several studies in this literature have pointed out that the cross-country income distribution has become increasingly bimodal, with probability mass concentrated at the two extremes. (See, for example, Azariadis and Stachurski (2005); Quah (1993)). In other words, while a handful of countries have grown to achieve high GDP per capita, many others have continued to be stuck in poverty. Poverty trap is one of the arguments proposed to explain this phenomenon. According to the poverty trap theory, economies clustering around the lower end

---

[6] In this chapter, we use the term "Gross Regional Domestic Product" to refer to the gross domestic product of the Indian sub-national economies, the Indonesian sub-national economies as well as the Greater China economies.

[7] The Greater China economies include the mainland China sub-national economies, Taiwan, Hong Kong and Macau while the Indonesia's sub-national economies refer to the Indonesian provinces. We exclude certain economies from the analysis because of data constraints. In total, our study covers 107 Asian developing economies (see Section 4.5 for more details).

of the income distribution are beset with self-reinforcing mechanisms which cause the persistence of poverty. These self-reinforcing mechanisms are the so-called traps.[8]

Both the theoretical and empirical literature about poverty trap are well developed. The theoretical models for poverty trap suggest the existence of multiple equilibria and elaborate the ways in which "bad" equilibria of low growth and low income may be selected. According to Azariadis and Stachurski (2005), there are in general two "canonical" classes of models. The first model is called *historical* self-reinforcement, a process whereby initial conditions of the endogenous variables, such as the stocks of physical and human capital or technological progress, can shape long-run outcomes. The second is the *inertial* self-reinforcement hypothesis which emphasises the role of beliefs and expectations in selecting "bad" equilibria and the role of societal conventions, norms and institutions in perpetuating poverty by preserving expectations and beliefs. In terms of the empirics, there have been efforts to test for the existence of poverty trap (Bloom *et al.*, 2003). There have also been many studies which empirically examine specific trap mechanisms (Azariadis and Stachurski, 2005, pp. 339–340) or traps which occur at the individual or group level.[9]

In contrast to poverty trap, the term middle-income trap has only gained currency in academic and policy discourses in recent years. Over the past few years, a debate has arisen around the observation that there are countries which have attained middle-income status for an extended period of time but have yet been able to catch up to the high-income economies. Some authors, such as Gill and Kharas (2007), Felipe (2012a), and Aiyar *et al.* (2013) claimed that these economies have fallen into a "middle-income trap" while others, such as Im and Rosenblatt (2013) and Bulman *et al.* (2014) disputed the existence of such trap. More recently, Ye and Robertson (2016) concluded that if middle-income traps do exist, they are not very common. In fact, much remains to be clarified about the concept. As Gill and Kharas (2015) have noted, different authors define "middle-income traps" in various ways. Despite the lack of consensus about the definition and existence of middle-income traps in the academic literature, policymakers tend to be concerned about them nonetheless. This has motivated a rich body of research into factors which are key in helping an economy avoid being trapped at the middle-income level.[10]

Our research has important differences with both the poverty trap and middle-income trap literature. We focus on growth slowdown at different levels of development.[11] In other words, unlike the poverty trap literature, we do not investigate mechanisms and factors which hamper

---

[8] Definition is adopted from Azariadis and Stachurski (2005).

[9] For instance, Jalan and Ravallion (2002) investigate geographical poverty traps arising from factor endowments among rural households from post-reform rural China.

[10] See, for example, Yusuf and Nabeshima (2009); Felipe (2012b); Bulman *et al.* (2014); Zhang (2014); Kasenda (2015); Agenor (2015); and Gill and Kharas (2015).

[11] Our study classifies economies into low-income, lower-middle-income, upper-middle-income, and high-income economies. See Section 4.3 for details.

the ability of low-income economies to generate growth. Instead, we are interested in episodes of reversals in growth rate *after the economy has enjoyed extended periods of fast growth.* We feel that the focus on growth slowdown is more relevant for low-income economies of our interest in ASEAN and Greater China, India and Indonesia as the main challenge for these economies is not so much how to generate but how to sustain growth. Meanwhile, in contrast to most of the middle-income trap literature, we do not wade into the debate on the trap existence. Instead, our research sharply focuses on factors which may make growth slowdown more likely at the middle-income level. Regardless of whether the middle-income trap exists, policymakers in middle-income economies should be concerned with potential weaknesses which may cause their economies to slow down.

In essence, our study is in line with the budding literature focusing on growth dynamics which has emerged in the wake of Pritchett (2000). Pritchett (2000) observed that instability is a fundamental property of the growth series of developing countries as there were many upturns and downturns over time. Because of this instability, Pritchett argues, studies which focus on the long-term growth rates are unlikely to be able to offer any useful insights. Instead, it is far more important to examine the "hills, plateaus, mountains, and plains" — the various growth patterns — in the data series. In recent years, an increasing number of empirical research has emerged to chart this territory.[12] Works which are most similar to ours include Eichengreen *et al.* (2012, 2013), Aiyar *et al.* (2013), and Zhang and Puy (2015). The first three examined episodes of growth slowdown in middle-income economies while the fourth analysed growth slowdown in low-income economies. As compared to these studies, ours is more comprehensive as we analyse economies at all levels of development, including low-income, lower-middle-income, upper-middle-income and high-income economies.

4.1.3 Motivation and Expected Contributions

Our study makes several significant contributions. We are among the first to provide a systematic quantitative analysis on the issue of growth slowdown at the high-income level, on top of investigating growth slowdown for economies in other income groups. The subject of high-income slowdown has only begun to garner attention in public and policy discourses in recent years (for example, see Neumann, 2015; Dehn, 2014). Nevertheless, it is highly relevant. As Japan's anaemic economic performance over the past 20 years demonstrates, further development after an economy attained high-income status is hardly assured and the failure to address the impediments to growth can be costly. As such, high-income economies, as well as those who are about to progress into this income group, also need to be mindful of the risk of growth slowdown.

[12] Examples of such research include Hausmann et al. (2005) which studied factors that trigger growth accelerations; Hausmann et al. (2006) which studied growth collapses; Jerzmanowski (2006) which highlighted the importance of institutions in determining the probability of economies switching between different regimes of growth; Reddy and Minoiu (2008) which investigated real income stagnations; Aiyar *et al.* (2013), Zhang and Puy (2015), Eichengreen *et al.* (2012, 2013) which examined growth slowdowns.

In addition, our research enhances the understanding on growth dynamics of India's sub-national economies. Current research on growth slowdown and in fact, most of the empirical growth literature, have focussed on India as a whole in their analyses. However, national aggregates may mask the remarkable diversity between the different sub-national economies of India. The Indian sub-national economies are very different from each other in terms of their levels of development, as reflected by the great variations in their GRDP per capita.[13] As a result, they are likely to face dissimilar growth problems and challenges, which need to be highlighted and discussed.

Furthermore, as mentioned in Section 4.1.1, we benchmark India's sub-national economies against ASEAN economies, Greater China economies and Indonesia's sub-national economies.[14] We track their development progress and assess the risk of these economies experiencing growth slowdown. In doing so, we have created a dataset of internationally comparable data on real GRDP per capita for Greater China economies and sub-national economies of India and Indonesia. To the best of our knowledge, we are the pioneers in this respect as such data is not available elsewhere in the literature. Our dataset presents GRDP per capita in 1990 constant prices Purchasing Power Parity dollar data for 33 Greater China economies, 32 Indian sub-national economies and 33 Indonesian sub-national economies from the early 1990s to the presence. The dataset is reported in Tan *et al.* (2016b) for Greater China economies and Tan *et al.* (2016c) for Indonesian sub-national economies and while the method to obtain it is detailed in Section 4.4.1. The method can easily be applied to calculate the GRDP per capita in 1990 Purchasing Power Parity dollar for sub-national economies in any other countries, leaving great potential to expand our unique dataset.

Finally, our research has important policy implications. The empirical findings from our model specifications enable us to perform statistical predictions for each economy in our study on the probability of it experiencing growth slowdown in the near future. This probability can be interpreted as preliminary caution for national and local governments so that they could take targeted actions in order to minimise the risks of economic slowdown. Meanwhile, variables identified as determinants of growth slowdown by our models indicate areas where policy actions and supportive reforms are needed.

The rest of the chapter is organised as follows. Section 4.2 provides some stylised facts about the economic growth landscape of the Indian sub-national economies. Section 4.3 summarises existing literature on income thresholds classification, identification of growth slowdown, as well as drivers of growth and determinants of growth slowdown. Section 4.4 details the methodology adopted by our study while Section 4.5 discusses data description and sources. Section 4.6 reveals our empirical findings, followed by Section 4.7 which talks about relative strengths and weaknesses for each Indian sub-national economy based on our results. Lastly, Section 4.8 draws relevant policy implications for each Indian sub-national economy and concludes the chapter.

---

[13] See Section 4.2 for more details.

[14] For a more comprehensive discussion of the dataset, see Tan *et al.* (2016a, 2016b, 2016c, 2017).

4.2 Stylised Facts on the Economic Growth Landscape of India

In order to understand the transitions across various income groups for India's sub-national economies, which in turn gives us a better picture of India's position in the world, we have adopted an income classification approach which is based on the absolute level of GRDP per capita. The sub-national economies of India are categorised according to the thresholds proposed by Felipe (2012a). We classify economies into four groups, namely low-income if the economy's GRDP per capita in 1990 Purchasing Power Parity dollar is below $2,000; lower-middle-income if the economy's GRDP per capita is at least $2,000 but less than $7,250; upper-middle-income if its GRDP per capita is at least $7,250 but less than $11,750; and high-income if its GRDP per capita is $11,750 or higher. In line with the World Bank's income classification method, these thresholds are held constant over time.[15] As the GRDP per capita for all Indian sub-national economies is denoted in current values of local currency unit (i.e. rupees (₹)), the method on converting the original data collected into the required 1990 Purchasing Power Parity dollar will be discussed later in Section 4.4.1.

Tables 4.2 and 4.3 show the GRDP per capita (in 1990 Purchasing Power Parity dollar) for each Indian sub-national economy during periods 1993–2002 and 2003–2013, respectively. For ease of reference, the GRDP per capita for all sub-national economies is colour-coded with red representing economies in the low-income group; yellow for lower-middle-income economies; green for upper-middle-income economies; and blue for high-income economies. We are unable to track the economic growth for Dadra and Nagar Haveli, Daman and Diu, and Lakshadweep over the years as the GRDP per capita figures for these three economies are unavailable. Since Telangana was formed fairly recently in 2014, data limitation restricts our analysis to treat Telangana and Andhra Pradesh as a single economy. All subsequent mentions of Andhra Pradesh in this chapter will therefore refer to the combined state of Telangana and Andhra Pradesh.

Since the inception of economic liberalisation and reforms undertaken by India in 1991, majority of the sub-national economies have graduated from the low-income group into the lower-middle-income group according to the GRDP per capita thresholds that we defined above. As depicted in Table 4.2, only six economies were in the lower-middle-income group in 1993, including Andaman and Nicobar Islands, Chandigarh, Delhi, Goa, Maharashtra, and Punjab. The rest were in the low-income group. In the next two decades, transition of economies from the low-income group to the lower-middle-income group has occurred at a gradual pace where a gentle decline in the red shaded area is observed in Figure 4.1. This is reflected in the reduction of number of people living below the poverty line, from 424.2 million people in 1993 to 259.5 million in 2010.[16] By 2013, there were

[15] The World Bank's Atlas method takes into account inflation when defining the thresholds for various income groups annually, thereby ensuring the thresholds to remain constant in real terms over time. More details on the World Bank's Atlas method can be found at https://datahelpdesk.worldbank.org/knowledgebase/articles/378832-what-is-the-world-bank-atlas-method. (last accessed on February 16, 2017).

[16] According to the poverty and equity data published by the World Bank, India's number of people living below the international poverty line, defined to be subsisting below US$1.90 per day (in 2011 prices), has decreased from 424.2 million people in 1993 to 259.5 million in 2010. More details on the poverty data can be found at http://povertydata.worldbank.org/poverty/country/IND (last accessed on February 16, 2017).

Table 4.2: GRDP per Capita for India's Sub-National Economies (in 1990 Purchasing Power Parity Dollar), 1993–2002

Economy	1993	1994	1995	1996	1997	1998	1999	2000	2001	2002
Andaman and Nicobar Islands	2,522	2,697	2,657	2,825	2,961	2,540	2,596	2,615	2,694	2,957
Andhra Pradesh	1,232	1,315	1,376	1,431	1,413	1,552	1,626	1,768	1,824	1,873
Arunachal Pradesh	1,439	1,388	1,516	1,416	1,435	1,473	1,448	1,535	1,700	1,589
Assam	950	983	978	972	977	998	1,267	1,291	1,275	1,381
Bihar	490	493	416	503	478	501	596	650	616	659
Chandigarh	3,112	3,262	3,496	3,789	3,966	4,166	4,611	5,059	5,406	6,109
Chhattisgarh	1,134	1,113	1,106	1,147	1,186	1,202	1,268	1,159	1,257	1,317
Dadra and Nagar Haveli	NA	NA	NA	NA	NA	NA	NA	NA	NA	NA
Daman and Diu	NA	NA	NA	NA	NA	NA	NA	NA	NA	NA
Delhi	3,005	3,235	3,130	3,350	3,703	3,806	4,036	4,145	4,164	4,366
Goa	2,907	3,087	3,261	3,587	4,134	4,667	4,540	4,679	4,671	5,157
Gujarat	1,664	1,913	1,942	2,122	2,080	2,184	2,116	2,056	2,163	2,366
Haryana	1,862	1,957	1,984	2,162	2,154	2,201	2,395	2,593	2,748	2,906
Himachal Pradesh	1,303	1,419	1,470	1,564	1,652	1,826	2,246	2,405	2,502	2,649
Jammu and Kashmir	1,117	1,088	1,126	1,155	1,195	1,200	1,521	1,551	1,577	1,691
Jharkhand	1,040	1,035	1,014	996	1,201	1,201	1,251	1,120	1,154	1,190
Karnataka	1,288	1,343	1,420	1,513	1,571	1,725	1,854	1,914	1,894	1,944
Kerala	1,294	1,411	1,557	1,653	1,717	1,793	2,073	2,116	2,170	2,363
Lakshadweep	NA	NA	NA	NA	NA	NA	NA	NA	NA	NA
Madhya Pradesh	1,090	1,081	1,094	1,150	1,157	1,210	1,299	1,232	1,275	1,217

Maharashtra	2,007	2,050	2,232	2,320	2,330	2,276	2,498	2,442	2,501	2,626
Manipur	992	947	982	1,047	1,096	1,120	1,392	1,274	1,303	1,289
Meghalaya	1,176	1,146	1,224	1,227	1,278	1,358	1,526	1,612	1,713	1,727
Mizoram	1,431	1,317	1,490	1,554	1,494	1,499	1,722	1,844	1,943	2,056
Nagaland	1,500	1,505	1,490	1,478	1,520	1,377	1,459	1,650	1,770	1,942
Odisha	827	887	976	878	990	999	1,127	1,098	1,127	1,149
Puducherry	1,704	1,745	1,837	2,432	3,095	3,201	3,230	3,712	3,877	4,256
Punjab	2,094	2,113	2,144	2,250	2,293	2,391	2,681	2,869	2,899	2,874
Rajasthan	1,036	1,155	1,176	1,303	1,333	1,378	1,441	1,373	1,440	1,325
Sikkim	1,364	1,317	1,385	1,432	1,504	1,569	1,645	1,773	1,863	2,022
Tamil Nadu	1,471	1,579	1,629	1,717	1,856	1,943	2,066	2,189	2,116	2,155
Tripura	911	863	950	1,050	1,166	1,233	1,469	1,603	1,766	1,793
Uttar Pradesh	846	878	887	974	965	979	1,033	1,026	1,015	1,053
Uttarakhand	1,133	1,230	1,204	1,209	1,218	1,228	1,449	1,600	1,653	1,844
West Bengal	1,106	1,148	1,231	1,257	1,390	1,496	1,635	1,674	1,738	1,784

■ Low-Income (Y_t < \$2,000) □ Lower-Middle-Income (\$2,000 ≤ Y_t <\$ 7,250)
■ Upper-Middle-Income (\$7,250 ≤ Y_t < \$11,750) ■ High-Income (\$11,750 ≤ Y_t)
■ Not Available

Note: Y_t denotes GRDP per capita (in 1990 Purchasing Power Parity dollar) of an economy in year t.

Source: Asia Competitiveness Institute's calculations based on data obtained from the Central Statistics Office, Census of India (1991, 2001, 2011), the World Bank's World Development Indicators and the Total Economy Database (May 2015).

Table 4.3: GRDP per Capita for India's Sub-National Economies (in 1990 Purchasing Power Parity Dollar), 2003–2013

Economy	2003	2004	2005	2006	2007	2008	2009	2010	2011	2012	2013
Andaman and Nicobar Islands	3,197	3,925	4,173	4,847	5,348	5,908	6,424	6,109	6,603	6,834	6,805
Andhra Pradesh	2,022	2,247	2,404	2,635	2,980	3,297	3,371	3,709	3,974	4,117	4,227
Arunachal Pradesh	1,701	2,322	2,317	2,332	2,517	2,780	3,304	3,543	3,919	3,892	4,005
Assam	1,420	1,497	1,554	1,569	1,600	1,718	1,853	1,947	2,030	2,034	2,123
Bihar	629	685	674	757	788	922	955	1,061	1,176	1,285	1,354
Chandigarh	6,650	7,133	7,984	8,917	9,208	9,703	10,106	10,266	10,883	10,833	11,339
Chhattisgarh	1,477	1,694	1,755	2,029	2,250	2,547	2,366	2,533	2,844	2,959	2,990
Dadra and Nagar Haveli	NA	NA	NA	NA	NA	NA	NA	NA	NA	NA	NA
Daman and Diu	NA	NA	NA	NA	NA	NA	NA	NA	NA	NA	NA
Delhi	4,579	5,386	5,766	6,259	6,743	7,582	7,894	8,164	8,606	9,094	9,563
Goa	5,647	7,277	7,726	8,326	9,221	11,348	11,919	12,372	14,924	13,379	14,016
Gujarat	2,647	2,985	3,348	3,591	3,862	4,053	4,320	4,665	4,986	4,983	5,234
Haryana	3,128	3,370	3,569	3,902	4,255	4,808	5,351	5,564	5,929	6,150	6,323
Himachal Pradesh	2,749	2,994	3,161	3,281	3,429	3,956	4,201	4,499	4,762	4,939	5,030
Jammu and Kashmir	1,733	1,980	2,015	2,063	2,126	2,270	2,351	2,512	2,736	2,796	2,867
Jharkhand	1,249	1,634	1,548	1,570	1,820	1,783	1,854	2,090	2,069	2,099	2,156
Karnataka	1,991	2,370	2,603	2,803	3,102	3,351	3,325	3,623	3,750	3,924	4,182
Kerala	2,527	2,958	3,215	3,390	3,621	3,976	4,168	4,255	4,710	4,767	4,901

Lakshadweep	NA	NA	NA	NA	NA	NA	NA	NA	NA	NA	NA
Madhya Pradesh	1,356	1,387	1,421	1,528	1,580	1,811	1,899	1,961	2,114	2,274	2,472
Maharashtra	2,821	3,216	3,522	3,923	4,271	4,429	4,584	5,033	5,240	5,397	5,586
Manipur	1,371	1,641	1,696	1,677	1,710	1,745	1,763	1,736	2,170	2,026	2,058
Meghalaya	1,789	2,056	2,107	2,298	2,387	2,657	2,626	2,673	2,917	2,913	3,018
Mizoram	2,071	2,219	2,283	2,330	2,496	2,803	2,919	3,157	3,160	3,476	3,857
Nagaland	2,011	2,321	2,488	2,583	2,712	3,028	3,123	3,165	3,525	3,676	3,811
Odisha	1,333	1,590	1,630	1,813	2,142	2,321	2,327	2,531	2,645	2,751	2,716
Puducherry	4,389	4,298	5,514	5,293	5,405	5,476	6,052	5,711	5,912	6,113	6,884
Punjab	2,980	3,000	3,151	3,427	3,821	4,121	4,271	4,388	4,650	4,721	4,772
Rajasthan	1,569	1,671	1,731	1,922	2,026	2,252	2,353	2,671	3,041	3,134	3,114
Sikkim	2,157	2,468	2,657	2,683	2,898	3,520	6,089	6,573	7,341	7,817	8,302
Tamil Nadu	2,258	2,637	2,903	3,244	3,406	3,671	4,001	4,370	4,654	4,736	4,923
Tripura	1,905	2,104	2,174	2,243	2,255	2,444	2,529	2,625	2,736	2,828	3,020
Uttar Pradesh	1,087	1,164	1,218	1,291	1,362	1,484	1,587	1,625	1,726	1,786	1,783
Uttarakhand	1,922	2,174	2,450	2,785	3,217	3,693	4,241	4,498	4,882	4,911	5,041
West Bengal	1,902	1,964	2,030	2,144	2,284	2,461	2,622	2,718	2,913	3,036	3,228

■ Low-Income ($Y_t < \$2{,}000$) □ Lower-Middle-Income ($\$2{,}000 \le Y_t < \$7{,}250$)
■ Upper-Middle-Income ($\$7{,}250 \le Y_t < \$11{,}750$) ■ High-Income ($\$11{,}750 \le Y_t$)
■ Not Available

Note: Y_t denotes GRDP per capita (in 1990 Purchasing Power Parity dollar) of an economy in year t.

Source: Asia Competitiveness Institute's calculations based on data obtained from the Central Statistics Office, Census of India (1991, 2001, 2011), the World Bank's World Development Indicators and the Total Economy Database (May 2015).

Figure 4.1: Area Chart for Distribution of India's Sub-National Economies by Income Categories, 1993–2013

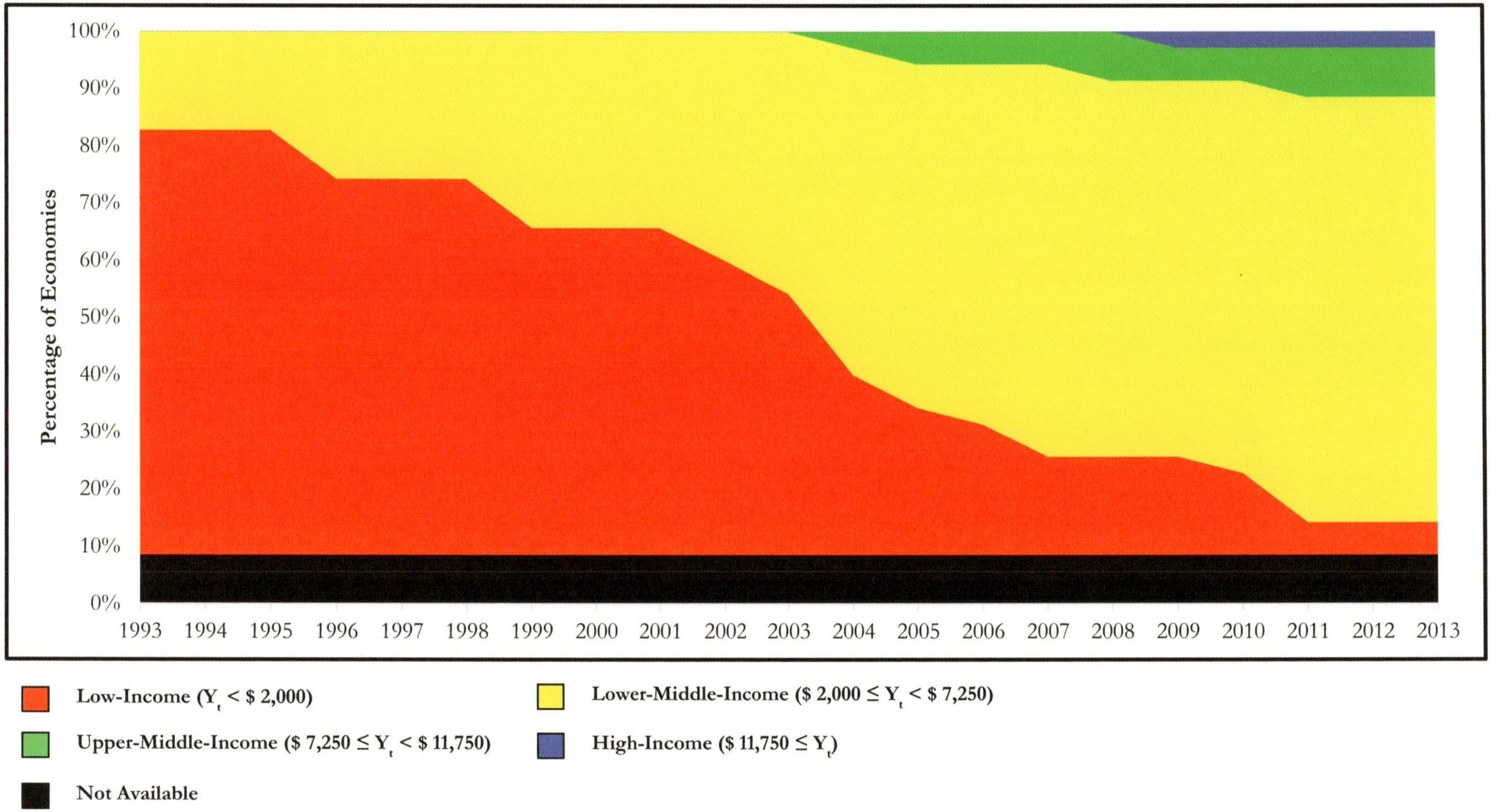

Note: Y_t denotes GRDP per capita (in 1990 Purchasing Power Parity dollar) of an economy in year t.

Source: Asia Competitiveness Institute's calculations based on data obtained from the Central Statistics Office, Census of India (1991, 2001, 2011), the World Bank World Development Indicators and the Total Economy Database (May 2015).

still two economies which were stuck in the low-income group, namely Bihar and Uttar Pradesh. Their progress in raising GRDP per capita has been slow over the years and if we assume that the economies continue on their current economic growth trajectories, it may take several more years before they can graduate into the lower-middle-income group. In particular, Bihar's GRDP per capita (in 1990 Purchasing Power Parity dollar) was $1,354 in 2013, far below the $2,000 threshold denoting the lower-middle-income group.

As the economies moved from the low-income to lower-middle-income group, we observe a continued rise in the number of economies within the lower-middle-income group. As illustrated in Figure 4.2, this number has increased from six in 1993 to 26 in 2013. However, there have been very few economies making the transition from the lower-middle-income group to the upper-middle-income group, with even fewer joining the high-income group. The first to graduate from being a lower-middle-income sub-national economy to an upper-middle-income sub-national economy was Goa in 2004. It was followed by Chandigarh in 2005, Delhi in 2008 and Sikkim in 2011. Apart from Sikkim, the other three economies were already in lower-middle-income group at the beginning of our study period (i.e. 1993). In comparison, Sikkim has achieved remarkable growth by traversing from low-income to lower-middle-income and then onwards to upper-middle-income within a short span of 21 years. Interestingly, these four economies that have relatively higher GRDP per capita (i.e. Goa, Chandigarh, Delhi, and Sikkim) are small in terms of population and land size,[17] indicating that the benefits brought along by the promising economic growth in these economies may not be widely enjoyed by most in India.

Out of the four economies that have successfully made the transition to the upper-middle-income group, only Goa joined the high-income league in 2009 and it has continued to grow since then. Hopes are high for Chandigarh to attain the high-income status soon as its GRDP per capita (in 1990 Purchasing Power Parity dollar) in 2013, at $11,339, was just slightly below the high-income thresholds (i.e. $11,750). In summary, as shown in Figure 4.2, there were two low-income economies, 26 lower-middle-income sub-national economies, three upper-middle-income economies and one high-income economy in India as of 2013.

For those sub-national economies of India which have transited from one income group to another during the period 1993–2013, they have only experienced upward movement, such as from the lower-middle-income to upper-middle-income group and then from the upper-middle-income to high-income group. In addition, most of the economies (78.13 percent out of the 32 economies) made only one transition during the study period with the most common movement being from the low-income group to the lower-middle-income group. Based on the 2013 GRDP per capita figures listed in Table 4.3 and the current economic growth trajectory, these sub-national economies still have a long way to go before becoming upper-middle-income

[17] Based on estimates by the Asia Competitiveness Institute, the populations of Chandigarh, Delhi, Goa and Sikkim in 2013 were 1,101,361, 17,567,772, 1,498,502 and 640,377, respectively, ranking (in ascending order) sixth, 18th, 10th and fifth, respectively among 35 sub-national economies of India. The land area of Chandigarh, Delhi, Goa and Sikkim as of 2013 were 114 square kilometre, 1,483 square kilometre, 3,702 square kilometre and 7,096 square kilometre, respectively, ranking (in ascending order) third, sixth, seventh and eighth, respectively, out of 35 sub-national economies of India.

Figure 4.2: Bar Chart for Distribution of India's Sub-National Economies by Income Categories, 1993–2013

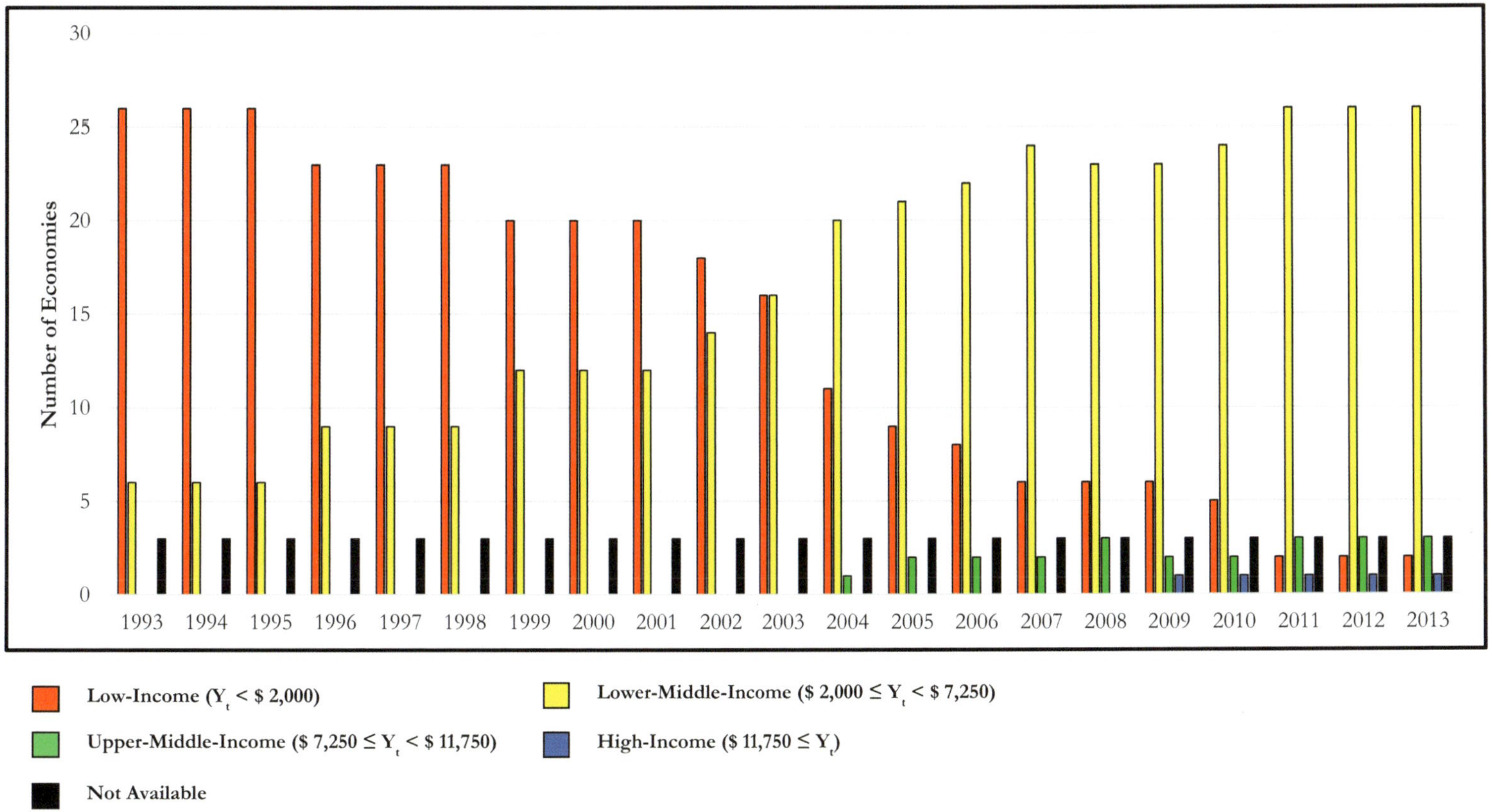

Note: Y_t denotes GRDP per capita (in 1990 Purchasing Power Parity dollar) of an economy in year t.

Source: Asia Competitiveness Institute's calculations based on data obtained from Central Statistics Office, Census of India (1991, 2001, 2011), the World Bank's World Development Indicators and the Total Economy Database (May 2015).

sub-national economies. We have also witnessed a handful of economies which have experienced astonishing growth in GRDP per capita where they moved across three income groups. They are Goa and Sikkim. On the other hand, there were five economies (15.63 percent of the economies) which have stagnated within their income groups throughout the study period, including Andaman and Nicobar Islands, Bihar, Maharashtra, Punjab, and Uttar Pradesh. Generally, sub-national economies of India have grown at a slower pace as compared to those in Greater China. In contrast to the one upward movement in terms of income group that most sub-national economies of India experienced, majority of the Greater China economies have made two transitions during roughly similar period. In other words, economies of India tend to stay longer in their respective income groups before graduating to the next one.

Table 4.4 lists the compound annual growth rate of GRDP per capita (in 1990 Purchasing Power Parity dollar) for India's sub-national economies during the 1993–2013 period. Sikkim achieved the highest growth rate of 9.45 percent while Jharkhand recorded the lowest growth rate of 3.71 percent. On average, Southern region has attained the highest growth rate of

Table 4.4: Compound Annual Growth Rates of GRDP per Capita (in 1990 Purchasing Power Parity Dollar) for India's Sub-National Economies, 1993–2013

Economy	Percent
Andaman and Nicobar Islands	5.09
Andhra Pradesh	6.36
Arunachal Pradesh	5.25
Assam	4.10
Bihar	5.22
Chandigarh	6.68
Chhattisgarh	4.97
Delhi	5.96
Goa	8.18
Gujarat	5.90
Haryana	6.30
Himachal Pradesh	6.99
Jammu and Kashmir	4.82
Jharkhand	3.71
Karnataka	6.07
Kerala	6.89
Madhya Pradesh	4.18
Maharashtra	5.25
Manipur	3.72
Meghalaya	4.83

(*Continued*)

Table 4.4: (*Continued*)

Economy	Percent
Mizoram	5.08
Nagaland	4.77
Odisha	6.13
Puducherry	7.23
Punjab	4.21
Rajasthan	5.66
Sikkim	9.45
Tamil Nadu	6.23
Tripura	6.18
Uttar Pradesh	3.80
Uttarakhand	7.75
West Bengal	5.50

Source: Asia Competitiveness Institute's calculations based on data obtained from the National Bureau of Statistics of China database, various provincial statistical yearbooks, the World Bank's World Development Indicators and the Total Economy Database (May 2015).

6.55 percent, followed by Western region of 5.88 percent, Northern region of 5.80 percent, North Eastern region of 5.42 percent and lastly, Eastern region of 5.10 percent.[18]

4.3 Literature Review

In this section, we review existing literature on works related to growth slowdown, including various ways of classifying economies into income groups and defining a growth slowdown episode. We will also discuss drivers of growth and determinants of growth slowdown used in other similar studies.

4.3.1 Income Threshold Classification

In current literature, there are two main approaches to income classification. The first is based on absolute levels of income. The World Bank's categorisation of economies into low-income, lower-middle-income, upper-middle-income and high-income economies based on the economies'

[18] The five regions of India are based on the regional classifications defined by the Confederation of Indian Industry (CII). Eastern region comprises the sub-national economies of Bihar, Chhattisgarh, Jharkhand, Odisha and West Bengal and the sub-national economies of Andaman and Nicobar Islands; Northern region comprises the sub-national economies of Haryana, Himachal Pradesh, Jammu and Kashmir, Punjab, Rajasthan, Uttar Pradesh and Uttarakhand and the sub-national economies of Delhi and Chandigarh; North Eastern region comprises the sub-national economies of Assam, Arunachal Pradesh, Manipur, Tripura, Mizoram, Meghalaya, Nagaland and Sikkim; Southern region comprises the sub-national economies of Andhra Pradesh, Karnataka, Kerala and Tamil Nadu and the sub-national economies of Puducherry; and the Western region comprises the sub-national economies of Goa, Gujarat, Madhya Pradesh, and Maharashtra and the sub-national economies of Daman and Diu and Dadra and Nagar Haveli (Tan *et al.*, 2015).

nominal Gross National Income (GNI) per capita exemplifies this approach. The World Bank adopts GNI per capita as a classification criterion because it is a useful and readily available indicator which is also correlated with other, non-income measures of welfare such as life expectancy at birth, mortality rates of children and enrolment rates in school. As of 2016, the World Bank defined low-income economies as those with GNI per capita of US$1,045 or less in 2014; lower-middle-income economies as those whose GNI per capita lies between US$1,045 and US$4,125; upper-middle-income economies as those with GNI per capita between US$4,125 and US$12,736 and high-income economies as those with GNI per capita of US$12,736 or more.[19] The GNI thresholds are adjusted for inflation and thus remain constant in real terms over time.

Felipe (2012a) also followed the absolute income level approach. However, the author proposed thresholds of GDP per capita in constant 1990 Purchasing Power Parity dollar. He first defined different sets of GDP per capita in 1990 Purchasing Power Parity dollar thresholds, where each set was made up of three different thresholds $t_0 < t_1 < t_2$. The t_0 distinguished low-income and lower-middle-income economies; t_1 separated lower-middle-income economies from upper-middle-income economies; while t_2 differentiated the upper-middle-income group from the high-income group. The three thresholds t_0, t_1 and t_2 could take different values at $250 intervals, where $\$1,500 \le t_0 \le \$4,750$; $\$5,000 \le t_1 \le \$8,750$; and $\$9,000 \le t_2 \le \$20,000$. Thus, for example, a set of thresholds might contain $t_0 = \$1,500$; $t_1 = \$5,000$; and $t_2 = \$9,000$ and another set may contain $t_0 = \$1,750$; $t_1 = \$5,000$; $t_2 = \$9,000$. In total, 10,080 sets were produced. Felipe used these sets of thresholds to classify all economies which the World Bank also classified over the period 1987–2010. He then calculated the pairwise correlation between the World Bank's classification and the 10,080 classifications using polychoric correlation. The set which yielded the highest correlation was selected as each income group classified according to these criteria was likely to retain the same underlying information (both income and non-income measures of well-being) encapsulated in the corresponding World Bank's income category. The author eventually selected the set with $t_0 = \$2,000$, $t_1 = \$7,250$ and $t_2 = \$11,750$.

Employing similar methodology as Felipe (2012a), Aiyar *et al.* (2013) also used the World Bank's GNI per capita thresholds as benchmarks to create income thresholds measured in GDP per capita in 2005 Purchasing Power Parity dollar. However, unlike Felipe (2012a), each potential set of thresholds in Aiyar *et al.* (2013) consisted of only two thresholds t_1 and t_2 ($t_1 < t_2$) where t_1 separated low-income from middle-income while t_2 distinguished middle-income from high-income. Both t_1 and t_2 could take a set of values at $1,000 intervals, where $\$1,000 \le t_1 \le \$3,000$ and $\$12,000 \le t_2 \le \$16,000$, creating in total 15 combinations. The authors eventually selected the set with $t_1 = \$2,000$ and $t_2 = \$15,000$ as the classification resulted from this set overlapped the most with the World Bank's classification. Clearly, as compared to Aiyar *et al.* (2013), the set of classification criteria in Felipe (2012a) provided a finer differentiation of the economies as it distinguished the lower-middle-income group from the upper-middle-income group. Furthermore, Felipe (2012a)'s thresholds were more precisely defined as the gap between each threshold was much smaller.

The second approach to income classification is based on relative levels of income. The Catch-Up Index (CUI) proposed by Woo (2012) exemplifies this approach. The CUI of an economy was expressed the percentage of the economy's income level relative to that of the

[19] See http://data.worldbank.org/about/country-and-lending-groups (last accessed on February 16, 2017).

United States in the same year. Countries were classified as high-income if their CUIs were more than 55 percent; middle-income if their CUIs were between 55 percent and 20 percent; and low-income if their CUIs were less than 20 percent (Woo, 2012). Fundamentally, classification based on relative level of income is problematic as it is subjected to economic fluctuations in the benchmark economy. For example, the CUI values of the ASEAN economies during the 2008 Global Financial Crisis and its aftermaths could have been artificially inflated. This is because, on the one hand, the United States experienced severe contractions in output and could only manage a slow recovery while on the other hand, ASEAN economies were much less affected and also recovered faster. As such, using CUI values to classify the ASEAN economies during this period risks mischaracterising (with an upward bias) their levels of development.

4.3.2 Growth Slowdown Identification

There are several definitions for growth slowdown in the existing literature. Aiyar *et al.* (2013) and Zhang and Puy (2015) characterised growth slowdown as "large, sudden and sustained deviations from the predicted growth path". These authors identified a country *i* as experiencing a growth slowdown in period *t* if the following two conditions were fulfilled simultaneously: (i) $\text{res}_t^i - \text{res}_{t-1}^i < p(0.20)$ and (ii) $\text{res}_{t+1}^i - \text{res}_{t-1}^i < p(0.20)$, where res_t^i is the residual of the country *i* in period *t* and *p*(0.20) denotes the 20th percentile of the empirical distribution of differences in residuals from one time period to another. Both authors defined $t = 5$. The residual res_t^i was defined as the gap between the actual growth rate and the predicted growth rate of economy *i* which was estimated based on a regression of per capita GDP growth against lagged income level and measures of human and physical capital. Condition (i) thus requires the difference of residual between period *t* and period $t-1$ to be smaller than the 20th percentile of the empirical distribution, indicating that the actual performance of the economy falls substantially below expectation. Condition (ii) requires the difference of residual between period $t+1$ and period $t-1$ to be smaller than the 20th percentile of the empirical distribution, thereby ensuring that the slowdown is sustained over a prolonged duration. This definition of growth slowdown requires estimation of predicted growth rates, which are difficult to be implemented in our context due to data constraints.

On the other hand, Eichengreen *et al.* (2012) defined growth slowdown as an episode where growth has hitherto been fast but has now slowed non-negligibly. The methodology, which was also adopted in Eichengreen *et al.* (2013), was based on the analysis of growth accelerations by Hausmann *et al.* (2005a). Formally, the authors identified a slowdown when three conditions were satisfied: (i) $g_{t,t-n} \geq 0.035$, (ii) $g_{t,t-n} - g_{t,t+n} \geq 0.02$ and (iii) $y_t > \$10{,}000$, where y_t is the GDP per capita in constant 2005 Purchasing Power Parity dollar in year *t*, while $g_{t,t-n}$ and $g_{t,t+n}$ are the average growth rate of the GDP per capita from year $t-n$ to *t* and the average growth rate of the GDP per capita from year *t* to $t+n$, respectively. In both Eichengreen *et al.* (2012, 2013), $n = 7$. Intuitively, the three conditions can be interpreted as follows. First, condition (i) requires that the average growth rate of GDP per capita of an economy to be at least 3.5 percent or greater before the slowdown. Next, condition (ii) identifies slowdown episodes when the average growth rate of GDP per capita declines by at least 2 percentage points, implying that the slowdown is non-negligible. Lastly, condition (iii) restricts identification of slowdown to those economies with GDP per capita that is larger than $10,000 (in 2005 Purchasing Power Parity dollar) as the authors wanted to rule out crises in not yet successful developing economies.

4.3.3 Drivers of Growth and Determinants of Growth Slowdown

Table 4.5 lists potential drivers of growth and determinants of growth slowdown based on various existing literature. The papers referred to in this table have empirically investigated the causes of growth slowdowns and key growth drivers of economies which might be income group-specific. Notable references include Aiyar *et al.* (2013), Eichengreen *et al.* (2012), Flaaen *et al.* (2013), Bloom *et al.* (2003), Jalan and Ravallion (2002).

4.4 Methodological Approach

In this section, we discuss our methodology. Section 4.4.1 describes the method through which we obtain GRDP per capita in 1990 Purchasing Power Parity dollar data for the economies in our sample. Next, Section 4.4.2 discusses the set of thresholds used to divide economies into income groups. Section 4.4.3 then describes what constitutes an episode of growth slowdown. Section 4.4.4 discusses the income group-specific regression analysis that we use to identify factors associated with the occurrences of growth slowdown at each level of development. When studying economies in the upper-middle-income and high-income groups, we also employ the Bayesian Model Averaging (BMA) technique which is outlined in Section 4.4.5. Lastly, Section 4.4.6 presents the approach taken to obtain predictive probability for each economy on its likelihood of experiencing growth slowdown in the near future.

4.4.1 Obtaining Gross Regional Domestic Product per Capita in 1990 Purchasing Power Parity Dollars

GRDP per capita of all economies in our study is measured in 1990 Purchasing Power Parity dollar. For the ASEAN economies, GRDP per capita in 1990 Purchasing Power Parity dollar is calculated by dividing GRDP in 1990 Purchasing Power Parity dollar data from the Total Economy Database, May 2015 version and Maddison (2010) to total population statistics reported by the World Bank. Meanwhile, GDRP per capita in 1990 Purchasing Power Parity dollar data for Hong Kong and Taiwan is obtained directly from the Total Economy Database.

However, data for the sub-national economies of mainland China, India and Indonesia are only reported in their respective local currency units. There is no existing database which compiles GRDP per capita in 1990 Purchasing Power Parity dollar for sub-national economies. Furthermore, there is no readily available conversion factor for 1990 Purchasing Power Parity dollar. Therefore, we take the following steps to obtain GRDP per capita data measured in 1990 Purchasing Power Parity dollar for the sub-national economies in mainland China, India and Indonesia.

Table 4.5: List of Potential Drivers of Growth and Determinants of Growth Slowdown

No.	Variable	Definition and explanation of the variable	Authors who use the variable
1	Size of Government index	This index measures the involvement of government in the economy. The index is made up of component indicators such as government investment and consumption spending, subsidies and transfers as a percentage of GDP, top marginal income tax rate and government ownership of enterprises.	Aiyar *et al.* (2013)
2	Rule of Law index	The index is made up of indicators for judicial independence, military interference in the rule of law, contract enforcement, the protection of property rights and regulatory restrictions on the sale of real property.	Aiyar *et al.* (2013)
3	Freedom to Trade Internationally index	The index is constructed from measures of trade taxes, non-tariff barriers, black market exchange rates and international capital market controls.	Aiyar *et al.* (2013)
4	Regulation index	The index measures the extent of credit market regulations, labour regulations and business regulations.	Aiyar *et al.* (2013)
5	Chinn–Ito Index for financial openness	The index is based on binary dummy variables codifying the tabulation of restrictions on cross-border financial transactions.	Aiyar *et al.* (2013); Eichengreen *et al.* (2012)
6	Total dependency ratio	Ratio of the number of old people (aged 65 and above) and young people (aged 15 and below) to the number of people of working age (ages between 15 and 64).	Aiyar *et al.* (2013); Eichengreen *et al.* (2012)
7	Old dependency ratio	Ratio of the number of old people (aged 65 and above) to the number of people of working age (ages between 15 and 64).	Eichengreen *et al.* (2012); Eichengreen (2013)
8	Young dependency ratio	Ratio of the number of young people (ages 15 and below) to the number of people of working age (ages between 15 and 64).	Eichengreen *et al.* (2012, 2013)
9	Fertility rate	Average number of births per woman.	Aiyar *et al.* (2013); Eichengreen *et al.* (2012)

10	Sex ratio	Ratio of total number of males in the population to the total number of females.	Aiyar *et al.* (2013)
11	Telephone lines per 100 people	Self-explanatory.	Aiyar *et al.* (2013)
12	Gigawatts of power generating capacity per 100 people	Self-explanatory.	Aiyar *et al.* (2013)
13	Length of road network per 100 people	Self-explanatory.	Aiyar *et al.* (2013)
14	Gross Domestic Product (GDP) per capita	Self-explanatory.	Eichengreen *et al.* (2012, 2013)
15	Pre-slowdown growth rate of GDP per capita	Growth rate of GDP per capita in the years preceding the slowdown.	Eichengreen *et al.* (2012, 2013)
16	Openness to trade	Ratio of the sum of imports and exports to GDP.	Aiyar *et al.* (2013); Eichengreen *et al.* (2012, 2013)
17	Terms of trade (TOT) shocks	Terms of trade is defined as the ratio of export price index to import price index. The specification of "shock" is based on the difference between the current value of the TOT and past values.	Aiyar *et al.* (2013); Eichengreen *et al.* (2012, 2013)
18	Commodity price shocks	Shocks in world oil price and food price.	Aiyar *et al.* (2013)
19	Ratio of gross capital inflows to gross domestic product	Self-explanatory.	Aiyar *et al.* (2013)
20	Ratio of public debt to gross domestic product	Self-explanatory.	Aiyar *et al.* (2013)
21	Banking crisis dummy	A binary variable which identifies if the economy has experienced at least one banking crisis (= 1 if yes, = 0 if no) in recent times.	Aiyar *et al.* (2013)
22	Financial crises dummy	A binary variable which identifies if the economy has experienced at least one financial crisis, of any kind (banking crisis, currency crisis, etc.) in recent times; variable = 1 if yes, = 0 if no.	Eichengreen *et al.* (2012, 2013)

(Continued)

Table 4.5: (*Continued*)

No.	Variable	Definition and explanation of the variable	Authors who use the variable
23	Inflation rate	Self-explanatory.	Aiyar *et al.* (2013); Eichengreen (2012, 2013)
24	Nominal exchange rate	Standard deviation of past nominal exchange rate over a certain past period (e.g. seven periods preceding the current one).	Eichengreen *et al.* (2012, 2013)
25	Real exchange rate	Self-explanatory.	Aiyar *et al.* (2013); Eichengreen *et al.* (2012, 2013)
26	Share of employment in manufacturing in total employment	Self-explanatory.	Eichengreen *et al.* (2012)
27	Share of total value-added from agriculture sector in gross domestic product	Self-explanatory.	Aiyar *et al.* (2013)
28	Share of total value-added from services sector in gross domestic product	Self-explanatory.	Aiyar *et al.* (2013)
29	Government share in gross domestic product per capita	Self-explanatory.	Eichengreen *et al.* (2012, 2013)
30	Investment share in gross domestic product per capita	Self-explanatory.	Eichengreen *et al.* (2012, 2013)
31	Consumption share in gross domestic product per capita	Self-explanatory.	Eichengreen *et al.* (2012, 2013)
32	Variables measuring the extent of diversification of the export basket	The extent of diversification is measured either by an index or the number of exports with revealed comparative advantage ratio (RCA)[20] ≥ 1.	Aiyar *et al.* (2013); Felipe (2012b)

[20] Formally, the RCA ratio is given by:

$$RCA = \left(\frac{xval_{ci}}{\sum_i xval_{ci}}\right) \Bigg/ \left(\frac{\sum_c xval_{ci}}{\sum_i \sum_c xval_{ci}}\right)$$

where $xval_{ci}$ is the value of country c's export of product i.

33	Variables related to the sophistication of goods exports:			
	33.1	Share of high-tech exports in total manufactured exports	Definition of "high-tech exports" follows the World Bank. "High-tech exports" are products with high research and development intensity, such as aerospace, computers, pharmaceuticals, scientific instruments and electrical machinery.	Eichengreen *et al.* (2013)
	33.2	Index of sophistication of goods exports[21]	The index is proposed by Hausmann *et al.* (2005b). The index is a weighted average of the sophistication level of each good in the export basket. The sophistication level of the good, in turn, is determined based on the assumption that goods exported by rich country are sophisticated.	Flaaen *et al.* (2013); Felipe (2012b)
34	Variables related to the sophistication of service exports			
	34.1	Share of modern service exports in total service exports	"Modern services" are supposedly impersonal, hence less labour-intensive and therefore more productive. The authors pick out five among 11 service categories reported in the International Monetary Fund's Balance of Payments data to be modern services: communications, insurance, financial, computer and information and other business services.	Flaaen *et al.* (2013)

(*Continued*)

[21] Formally, the export sophistication index for country c is given by:

$$Index_c = \sum_i \frac{xval_{ci}}{\sum_i xval_{ci}} * PRODY_i$$

where $xval_{ci}$ is the value of country c's export of product i, and

$$PRODY_i = \sum_c \left[\left(\frac{xval_{ci}}{\sum_i xval_{ci}} \right) \Big/ \sum_c \left(\frac{xval_{ci}}{\sum_i xval_{ci}} \right) \right] * GDPPC_c$$

with $GDPPC_c$ = gross domestic product per capita of country c.

Table 4.5: *(Continued)*

No.	Variable		Definition and explanation of the variable	Authors who use the variable
	34.2	Index of sophistication of service exports	An imitation of the index of sophistication of goods exports.	Flaaen *et al.* (2013)
35	Variables related to FDI:			
	35.1	Ratio of total foreign direct investment inflow to gross domestic product	Self-explanatory.	Zhang (2014)
	35.2	Foreign Direct Investment Regulatory Restrictiveness Index	The index is constructed by the OECD, at the sectorial (e.g. manufacturing, tertiary) and sub-sectorial (e.g. business services, communication) levels for national economies. The higher the index value, the more restrictive to foreign direct investment the country is.	Flaaen *et al.* (2013)
36	Growth rate of real gross domestic product of the world		Self-explanatory.	Eichengreen *et al.* (2013)
37	Gross domestic product weighted distance to other countries		Weighted sum of distance from the country in question to the rest in the sample. The weight is the percentage of the destination country in global GDP.	Aiyar *et al.* (2013)
38	Total amount of intra-regional trade (exports and imports to economies in the same region)		Self-explanatory.	Aiyar *et al.* (2013)
39	Variables related to the political conditions:			
	39.1	"Positive changes" — from authoritarian to more democratic	A binary variable which identifies if the country became more democratic in the preceding periods (= 1 if yes, = 0 if no). This is done by observing the change in value of the Polity Index, an index constructed by the Centre for Systemic Peace to measure the degree of authority of a political regime.	Eichengreen *et al.* (2012, 2013)
	39.2	"Negative changes" — from democratic to more authoritarian	A binary variable which identifies if the country became more authoritarian in the preceding periods (= 1 if yes, = 0 if no). This is the counterpart to the "positive changes" variable.	Eichengreen *et al.* (2012, 2013)

40	Wars and civil conflicts dummy	A binary variable which identifies if the country has experienced wars or civil conflicts in recent times (= 1 if yes, = 0 if no).	Aiyar *et al.* (2013)
41	Natural disaster dummy	A binary variable which identifies if the country has experienced natural disaster in recent times (= 1 if yes, = 0 if no).	Aiyar *et al.* (2013)
42	Fraction of country's land area in the tropic zone	Self-explanatory.	Aiyar *et al.* (2013)
43	Ethno-linguistic fractionalization index	Index measuring the probability of two random people in a country speaking different languages.	Aiyar *et al.* (2013)
44	Fraction of Buddhist population in total population	Self-explanatory.	Aiyar *et al.* (2013)
45	Spanish colony dummy	Variable = 1 if country was a Spanish colony in the past, = 0 if not.	Aiyar *et al.* (2013)
46	Variables related to the education level of the population:		
	46.1 Years of schooling	Average number of years of schooling for population aged 15 and above.	Eichengreen *et al.* (2013)
	46.2 Years of schooling at secondary and higher level	Average number of years of schooling at secondary and higher level for population aged 15 and above.	Eichengreen *et al.* (2013)
47	Scientific journal articles per 10,000 people	Self-explanatory.	Zhang (2014)
48	Latitude	Absolute value of latitude of approximate centre of country.	Bloom *et al.* (2003)
49	Landlocked	Dummy variable = 1 for landlocked countries and = 0 for all others.	Bloom *et al.* (2003)
50	Percent Land coastal	Percentage of land within 100 km of coast.	Bloom *et al.* (2003)

(Continued)

Table 4.5: (*Continued*)

No.	Variable	Definition and explanation of the variable	Authors who use the variable
51	Maximum temperature	Average maximum temperature of capital city in degrees centigrade.	Bloom *et al.* (2003)
52	Rainfall	Average annual rainfall in capital city in centimetres.	Bloom *et al.* (2003)
53	Homogeneity	Percentage of population in largest single group that shares the same ethnic, linguistic, and religious characteristics.	Bloom *et al.* (2003)
54	Proportion of villages that have a mountainous terrain	Self-explanatory.	Jalan and Ravallion (2002)
55	Cultivated area per 10,000 persons per km^2	Self-explanatory.	Jalan and Ravallion (2002)
56	Infant mortality rate	Infant mortality rate per 1,000 live births.	Jalan and Ravallion (2002)
57	Medical personnel per 10,000 persons	Self-explanatory.	Jalan and Ravallion (2002)
58	Proportion of population living in the urban areas	Self-explanatory.	Jalan and Ravallion (2002)

Source: Asia Competitiveness Institute's compilation.

First, GRDP data in current prices of local currency are collected and divided by the corresponding population data. All data sources are listed in Section 4.5. The resultant nominal GRDP per capita in local currency is then converted to constant 1990 Purchasing Power Parity dollar by multiplying them with a year-specific conversion factor, which is calculated as follows:

$$\textit{Conversion factor for Country C in year t} = \frac{\textit{Country C's GDP per capita in 1990 Purchasing Power Parity dollar in year t}}{\textit{Country C's GDP per capita in current prices of local currency unit in year t}}$$

where country C can be either China, India or Indonesia, depending on the sub-national economy concerned and year t spans between 1993 and 2013 which is the study period.

All sub-national economies of the same country therefore share a common conversion factor for each year. By doing so, we assume that the ratio of GRDP per capita expressed in 1990 Purchasing Power Parity dollar to that of in the current prices of local current unit for a sub-national economy is the same as that at country level. All data for national GDP per capita in 1990 Purchasing Power Parity dollar are retrieved from the Total Economy Database, May 2015 version while national GDP per capita in current prices of local currency units are collected from the World Bank's World Development Indicators.

4.4.2 Classification of Income Thresholds

To classify the economies into different income groups, we adopt the classification criteria based on the absolute level of GRDP per capita in 1990 Purchasing Power Parity dollar as proposed by Felipe (2012a). The classification thresholds are outlined in Table 4.6 and are held constant over time.

Felipe (2012a)'s thresholds are ideal for our study for at least two reasons. Firstly, the income thresholds proposed are defined based on GDP per capita rather than the GNI per capita. Although the World Bank's income classification, measured in current GNI per capita, is the most widely used to divide economies into income groups, it cannot be applied directly

Table 4.6: Income Thresholds Classification Adopted

Income Group	Classification Thresholds
Low-income	GRDP per capita < Purchasing Power Parity dollar 2,000
Lower-middle-income	Purchasing Power Parity dollar 2,000 ≤ GRDP per capita < Purchasing Power Parity dollar 7,250
Upper-middle-income	Purchasing Power Parity dollar 7,250 ≤ GRDP per capita < Purchasing Power Parity dollar 11,750
High-income	GRDP per capita ≥ Purchasing Power Parity dollar 11,750

Source: Asia Competitiveness Institute's compilation.

to our work as most of the economies included in our study are sub-national economies for which GNI per capita data are not available. Secondly, income thresholds by Felipe are obtained through finding the closest threshold values defined in terms of GDP per capita (in 1990 Purchasing Power Parity dollar) to those of the World Bank. This ensures that each income category still retain the same underlying information as their World Bank's counterparts.

Due to data constraints whereby we have insufficient observations to run separate regression analyses for the upper-middle-income and high-income economies, we have merg economies from these two groups into a single category, namely the combined group of upper-middle-income and high-income economies, when investigating potential determinants that are associated with growth slowdown.

4.4.3 Identification of Growth Slowdowns

Following Eichengreen *et al.* (2012), which is based on the analysis of growth accelerations by Hausmann *et al.* (2005a), we define an episode as a growth slowdown if growth has hitherto been fast but has slowed non-negligibly. Episodes of slowdown are isolated according to income groups because we suspect that determinants of growth slowdown at various stages of development may be different from each other. Other empirical works, such as Aiyar *et al.* (2013) and Bulman *et al.* (2014), offer evidence supporting this hypothesis.

Formally, a slowdown is identified when conditions (1) and (2) below are fulfilled along with one of the conditions (3), depending on whether the economy at time t is in the low-income group (i.e. condition (3a)), lower-middle-income group (i.e. condition (3b)), or combined group of upper-middle-income and high-income economies (i.e. condition (3c)). The three conditions are as follows:

$$g_{t,t-n} \geq 0.035 \tag{1}$$

$$g_{t,t-n} - g_{t,t+n} \geq 0.02 \tag{2}$$

$$y_t < \text{Purchasing Power Parity dollar 2,000} \tag{3a}$$

$$\text{Purchasing Power Parity dollar 2,000} \leq y_t < \text{Purchasing Power Parity dollar 7,250} \tag{3b}$$

$$y_t \geq \text{Purchasing Power Parity dollar 7,250} \tag{3c}$$

where y_t is the GRDP per capita in 1990 Purchasing Power Parity dollar in year t while $g_{t,t-n}$ and $g_{t,t+n}$ are the least square growth rate of the GRDP per capita from year $t-n$ to t and the least square growth rate of the GRDP per capita from year t to $t+n$, respectively. Mathematically, $g_{t,t-n}$ takes the following form:

$$\ln\,(y_{t-n+i}) = a + \ln\,(1 + g_{t,t-n}) * i, \text{ where } i = 0,1,\ldots,n.$$

In this chapter, we set $n = 5$. Due to the structures of conditions (1) and (2), this means that growth slowdown cannot be identified for the first and last five years of the study period. As our analysis covers the period 1993–2013, slowdown episodes between 1998 and 2008 are identified.

The intuitive interpretations of the conditions are as follows. First, condition (1) requires that the least square growth rate of GRDP per capita of an economy to be at least 3.5 percent or greater before the slowdown. Economies satisfying this condition are those with high initial growth rates. Next, condition (2) identifies slowdown episodes when the least square growth rate of GRDP per capita declines by at least 2 percentage points, implying that the slowdown is non-negligible. Lastly, conditions (3a), (3b) and (3c) separate the occurrences of slowdown by their income groups. For instance, if GRDP per capita for an economy satisfies conditions (1), (2) and (3a), the economy is said to have experienced growth slowdown as a low-income economy. On the other hand, if another economy's GRDP per capita satisfies conditions (1), (2) and (3b) instead, that economy is deemed to undergo growth slowdown as a lower-middle-income economy.

In any particular year t, we assign value 1 to economies for which a slowdown episode is identified. Economies which belong to the same income group but do not experience slowdown are coded as 0. In this way, we create income group-specific dummy variables representing the

Figure 4.3: Frequency of Growth Slowdown in Each Income Group for ASEAN, Greater China, India and Indonesian Economies

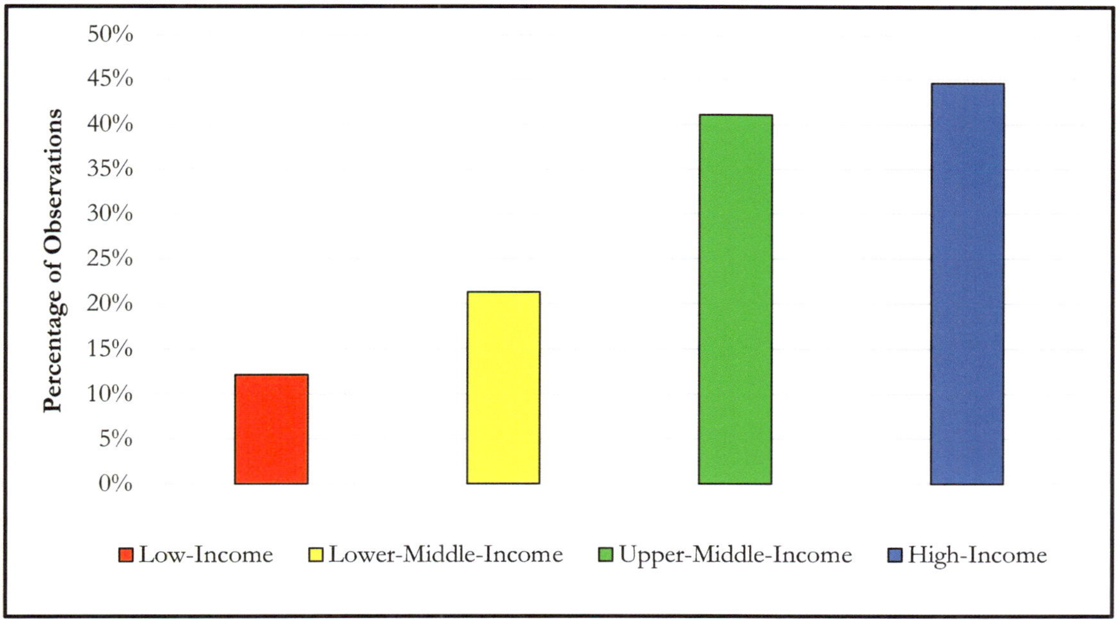

Note: Frequency of growth slowdown in each income group is calculated by dividing the number of slowdown occurrences by the total number of observations in that particular income group.

Source: Asia Competitiveness Institute's calculations.

occurrence (or lack thereof) of growth slowdown. These dummies will serve as the dependent variables in the regression analysis.

Generally, economies in our sample do not stay within a single income group over the entire study period. As a result, the slowdown dummies generated for an economy over the years may be treated as observations for analyses of different income groups. For example, during the period 1993–2002, Thailand was a lower-middle-income economy. It subsequently graduated to the upper-middle-income group in 2003 and continued to stay in that group until the end of the study period. In this case, the slowdown dummies generated using data between 1993 and 2002 contribute to the analysis of growth slowdown in the lower-middle-income group while those generated using data from 2003 onwards are part of the analysis for the combined group of upper-middle-income and high-income economies.

Figure 4.3 shows the frequency of growth slowdown in each income group in the sample as identified by our approach. As the economies move across the income groups from low-income to lower-middle-income to upper-middle-income and lastly high-income group, the frequency of slowdown increases.

4.4.4 Regression Analysis on Determinants of Growth Slowdown

Having identified growth slowdown episodes, we now turn to studying their determinants. We specify income group-specific logistic regression models using the slowdown dummy created as the dependent variable to examine the impact of various determinants on the probability of an economy experiencing growth slowdown. We are guided by economic theories when picking potential independent variables. In other words, we specify three models of growth slowdown: one for the low-income economies, another for the lower-middle-income economies and a third for the combined group of upper-middle-income and high-income economies. Regressors in our model include GRDP per capita (in 1990 Purchasing Power Parity dollar) as well as measures for demographic, infrastructure, human capital, macroeconomic conditions and exogenous factors. As robustness check, we have also performed probit regressions on the same set of determinants as those by logistic models.

When conducting the regressions, we also pool all the observations of the same income group from economies in ASEAN, Greater China, India, and Indonesia together. Although the regional traits are omitted as a result, this approach provides substantially more observations for each income group. Consequently, more precise estimates tend to be produced coupled with better probability predictive power of the regressions. Combining observations for economies from different geographical regions when running regressions to identify determinants of growth slowdown is a common approach in the literature. For instance, Aiyar *et al.* (2013) used annual data of 138 countries and segregated them according to income groups when performing separate regressions. Meanwhile, Eichengreen *et al.* (2012) estimated a single regression using annual data of countries with GDP per capita that are greater than $10,000 in Purchasing Power Parity dollar in 2005.

Since a relatively large number of potential regressors are examined in our study, model uncertainty is one major problem that we have to contend with. In an attempt to tackle this issue, we employ the Bayesian Model Averaging (BMA) technique which is discussed in Section 4.4.5.

4.4.5 Bayesian Model Averaging as Robustness Check

The BMA technique is mainly employed to solve the "open-endedness of theories" problem. This is a fundamental challenge with growth regressions, in particular, when determining which variables to be included in the analysis (Brock, 2001). Open-endedness means that with the validation of one economic theory or model of growth, it does not simply imply that the others are false. BMA offers an alternative by considering all possible combinations of variables and assigns each combination a posterior model probability of being the "true" model based on Bayesian inference (Benkovskis *et al.*, 2015). BMA techniques will not generate the "best model". Instead, it generates a posterior inclusion probability (PIP) attached to each variable which can be interpreted as the probability of that variable belonging in the true empirical model. In other words, variables with high PIPs are considered robust determinants of growth slowdown (González-Aguado and Moral-Benito, 2013).

We mainly refer to the work by González-Aguado and Moral-Benito (2013) to develop the theoretical foundation for performing BMA techniques. In particular, the following equation shows a generic form of an empirical model:

$$\Psi = \theta X + \varepsilon$$

where Ψ is the dependent variable which in our case is the slowdown dummy, X represents a set of independent variables, θ is the vector of parameters, and ε is the error term. Suppose we have K possible independent variables to be selected. In this case, there will be 2^K different potential models which seek to explain the data, y, or 2^K different choices of X, indexed by $j = 1, 2, \ldots, 2^K$.

Next, we specify a prior mean model size $\bar{k}$ excluding the dependent variable. This is the prior belief of the right model size before seeing the data. In our case, we set $\bar{k} = 3$. Each variable then has a prior inclusion probability $\bar{k}/K$, and for a model, M_j, with m variables ($0 \le m \le K$), its prior model probability is calculated as follows:

$$P(M_j) = \left(\frac{\bar{k}}{K}\right)^m \left(1 - \frac{\bar{k}}{K}\right)^{K-m}$$

By Bayes' Rule, we can calculate the posterior model probability as follows:

$$P(M_j|y) = \frac{f(y \mid M_j)P(M_j)}{f(y)}$$

Here, $f(y \mid M_j)$ is usually called the marginal likelihood. It can be calculated using the following equation:

$$g(\theta^j|y, M_j) = \frac{f(y \mid \theta^j, M_j)g(\theta^j \mid M_j)}{f(y \mid M_j)}$$

where θ^j is the parameter set for the model M_j. If we integrate both sides of the equation above with respect to θ^j and use the fact that $\int g\left(\theta^j | y, M_j\right) d\theta^j = 1$ since g is a probability density function, we can obtain the following equation:

$$f\left(y | M_j\right) = \int f(y | \theta^j, M_j) g\left(\theta^j | M_j\right) d\theta^j$$

Moreover, considering θ a function of θ^j over $j = 1, \ldots, 2^K$, then the posterior density of the parameters for all the models is as follows:

$$g(\theta | y) = \sum_{j=1}^{2^K} P\left(M_j | y\right) g(\theta | y, M_j)$$

By taking expectations on both sides, we obtain the estimation of the parameters,

$$E(\theta | y) = \sum_{j=1}^{2^K} P\left(M_j | y\right) E(\theta | y, M_j)$$

and the posterior variance is as follows:

$$Var(\theta | y) = \sum_{j=1}^{2^K} P\left(M_j | y\right) Var\left(\theta | y, M_j\right) + \sum_{j=1}^{2^K} P\left(M_j | y\right)\left(E(\theta | y, M_j) - E(\theta | y)\right)^2$$

Lastly, we can compute the posterior inclusion probability, or robustness, of each variable x by

$$posterior\ inclusion\ probability = P\left(\theta_x \neq 0 | y\right) = \sum_{\theta_h \neq 0} P\left(M_j | y\right)$$

Following Benkovskis *et al.* (2015), we identify variables as robust if two criteria are met. Firstly, the posterior inclusion probability (PIP) should exceed the prior inclusion probability. For example, if the total number of variables considered is $K = 17$ and the prior mean model size is $\bar{k} = 3$, the prior inclusion probability $= \bar{k}/K = 3/17$. So, in order for a variable to be deemed as robust determinant of growth slowdown, its posterior inclusion probability should be at least 3/17 in addition to fulfilling the second criterion. Secondly, the ratio of conditional posterior mean to conditional posterior standard deviation is larger than 1.65 in absolute value, which corresponds to a 90 percent coverage interval under Gaussian posterior parameter distribution. The mathematical representation is as follows:

$$\left| \frac{E(\theta | y)}{\sqrt{Var(\theta | y)}} \right| > 1.65$$

The two criteria need to be simultaneously satisfied for a variable to be considered robust.

In our study, we apply BMA techniques to the combined group of the upper-middle-income and high-income economies after logistic and probit estimations are conducted. The issue of model uncertainty is most acute in this case as growth slowdown in high-income economies is relatively unexplored in the literature. The BMA results are presented in Section 4.6.2.[22]

4.4.6 Obtaining Predictive Probability of an Economy Falling into a Slowdown

Based on the income group-specific models which link the probability of growth slowdown with the various determinants, we can compute the predictive probability of a particular economy experiencing growth slowdown in the near future by applying the relevant estimated logistic regression coefficients to the latest available data for that economy. This exercise enables us to identify high-risk economies which may require urgent policy intervention to help averting the prospect of slowing down. Since we set $n = 5$, the predictive probability of growth slowdown generated covers the next five-year period starting from the year which the data represent.

Formally, suppose the logistic regression model for a particular income group includes the variables X_1, X_2, X_3, and X_4 with their respective coefficient estimates being $\widehat{\beta_1}, \widehat{\beta_2}, \widehat{\beta_3}$, and $\widehat{\beta_4}$ and the constant is estimated to be $\widehat{\beta_0}$. If the values of the four variables for an economy in that income group in year t are x_1, x_2, x_3, and x_4 the probability p of this economy experiencing growth slowdown during the period from year t to year $t + 5$ is given by

$$p = \frac{\delta}{1+\delta}$$

where

$$\delta = \exp\left(\widehat{\beta_0} + \widehat{\beta_1}x_1 + \widehat{\beta_2}x_2 + \widehat{\beta_3}x_3 + \widehat{\beta_4}\, x_4\right)$$

Since δ is positive, p is strictly between 0 and 1. As the latest year with available data for all determinants in the logistic models is 2012, we are able to generate predictive probabilities reflecting the likelihood of growth slowdown during the 2012–2017 period. Economies with higher probabilities face greater risks of growth slowdown over these years.

The interpretation of a low probability number is less straightforward. Low predictive probability does not necessarily imply a bright prospect for the economy. For a slowdown to be defined in our methodological framework, we first require the least square growth rate of GDP per capita (in 1990 Purchasing Power Parity dollar) to be at least 3.5 percent in the five years preceding the slowdown period (condition 1 presented in Section 4.4.3). Thus, low predictive

[22] Asia Competitiveness Institute would like to express our heartfelt gratitude to Dr. Carlos Gonzalez-Aguado and Dr. Enrique Moral-Benito for sharing their BMA programme.

probability may reflect either of the two following scenarios: the economy is indeed a fast growing economy which is likely to sustain its growth momentums or that the economy's growth rate is low to begin with and is therefore not identified as experiencing slowdown by definition. In other words, it is possible that economies with low predictive probability suffers from stagnation, which is beyond the scope of this chapter.

4.5 Data Description, Statistical Computation and Sources

Our dataset covers 107 economies, containing nine ASEAN countries, 33 Greater China economies, 32 sub-national economies of India and 33 sub-national economies of Indonesia,[23] and spans the 1993–2013 period.[24] Following the methods outlined in Sections 4.4.1–4.4.3, we generate the growth slowdown dummy using data on GRDP and population. Various potential determinants of growth slowdown such as demographic, infrastructure, human capital, macroeconomic conditions and exogenous factors are also collected for each economy as the independent variables. Regression analysis is then conducted based on the independent and dependent variables collected in order to identify potential determinants of growth slowdown for economies in each income group. Annual data is used in this study.

As mentioned in previous sections, our analysis is conducted based on GRDP per capita data denoted in 1990 Purchasing Power Parity dollar. For the ASEAN economies, including Cambodia, Indonesia, Laos, Malaysia, Myanmar, the Philippines, Singapore, Thailand, and Vietnam, we are able to collect the data on GRDP in 1990 Purchasing Power Parity dollar directly from the Total Economy Database, May 2015 version.[25] GRDP per capita in 1990 Purchasing Power Parity dollar is therefore obtained by dividing the GRDP (in 1990 Purchasing Power Parity dollar) for each economy in each year with the corresponding total population number for the year. We use the population statistics published in the World Bank's World Development Indicators.

For Hong Kong and Taiwan, we collect GRDP per capita in 1990 Purchasing Power Parity dollar directly from the Total Economy Database, May 2015 version. As for the 31 mainland China economies, we first collect nominal GRDP in yuan and then divide the GRDP data by the total population in order to obtain each economy's nominal GRDP per capita in yuan.

[23] The nine ASEAN economies included in our study are Cambodia, Indonesia, Laos, Malaysia, Myanmar, the Philippines, Singapore, Thailand, and Vietnam. The 33 Greater China economies covered in our study are the 31 mainland China sub-national economies, Hong Kong and Taiwan. The 32 sub-national economies of India included in our study are all the sub-national economies of India excluding Dadra and Nagar Haveli, Daman and Diu, and Lakshadweep. As mentioned in Section 4.2, Andhra Pradesh and Telangana are treated as a single economy using the name Andhra Pradesh. The 33 sub-national economies of Indonesia refer to all the sub-national economies of Indonesia.

[24] Unlike the rest of the economies, data for Laos are available from 1993 to 2008 only.

[25] All GRDP data for the economies listed above are obtained from the Total Economy Database, May 2015 version (The Conference Board, 2015) except for Laos, which are unavailable in the database and are therefore retrieved from the Maddison (2010).

The nominal GRDP data (in yuan) is collected from various provincial statistical yearbooks and from the website of the National Bureau of Statistics of China, while the population data are from the China Population and Employment Statistics Yearbook 2013, the China Statistical Yearbook 2014 and from the website of the National Bureau of Statistics of China. GRDP per capita in 1990 Purchasing Power Parity dollar is then calculated using method described in Section 4.4.1.

Likewise, for the sub-national economies of India, we first collect nominal GRDP in current rupees (₹) and then divide the data by the total population to obtain each economy's nominal GRDP per capita (in ₹). The nominal GRDP data (in ₹) for the economies in India are retrieved from the website of the Ministry of Statistics and Programme Implementation (MOSPI), Central Statistics Office while the population data in census years (1991, 2001 and 2011) are collected from the Census of India. Population data for all other years during the 1993–2013 period are estimated based on census data. The conversion of nominal GRDP per capita data in rupees (₹) to that in 1990 Purchasing Power Parity dollar follows the procedure outlined in Section 4.4.1.

For sub-national economies of Indonesia, the GRDP per capita in 1990 Purchasing Power Parity dollar data are prepared in similar way as that for the 31 mainland China economies and the sub-national economies of India. The nominal GRDP data (in rupiahs) are collected from the World Bank Indo-Dapoer and PDRB Menurut Penggunaan while the population data are from the World Bank Indo-Dapoer. For the seven new Indonesian sub-national economies created after 1993, namely Maluku Utara, Papua Barat, Banten, Kepulauan Bangka Belitung, Gorontalo, Kepulauan Riau, and Sulawesi Barat, we have backtracked their GRDP and population data until 1990.[26] We first calculate the ratios of the data between the newly created sub-national economies and the sub-national economies which it was formed from and then fit an exponential trend on the ratios. The GRDP and population data between 1993 and the year of bifurcation are then estimated based on the fitted exponential trend.

Our study examines different potential determinants of growth slowdown for economies in the context of different income groups, ranging from dependency ratios, openness to trade, exchange rates, world's GDP growth rate, employment structure, literacy rate, economic structure, productivity, infrastructure and government consumption expenditure. Ideally, many other explanatory variables should be considered as reviewed in Section 4.3.3. However, working on sub-national economies in Greater China, India and Indonesia and the countries of ASEAN over the span of two decades demands consistency in definition of indicators, which implies inevitable data gaps. We have also included some other potential determinants of growth slowdown which are important but not used in existing works, including productivity measures of the primary, secondary and tertiary industries. Table 4.7 summarises the list of potential independent variables we consider with details on the units and sources of data for economies in the various regions.

[26] Maluku Utara was created out of Maluku on October 4th, 1999; Papua Barat was created out of Papua on October 4th, 1999; Banten was created out of Jawa Barat on October 17th, 2000; Kepulauan Bangka Belitung was created out of Sumatera Selatan on December 4th, 2000; Gorontalo was created out of Sulawesi Utara on December 22nd, 2000; Kepulauan Riau was created out of Riau on October 25th, 2002; and Sulawesi Barat was created out of Sulawesi Selatan on October 5th, 2004.

Table 4.7: Unit and Data Sources for Independent Variables

<table>
<tr><th rowspan="2">No.</th><th rowspan="2">Independent Variables</th><th rowspan="2">Unit</th><th colspan="4">Data Sources</th></tr>
<tr><th>ASEAN</th><th>Greater China</th><th>India</th><th>Indonesia</th></tr>
<tr><td>1</td><td>Total Dependency Ratio</td><td>Percent</td>
<td rowspan="9">• Abbas et al. (2010)
• Barro and Lee (2013)
• Bluedorn et al. (2013)
• Centre for Research on the Epidemiology of Disaster, The International Disaster Database
• Euromonitor International, Global Market Information Database
• Fraser Institute, Economic Freedom of the World database</td>
<td rowspan="9">• Almanac of China's Population
• China Compendium of Statistics 1949–2008
• China Energy Statistical Yearbook
• China Population and Employment Statistical Yearbook
• China Statistical Yearbook
• China Statistical Yearbook on Science and Technology</td>
<td rowspan="9">• CEIC database
• Census of India: 1991, 2001 and 2011
• Centre for Monitoring Indian Economy Pvt. Ltd. (CMIE): States of India database
• Indiastat
• Ministry of Statistics and Programme Implementation (MOSPI), Central Statistics Office
• Ministry of Statistics and Programme Implementation (MOSPI), National Sample Survey Office</td>
<td rowspan="9">• CEIC Database
• Indikator Kesejahteraan Rakyat
• Investment Coordinating Board (BKPM)
• Keuangan Pemerintah Provinsi
• PDRB Menurut Penggunaan
• PDRB Provinsi Menurut Lapangan Usaha
• Proyeksi Penduduk Indonesia
• Statistik Indonesia</td></tr>
<tr><td>2</td><td>Old Dependency Ratio</td><td>Percent</td></tr>
<tr><td>3</td><td>Young Dependency Ratio</td><td>Percent</td></tr>
<tr><td>4</td><td>Openness To Trade</td><td>Percent of GRDP</td></tr>
<tr><td>5</td><td>Percentage Change in Nominal Exchange Rate</td><td>Percent</td></tr>
<tr><td>6</td><td>World Gross Domestic Product Real Growth Rate</td><td>Percent</td></tr>
<tr><td>7</td><td>Foreign Direct Investment Inflows as Percent of GRDP</td><td>Percent of GRDP</td></tr>
<tr><td>8</td><td>Employment in Primary Industry as Percent of Total Employment</td><td>Percent of Total Employment</td></tr>
<tr><td>9</td><td>Employment in Secondary Industry as Percent of Total Employment</td><td>Percent of Total Employment</td></tr>
</table>

10	Employment in Tertiary Industry as Percent of Total Employment	Percent of Total Employment	• International Labour Organisation, Key Indicators of the Labour Market, 8th Edition • International Monetary Fund, World Economic Outlook Database, April 2015 • Maddison (2010) • The Conference Board, Total Economy Database, May 2015 version • United Nations Conference on Trade and Development • World Bank, World Development Indicators	• Global Market Information Database (GMID) • Hong Kong Annual Digest • Provincial Statistical Yearbook • Statistical Yearbook of the Chinese Investment in Fixed Assets • Taiwan Statistical Yearbook • Taiwan Statistical Data Book • The Conference Board, Total Economy Database, May 2015 version • World Bank, World Development Indicators	• The Conference Board, Total Economy Database, May 2015 version • World Bank, World Development Indicators	• Statistik Kesejahteraan Rakyat • Statistik Keuangan Pemerintah Provinsi • Statistik Perhubungan • Statistik Perhubungan • Statistik Transportasi • The Conference Board, Total Economy Database, May 2015 version • World Bank Indo-Dapoer • World Bank, World Development Indicators
11	Literacy Rate	Percent				
12	Overall Productivity	Constant 1990 Purchasing Power Parity dollar				
13	Primary Industry Value Added per Worker	Constant 1990 Purchasing Power Parity dollar				
14	Secondary Industry Value Added per Worker	Constant 1990 Purchasing Power Parity dollar				
15	Tertiary Industry Value Added per Worker	Constant 1990 Purchasing Power Parity dollar				
16	Length of Road	Kilometre				
17	Road Density	Kilometre per Square Kilometre				
18	Length of Road per Capita	Kilometre per 10,000 People				
19	Primary Industry Value Added as Percent of GRDP	Percent of GRDP				
20	Secondary Industry Value Added as Percent of GRDP	Percent of GRDP				
21	Tertiary Industry Value Added as Percent of GRDP	Percent of GRDP				
22	Government Consumption Expenditure as Percent of GRDP	Percent of GRDP				

Source: Asia Competitiveness Institute's compilation.

For certain independent variables which have a few years of missing data and display a clear linear trend, we employ linear interpolation or extrapolation to fill in the missing data. In the case whereby all the economies of the same region do not have data for the earlier years of the study period, we conduct estimation based on the exponential trend of available data.

In our dataset, there are a few sub-national economies which are created during the study period. For India, three bifurcations occurred during the study period: Chhattisgarh was separated from Madhya Pradesh on November 1, 2000, Uttarakhand (formerly known as Uttaranchal) was created from Uttar Pradesh on November 9, 2000, and Jharkhand was carved out of Bihar on November 15, 2000. Data for these three newly created economies are missing before 2000 for a few independent variables. For these missing data, we first calculate the ratios of the data between the newly created sub-national economy and the sub-national economy which it was formed from and then fit an exponential trend on the ratios. Data between 1993 and 2000 are then estimated based on the fitted exponential trend.

4.6 Empirical Findings

4.6.1 Determinants of Growth Slowdown by Income Thresholds

Table 4.8 summarises our research findings on determinants that are strongly associated with growth slowdown in the low-income group, lower-middle-income group and combined group of upper-middle-income and high-income economies. These results are generated by employing logistic regression model. In all three models, we employ GRDP per capita (in 1990 Purchasing Power Parity dollar) as a control variable to guard against omitted variable bias.

As illustrated in Table 4.8, growth slowdown in low-income group is mainly associated with the level of GRDP per capita, literacy rate, foreign direct investment inflows as percentage of GRDP, and length of road per capita with the first two determinants being significant at the 5 percent level, while the last two at 10 percent level.

On the other hand, growth slowdown in the lower-middle-income group is associated with the level of GRDP per capita, foreign direct investment inflows as percentage of GRDP, old dependency ratio, employment in tertiary industry as percentage of total employment, and literacy rate with the first three determinants being significant at 1 percent level, employment in tertiary industry as percentage of total employment at 5 percent level, and literacy rate at 10 percent level.

Meanwhile, growth slowdown in the combined group of upper-middle-income and high-income economies is associated with GRDP per capita, openness to trade, literacy rate, employment in tertiary industry as percentage of total employment, and secondary industry value added per worker with the first two determinants being significant at 1 percent level while the last three determinants are significant at 5 percent level. The next few paragraphs discuss each determinant in the three models, with the exception of the control variable GRDP per capita, in further detail. It is worth noting that some determinants are associated with the occurrence of growth slowdown in more than one income group.

Table 4.8: Determinants of Growth Slowdown for the Low-Income Group, Lower-Middle-Income Group and the Combined Group of Upper-Middle-Income and High-Income Economies, Logistic Model

	Growth Slowdown Models		
Income Groups	**Low-Income**	**Lower-Middle-Income**	**Combined Group of Upper-Middle-Income and High-Income Economies**
GRDP per Capita	0.0013** (0.0005)	0.0005*** (0.0001)	0.0003*** (0.0001)
Literacy Rate	–0.0304** (0.0133)	–0.0197* (0.0114)	–0.1481** (0.0597)
Foreign Direct Investment Inflows as Percent of GRDP	–0.5082* (0.2629)	–0.1935*** (0.0523)	
Length of Road per Capita	–0.0126* (0.0072)		
Employment in Tertiary Industry as Percent of Total Employment		–0.0287** (0.0115)	–0.0426** (0.0172)
Old Dependency Ratio		0.0750*** (0.0287)	
Openness To Trade			–0.0091*** (0.0030)
Secondary Industry Value Added per Worker			–0.00002** (7.89 e^{-6})
Constant	–1.0075 (1.0799)	–0.9246 (1.0452)	14.5001*** (5.5816)
No. of Observations	358	667	147
Pseudo R^2	0.0680	0.0876	0.1215

Note: Numbers in the parentheses are standard errors. *, ** and *** denote the coefficient is significant at 10 percent level, 5 percent level and 1 percent level, respectively.
Source: Asia Competitiveness Institute's calculations.

Literacy rate appears as a significant variable in growth slowdown models for all three income groups, including the low-income group, lower-middle-income group, and the combined group of upper-middle-income and high-income economies. The signs of the coefficients are consistently negative, indicating that literacy is negatively associated with the probability of slowdown in all income groups. Basic literacy is the prerequisite for further educational attainment, and it facilitates and enables learning throughout a person's lifecycle after becoming literate. Thus, high literacy rate is necessary for an economy to achieve a high degree of human capital accumulation which is important for sustaining growth.

Foreign direct investment inflows as percentage of GRDP is a significant variable in the slowdown model for the low-income and lower-middle-income economies. The signs of the coefficients in both models are negative, indicating an inverse relation between foreign direct investment inflows and the probability of slowdown for economies in the low-income and lower-middle-income groups. The result is intuitive. The influx of capital through foreign direct investment increases capital accumulation in the host economy. More importantly, foreign direct investment promotes technological development through technological transfer and diffusion. It may also help augment managerial expertise in the host economy. Thus, foreign direct investment is an important driver of continued growth in low-income and lower-middle-income economies as growth in these economies is usually hampered by capital inadequacies and technological backwardness.

Length of road per capita appears as a significant determinant of growth slowdown for the low-income group. The negative sign of the coefficient points to an inverse relation between road per capita and the probability of low-income economies experiencing growth slowdown. This result suggests that basic infrastructure development is important for low-income economies to sustain growth. Improving road networks and transport infrastructure in general grants producers in low-income economies access to new markets. At the same time, it also connects firms from more developed regions to labour in low-income economies, creating more opportunities for growth.

Employment in tertiary industry as percentage of total employment is a significant variable in the slowdown models for lower-middle-income economies as well as the upper-middle- and high-income economies. The sign of the coefficients is consistently negative, indicating an inverse relation between employment in tertiary industry and the probability of slowdown for these economies. As an economy progresses, it becomes increasingly hard to sustain growth through exporting manufacturing products. This is because the economy slowly loses its cost advantage to less developed competitors. Thus, it is important for more advanced economies to diversify into the tertiary sector so that they can move up the value chain and create more opportunities for sustainable growth. Furthermore, certain high value added industries such as research and development, financial services and consultancy services also help boost the potentials, productivity and performance of other sectors and industries of the economy.

Old age dependency ratio is positively associated with the probability of growth slowdown for lower-middle-income economies. A high old dependency ratio means that the labour force has to support a higher number of elderlies. With fewer people of working age, the pool of productive labour shrinks. Furthermore, a smaller working-age population also means less domestic resources for productive investments as this group tends to save while the older population tends to dissave. Economies with high old dependency ratio are thus more prone to slowdown.

Openness to trade is negatively associated with the probability of slowdown for the upper-middle-income and high-income economies. Having access to foreign markets provides the economy with more opportunities for growth. Trade with multiple international partners might also help diversify the demand risks from sole reliance on domestic market demand to a mix between domestic and external consumers. Furthermore, the exposure to global competition provides the impetus for domestic economic restructuring and other reform initiatives to address existing weaknesses and inefficiencies in the domestic economy which may otherwise hamper growth.

Finally, secondary industry value added per worker is negatively associated with the probability of slowdown for upper-middle-income and high-income economies. The result underscores the importance of improving productivity for continued growth in upper-middle-income and high-income economies. As an economy matures, it becomes increasingly difficult to grow by expanding industrial production as idle or underemployed factors of production become scarcer. Thus, productivity enhancement is necessary for sustaining growth and economies with lower productivity are more prone to slowdown.

As a robustness check, we have also performed probit regressions using the same set of determinants as shown in Table 4.8 for the three income groups and the results are included in Appendix 4. In short, these two sets of results are similar to each other.

4.6.2 Bayesian Model Averaging Results

In this section, we present three sets of Bayesian Model Averaging (BMA) results for the combined group of upper-middle-income and high-income economies. This is because among the list of possible determinants for growth slowdown considered in our study (see Table 4.7), we have variables related to the employment structure of the primary, secondary, and tertiary industries, the contribution of each sector to the economy's GRDP as well as value-added per worker for each sector. Considering these three types of data in a single BMA estimation will pose multicollinearity problem as they are highly correlated.

We have therefore conducted three rounds of BMA estimations for the combined group of upper-middle-income and high-income economies. For the first round of BMA estimation, we include only variables related to employment structure and value added per worker while leaving out variables on economic structure. All the other potential determinants such as dependency ratios, openness to trade, exchange rates, etc. still remain in our BMA estimation. The second round of BMA estimation is similar to that of the first with the only difference being that variables related to economic structure are used in place of those on value added per worker. As for the third round of BMA estimation, economic structure-related variables and value added per worker variables are used while employment structure-related variables are omitted. The results for these three rounds of BMA estimations are thus labelled as Result (I), Result (II) and Result (III), respectively, in Tables 4.9, 4.10 and 4.11.

Common to these three results, GRDP per capita, overall productivity, employment in tertiary industry as percentage of total employment, road density, tertiary industry value added per worker, and government consumption expenditure as percentage of GRDP are regarded as robust determinants of growth slowdown. Moreover, secondary industry value added per worker is considered a robust determinant in Results (I) (see Table 4.9). Note that three robust determinants identified through this BMA exercise are also in our logistic model for growth slowdown in the combined group of upper-middle-income and high-income economies, namely GRDP per capita, employment in tertiary industry as percentage of total employment, and secondary industry value added per worker.

Table 4.9: BMA Result (I) for the Combined Group of Upper-Middle-Income and High-Income Economies

Determinants	Posterior Inclusion Probability (PIP)	Posterior Mean	Posterior Standard Deviation (PSTD)	|Posterior Mean / PSTD|
GRDP per Capita	0.99999	0.00064	0.00015	4.12338
Total Dependency Ratio	0.09732	–0.05030	0.02734	1.83994
Openness To Trade	0.06949	–0.00504	0.00337	1.49807
Percent Change in Nominal Exchange Rate	0.04596	–0.02867	0.02289	1.25274
World Gross Domestic Product Real Growth Rate	0.04583	0.20967	0.15319	1.36868
Foreign Direct Investment Inflows as Percent of GRDP	0.02444	0.01589	0.03105	0.51174
Employment in Secondary Industry as Percent of Total Employment	0.03662	0.02284	0.02063	1.10711
Employment in Tertiary Industry as Percent of Total Employment	1.00000	–0.15190	0.03097	4.90544
Literacy Rate	0.03494	0.06195	0.06056	1.02297
Overall Productivity	0.21863	–0.00009	0.00004	2.35135
Primary Industry Value Added per Worker	0.07917	–0.00004	0.00002	1.71429
Secondary Industry Value Added per Worker	0.18367	–0.00002	0.00001	2.00000
Tertiary Industry Value Added per Worker	0.99996	–0.00015	0.00003	4.38235
Road Density	1.00000	0.72957	0.13929	5.23795
Length of Road per Capita	0.02424	–0.00521	0.01203	0.43301
Government Consumption Expenditure as Percent of GRDP	0.99996	0.41966	0.08587	4.88716
Old Dependency Ratio	0.02482	0.04029	0.05927	0.67980

Notes: Those highlighted in grey are considered robust determinants for growth slowdown in the combined group of upper-middle-income and high-income economies as they satisfy the two criteria simultaneously:

(i) The posterior inclusion probability (PIP) exceeds the prior inclusion probability (i.e. $\frac{3}{17} = 0.17647$) and

(ii) The ratio of conditional posterior mean to conditional posterior standard deviation is larger than 1.65 in absolute value, which corresponds to a 90 percent coverage interval under Gaussian posterior parameter distribution.

Source: Asia Competitiveness Institute's calculations.

Table 4.10: BMA Result (II) for the Combined Group of Upper-Middle-Income and High-Income Economies

Determinants	Posterior Inclusion Probability (PIP)	Posterior Mean	Posterior Standard Deviation (PSTD)	$\left\lvert\frac{\text{Posterior Mean}}{\text{PSTD}}\right\rvert$
GRDP per Capita	0.99998	0.00078	0.00014	5.63309
Total Dependency Ratio	0.05467	−0.04782	0.03672	1.30227
Openness To Trade	0.02569	−0.00181	0.00230	0.78472
Percentage Change in Nominal Exchange Rate	0.16702	−0.01240	0.00726	1.70756
World Gross Domestic Product Real Growth Rate	0.04764	0.19307	0.14079	1.37131
Foreign Direct Investment Inflows as Percent of GRDP	0.03552	−0.02699	0.02568	1.05081
Employment in Secondary Industry as Percent of Total Employment	0.02115	−0.00380	0.02091	0.18150
Employment in Tertiary Industry as Percent of Total Employment	0.20822	−0.05732	0.02624	2.18438
Literacy Rate	0.02056	−0.00564	0.06622	0.08515
Overall Productivity	0.99953	−0.00024	0.00005	5.22222
Road Density	1.00000	0.55152	0.10345	5.33114
Length of Road per Capita	0.02133	−0.00254	0.01219	0.20866
Secondary Industry Value Added as Percent of GRDP	0.06572	−0.02682	0.01872	1.43279
Tertiary Industry Value Added as Percent of GRDP	0.99937	−0.10876	0.02273	4.78558
Government Consumption Expenditure as Percent of GRDP	0.99939	0.37034	0.07734	4.78842
Old Dependency Ratio	0.02357	0.03587	0.05495	0.65280

Notes: Those highlighted in grey are considered robust determinants for growth slowdown in the combined group of upper-middle-income and high-income economies as they satisfy the two criteria simultaneously:

(i) The posterior inclusion probability (PIP) exceeds the prior inclusion probability (i.e. $\frac{3}{17} = 0.17647$) and

(ii) The ratio of conditional posterior mean to conditional posterior standard deviation is larger than 1.65 in absolute value, which corresponds to a 90 percent coverage interval under Gaussian posterior parameter distribution.

Source: Asia Competitiveness Institute's calculations.

Table 4.11: BMA Result (III) for the Combined Group of Upper-Middle-Income and High-Income Economies

Determinants	Posterior Inclusion Probability (PIP)	Posterior Mean	Posterior Standard Deviation (PSTD)	$\left|\frac{\text{Posterior Mean}}{\text{PSTD}}\right|$
GRDP per Capita	0.99876	0.00071	0.00014	4.93056
Total Dependency Ratio	0.10938	–0.06037	0.03222	1.87374
Openness To Trade	0.02969	–0.00237	0.00241	0.98218
Percentage Change in Nominal Exchange Rate	0.09032	–0.01107	0.00782	1.41635
World Gross Domestic Product Real Growth Rate	0.03916	0.18080	0.14454	1.25085
Foreign Direct Investment Inflows as Percent of GRDP	0.05383	–0.03809	0.02627	1.44978
Literacy Rate	0.02926	0.05384	0.06011	0.89569
Overall Productivity	0.99686	–0.00022	0.00005	4.71739
Primary Industry Value Added per Worker	0.01876	0.00000	0.00002	0.20000
Secondary Industry Value Added per Worker	0.01938	0.00000	0.00001	0.16667
Tertiary Industry Value Added per Worker	0.01988	0.00002	0.00004	0.41026
Road Density	1.00000	0.58675	0.11090	5.29069
Length of Road per Capita	0.03187	–0.01070	0.01042	1.02707
Secondary Industry Value Added as Percent of GRDP	0.02545	–0.01341	0.01715	0.78177
Tertiary Industry Value Added as Percent of GRDP	0.99999	–0.12373	0.02311	5.35436
Government Consumption Expenditure as Percent of GRDP	0.99990	0.41049	0.08471	4.84605
Old Dependency Ratio	0.01877	0.01127	0.05695	0.19795

Notes: Those highlighted in grey are considered robust determinants for growth slowdown in the combined group of upper-middle-income and high-income economies as they satisfy the two criteria simultaneously:

(i) The posterior inclusion probability (PIP) exceeds the prior inclusion probability (i.e. $\frac{3}{17} = 0.17647$) and

(ii) The ratio of conditional posterior mean to conditional posterior standard deviation is larger than 1.65 in absolute value, which corresponds to a 90 percent coverage interval under Gaussian posterior parameter distribution.

Source: Asia Competitiveness Institute's calculations.

4.6.3 Predictive Probability of Growth Slowdown

Using the income group-specific logistic models, we compute predictive probabilities of near-future slowdown for the economies of ASEAN, Greater China, India and Indonesia. The predictive probability for an economy is computed using its 2012 data for the relevant determinants (see Section 4.4.6 for details). It is illustrative of the risk that the economy will experience growth slowdown in the five years following 2012, or the period 2012–2017: the higher the probability, the higher the likelihood of growth slowdown.

Figure 4.4 shows the scatterplot of the predictive probabilities for 107 economies in ASEAN, Greater China, India and Indonesia against the initial level of GRDP per capita in 1990 Purchasing Power Parity dollar of each economy at the start of the prediction period in 2012. In general, upper-middle-income and high-income economies have higher probabilities of slowdown than lower-middle-income economies, which in turn are more likely to slow down than economies in the low-income group. In addition, within each income group, the likelihood of slowdown seems to increase with GRDP per capita level, as evident in the upward sloping trend line. Interestingly, the rate of increase is not uniform across income groups. The likelihood of slowdown seems to increase at decreasing rates as an economy graduates from one income group to another.

Figure 4.4: Scatterplot Showing Predictive Probabilities of Growth Slowdown for Economies in ASEAN, Greater China, Indonesia and India for the Period 2012–2017 (Based on Income Group Specific Logistic Models)

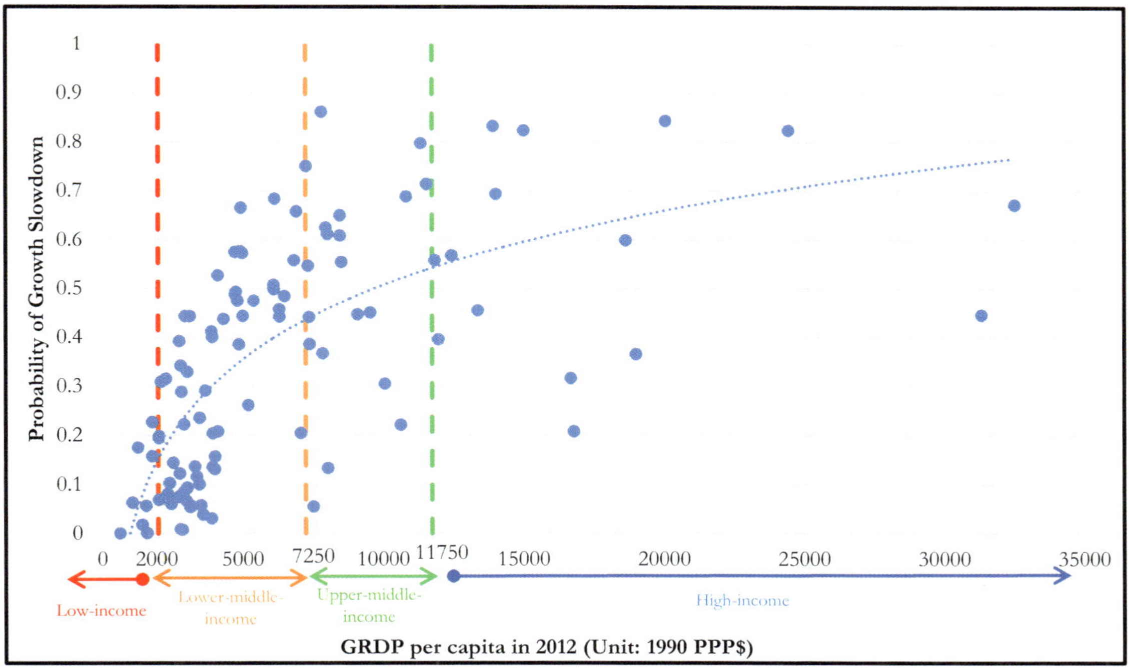

Source: Asia Competitiveness Institute's calculations.

The next section will discuss in detail the predictive probabilities for India's sub-national economies. For completeness, we have also calculated predictive probabilities using the probit specifications reported in Appendix 4. These probabilities are provided in Appendix 5.

4.6.3.1 *Predictive Probability of Growth Slowdown for India's Sub-National Economies*

By 2012, there are two low-income sub-national economies, 26 lower-middle-income sub-national economies, two upper-middle-income sub-national economies and one high-income sub-national economy in India.[27] Figure 4.5 paints a rather diverse picture on the near-future prospects of India's sub-national economies. The average predictive probability of growth slowdown is 0.43071, indicating that on average, India's sub-national economies have a 43 percent chance of experiencing growth slowdown in the 2012–2017 period. However, the average probability for the two low-income economies is only 0.20057 while the average for the combined group of India's upper-middle-income and high-income sub-national economies is much higher at 0.61294. The average for the lower-middle-income sub-national economies is 0.42038, close to the overall average.

There are also considerable variations in predictive probabilities within each income group. Table 4.12 displays the specific probability for each Indian sub-national economy. Probabilities of slowdown for Bihar and Uttar Pradesh, the only two low-income sub-national economies in 2012, are 0.17458 and 0.22656, respectively. Meanwhile, among the lower-middle-income sub-national economies, Manipur has the lowest probability at only 0.19382. However, the predictive probabilities of as many as eight sub-national economies, namely Andaman and Nicobar Islands, Andhra Pradesh, Gujarat, Haryana, Himachal Pradesh, Puducherry, Punjab, and Uttarakhand, are above 0.5. These sub-national economies thus have more than even odds of experiencing growth slowdown during 2012–2017. Among them, Haryana has the highest probability at 0.68371. Finally, within the combined group of upper-middle-income and high-income Indian sub-national economies, Delhi's probability at 0.44670 is the lowest. Surprisingly, Goa, the only high-income sub-national economy of India by 2012, is not the most likely to slow down in this group. Instead, it is Sikkim whose predictive probability stands at 0.86214. Also, Sikkim and Chandigarh are the two upper-middle-income sub-national economies whose probabilities of slowdown are greater than 0.5.

The general prospect of the India sub-national economies is less worrying than that of Greater China economies but bleaker than the outlook for economies in ASEAN and Indonesia. The average predictive probability for India is lower than the average probability for Greater China (0.56872) (Tan *et al.*, 2016b) but much higher than the averages for ASEAN (0.20890) (Tan *et al.*, 2017) and Indonesia (0.10264) (Tan *et al.*, 2016c). In addition, the fact that 10 economies, or almost a third of India's sub-national economies, have higher than even odds of slowing down is clearly a cause for concern. Our predictive probability results thus indicate that there are important weaknesses in India's sub-national economies which need to be addressed.

---

[27] GRDP per capita for Dadra and Nagar Haveli, Daman and Diu, and Lakshadweep are not available throughout the study period.

Figure 4.5: Bar Chart Showing Predictive Probabilities of Growth Slowdown for India's Sub-National Economies for the Period 2012–2017 (Based on Income Group-Specific Logistic Models)

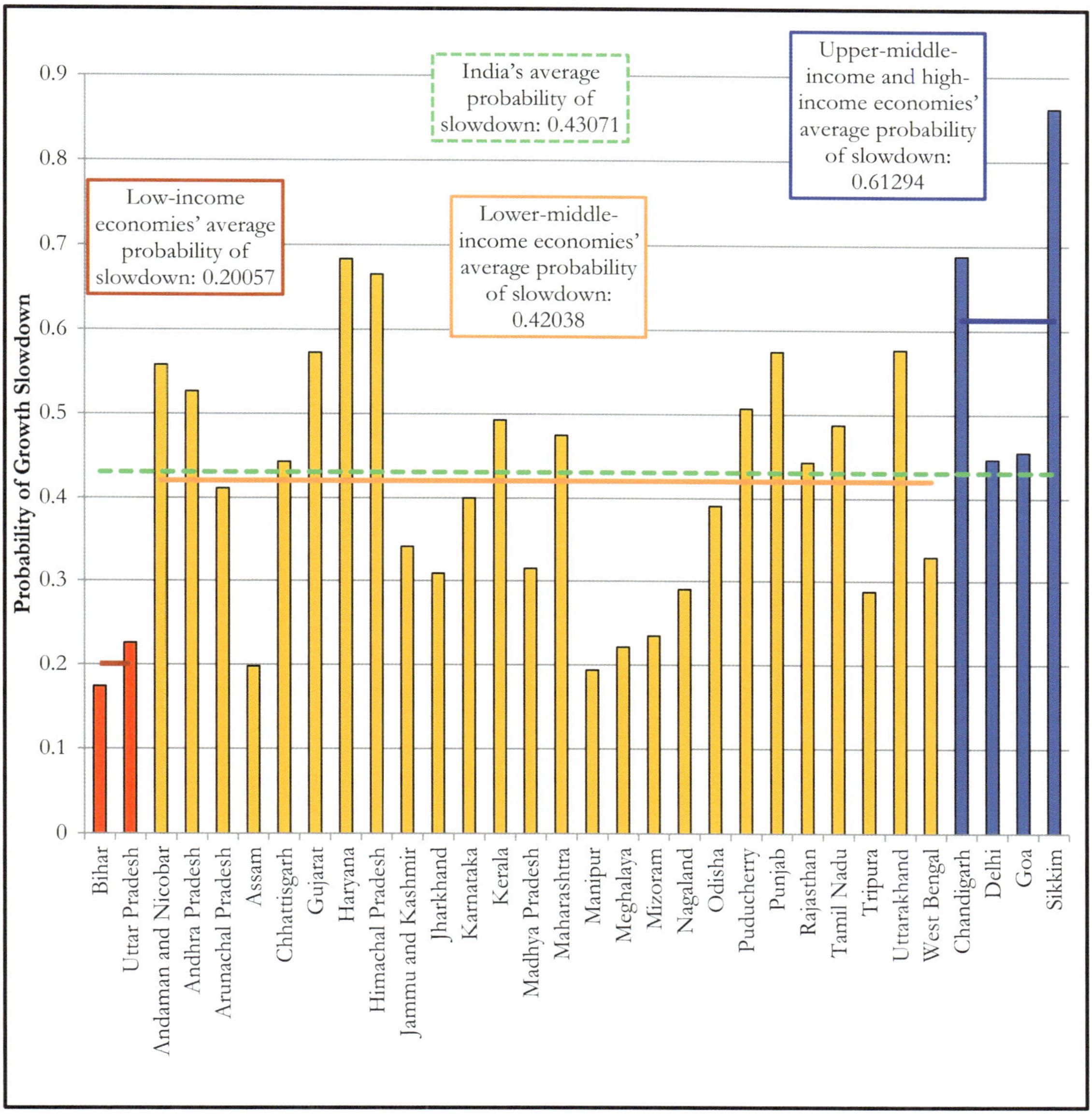

Notes: (i) Averages reported are simple averages.

(ii) Predictive probabilities for Dadra and Nagar Haveli, Daman and Diu, and Lakshadweep are not generated. This is because GRDP per capita for these economies are not available throughout the study period.

Source: Asia Competitiveness Institute's calculations.

Table 4.12: Predictive Probabilities of Growth Slowdown for India's Sub-National Economies for the Period 2012–2017 (Based on Income Group Specific Logistic Models)

Economy	Income Group Which Economy Belongs to in 2012	Probability of Experiencing Growth Slowdown during 2012–2017
Andaman and Nicobar Islands	Lower-middle-income	0.55783
Andhra Pradesh	Lower-middle-income	0.52651
Arunachal Pradesh	Lower-middle-income	0.41137
Assam	Lower-middle-income	0.19794
Bihar	Low-income	0.17458
Chandigarh	Upper-middle-income	0.68791
Chhattisgarh	Lower-middle-income	0.44297
Delhi	Upper-middle-income	0.44670
Goa	High-income	0.45501
Gujarat	Lower-middle-income	0.57284
Haryana	Lower-middle-income	0.68371
Himachal Pradesh	Lower-middle-income	0.66571
Jammu and Kashmir	Lower-middle-income	0.34159
Jharkhand	Lower-middle-income	0.30883
Karnataka	Lower-middle-income	0.39992
Kerala	Lower-middle-income	0.49291
Madhya Pradesh	Lower-middle-income	0.31460
Maharashtra	Lower-middle-income	0.47476
Manipur	Lower-middle-income	0.19382
Meghalaya	Lower-middle-income	0.22175
Mizoram	Lower-middle-income	0.23532
Nagaland	Lower-middle-income	0.29038
Odisha	Lower-middle-income	0.39116
Puducherry	Lower-middle-income	0.50693
Punjab	Lower-middle-income	0.57477
Rajasthan	Lower-middle-income	0.44297
Sikkim	Upper-middle-income	0.86214
Tamil Nadu	Lower-middle-income	0.48745
Tripura	Lower-middle-income	0.28789
Uttar Pradesh	Low-income	0.22656
Uttarakhand	Lower-middle-income	0.57689
West Bengal	Lower-middle-income	0.32905

Note: Predictive probabilities for Dadra and Nagar Haveli, Daman and Diu, and Lakshadweep are not generated. This is because GRDP per capita for these economies are not available throughout the study period.

Source: Asia Competitiveness Institute's calculations.

4.7 Relative Strengths and Weaknesses of India's Sub-National Economies

Equipped with the knowledge of the general risk level of each economy experiencing growth slowdown at its respective level of development as illustrated by the predictive probability results in Section 4.6.3, it would be meaningful if we could pinpoint the relative strengths and weaknesses of each sub-national economy, thereby aiding policymakers to identify areas in which further improvement could be made to reduce the risks of growth slowdown. To this end, we compute the standardised score for each sub-national economy in terms of the determinants of growth slowdown for the income groups they belong to. Standardised scores are calculated for all determinants of growth slowdown with the exception of the control variable GRDP per capita.

Formally, the standardised score for determinant D of economy E which is in income group I is defined as $Standardised\,score_{D,E,I} = \frac{X_{D,E,I} - \bar{X}_{D,I}}{SD_{D,I}}$, where $X_{D,E,I}$ is the value of determinant D of economy E which is in income group I, $\bar{X}_{D,I}$ is the mean value of determinant D for all economies within the income group I, and $SD_{D,I}$ is the standard deviation of determinant D for all economies within the income group I. The mean value of determinant D for all economies within the income group I is defined as $\bar{X}_{D,I} = \frac{1}{N}\sum_{e=1}^{N} X_{D,e,I}$, where N is the total number of economies within the income group I. The standard deviation of determinant D for all economies within the income group I is defined as $SD_{D,I} = \sqrt{\frac{1}{N}\sum_{i=1}^{N}\left(X_{D,E,I} - \bar{X}_{D,I}\right)^2}$. For all determinants except for old dependency ratio, a high value of $X_{D,E,I}$ would indicate a high $Standardised\,score_{D,E,I}$. In contrast, we reverse score old dependency ratio so that the standardised score is low if the original value of the ratio is high. This is because unlike the other determinants, high old dependency ratio is associated with increasing likelihood of growth slowdown.

Constructed in the manner described above, the standardised scores reflect the gaps between the economy's performance and the average performance of other economies in the same income group. If the standardised score of an economy is zero, it means that the economy is an average performer within its income group. On the other hand, if the standardised score is negative, it implies that the economy is performing more poorly than others; while positive standardised score indicates better than average performance. The farther away the standardised score is from zero, the farther away the performance of said economy from the average of that particular income group. For instance, a large negative standardised score means very poor performance, while a large positive standardised score denotes very strong performance.

Figures 4.6–4.37 provide a web analysis displaying the standardised scores of Indian sub-national economies in terms of the determinants of growth slowdown (with the exception of GRDP per capita). The larger the area under each economy's line, the better its performance in the particular dimension considered. To provide a better sense of the relative strengths and weaknesses of each economy, we also benchmark their standardised scores against the median scores and maximum scores of the income group they belong to. All data used in generating the web analysis are as of 2012. The dimensions/determinants chosen to be considered for each economy depends on the income group to which the economy belongs to in the same year.

Andaman and Nicobar Islands

Lower-Middle-Income Economy

Figure 4.6 shows the relative strengths and weaknesses of Andaman and Nicobar Islands which was a lower-middle-income economy in 2012 according to the income classification we adopt. As discussed in Section 4.6.1, we found four determinants which are associated with growth slowdown in this particular income group, namely old dependency ratio, literacy rate, foreign direct investment inflows as percentage of GRDP and employment in tertiary industry as percentage of total employment. The solid line shows the standardised score for Andaman and Nicobar Islands. The dashed line represents the median score for all economies in the lower-middle-income group across ASEAN, Greater China, India, and Indonesia, while the dotted line denotes the maximum score for those economies.

Andaman and Nicobar Islands performed well in terms of employment in tertiary industry as its score for employment in tertiary industry as percentage of total employment was 1.7780. Andaman and Nicobar Islands' score for old dependency ratio also exceeded the median score

Figure 4.6: Andaman and Nicobar Islands' Strengths and Weaknesses

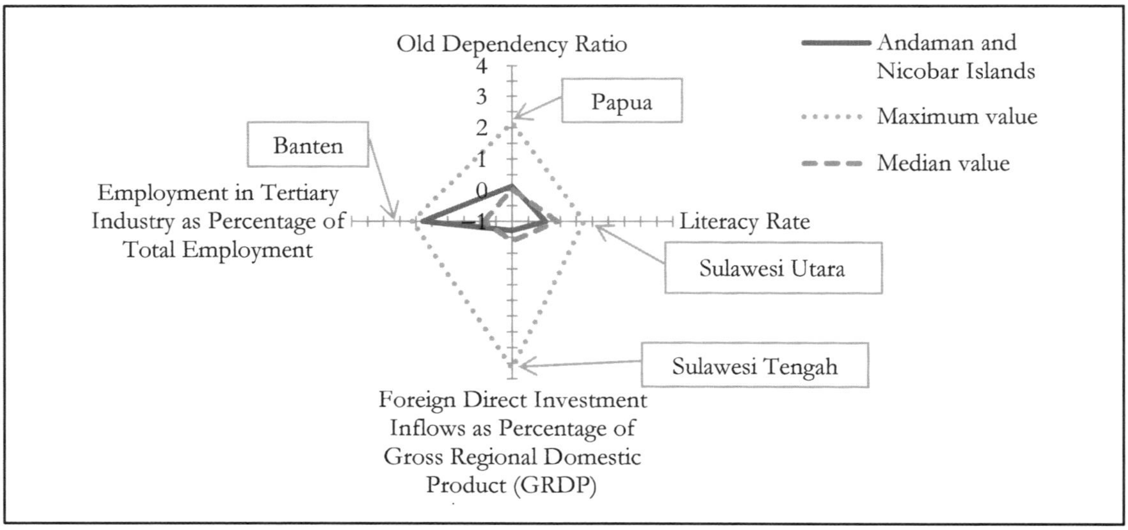

Source: Asia Competitiveness Institute's calculations.

for the lower-middle-income group. However, the economy's scores for literacy rate and foreign direct investment inflows as percentage of GRDP lagged behind the median. Going forward, Andaman and Nicobar Islands may utilise its advantage on tertiary industry employment to provide better services and attract more foreign direct investment inflows, as well as strengthening basic education to improve literacy rate.

Andhra Pradesh

Lower-Middle-Income Economy

Figure 4.7 shows the relative strengths and weaknesses of Andhra Pradesh which was a lower-middle-income economy in 2012 according to the income classification we adopt. As discussed in Section 4.6.1, we found four determinants which are associated with growth slowdown in this particular income group, namely old dependency ratio, literacy rate, foreign direct investment inflows as percentage of GRDP and employment in tertiary industry as percentage of total employment. The solid line shows the standardised score for Andhra Pradesh. The dashed line represents the median score for all economies in the lower-middle-income group across ASEAN, Greater China, India and Indonesia, while the dotted line denotes the maximum score for those economies.

Figure 4.7: Andhra Pradesh's Strengths and Weaknesses

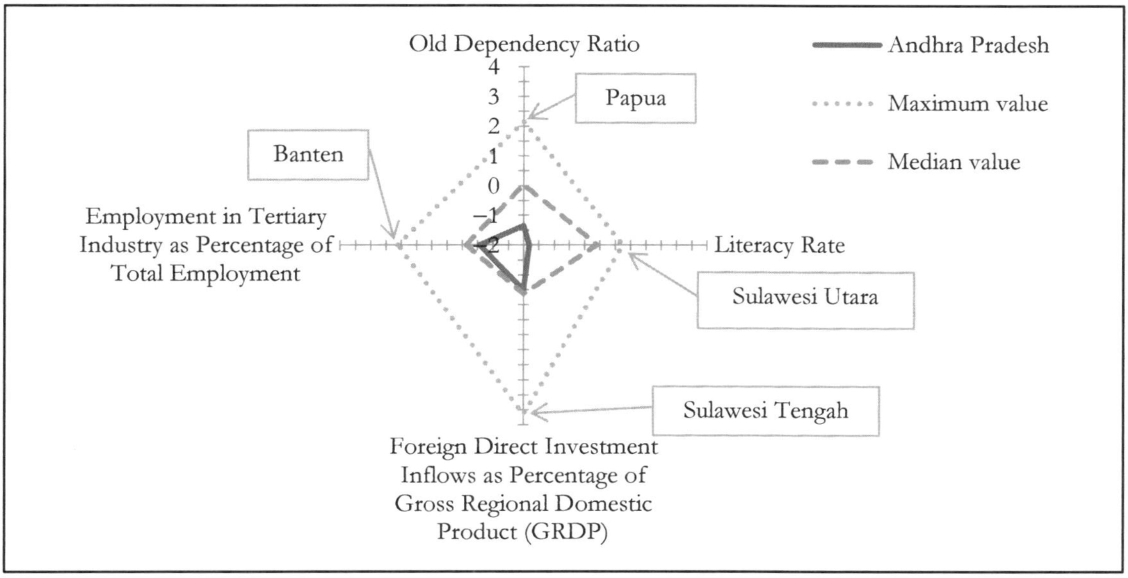

Source: Asia Competitiveness Institute's calculations.

In general, Andhra Pradesh's scores lagged behind the respective median scores for the lower-middle-income group in all aspects, especially in terms of old dependency ratio and literacy rate. These findings indicate that Andhra Pradesh needs to improve access to education. In addition, Andhra Pradesh may seek to encourage foreign direct investment and develop its tertiary industry to create more job opportunities. This will help retain the young workforce, which will help Andhra Pradesh to cope with the challenges of the ageing population.

Arunachal Pradesh

Lower-Middle-Income Economy

Figure 4.8 shows the relative strengths and weaknesses of Arunachal Pradesh which was a lower-middle-income economy in 2012 according to the income classification we adopt. As discussed in Section 4.6.1, we found four determinants which are associated with growth slowdown in this particular income group, namely old dependency ratio, literacy rate, foreign direct investment inflows as percentage of GRDP and employment in tertiary industry as percentage of total employment. The solid line shows the standardised score for Arunachal Pradesh. The dashed line represents the median score for all economies in the lower-middle-income group across ASEAN, Greater China, India, and Indonesia, while the dotted line denotes the maximum score for those economies.

Figure 4.8: Arunachal Pradesh's Strengths and Weaknesses

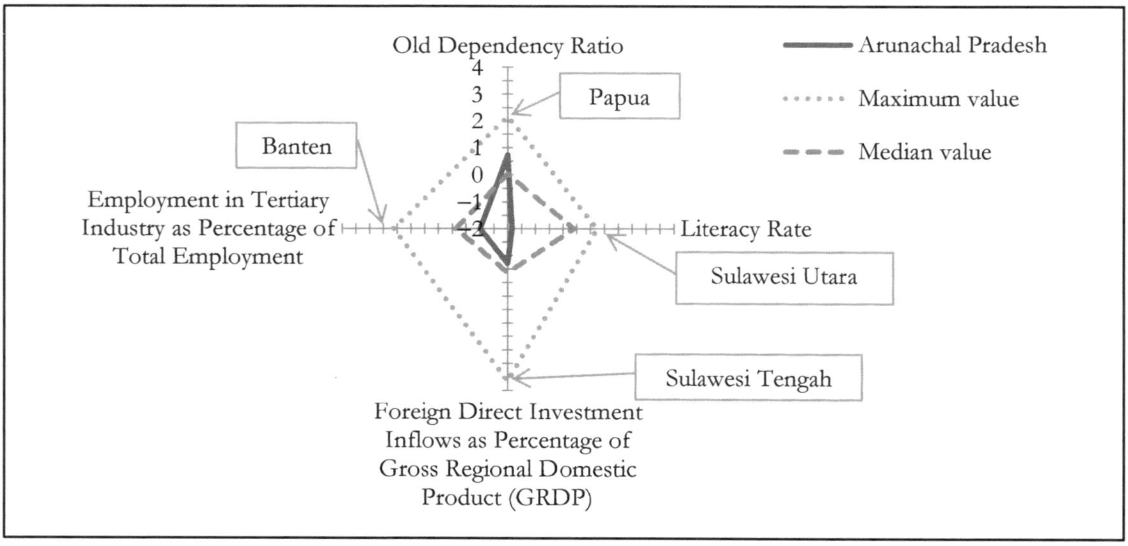

Source: Asia Competitiveness Institute's calculations.

As shown in Figure 4.8, Arunachal Pradesh's score for old dependency ratio was above the median score for the lower-middle-income economy. However, its scores for the other three determinants were below the median. Literacy rate is the most significant weakness of Arunachal Pradesh, as the economy's score for this determinant was −1.8304, which lagged very far behind the median score of 0.4026. Thus, more should be done to improve access to basic education.

Assam

Lower-Middle-Income Economy

Figure 4.9 shows the relative strengths and weaknesses of Assam which was a lower-middle-income economy in 2012 according to the income classification we adopt. As discussed in Section 4.6.1, we found four determinants which are associated with growth slowdown in this particular income group, namely old dependency ratio, literacy rate, foreign direct investment inflows as percentage of GRDP and employment in tertiary industry as percentage of total employment. The solid line shows the standardised score for Assam. The dashed line represents the median score for all economies in the lower-middle-income group across ASEAN, Greater China, India, and Indonesia, while the dotted line denotes the maximum score for those economies.

Figure 4.9: Assam's Strengths and Weaknesses

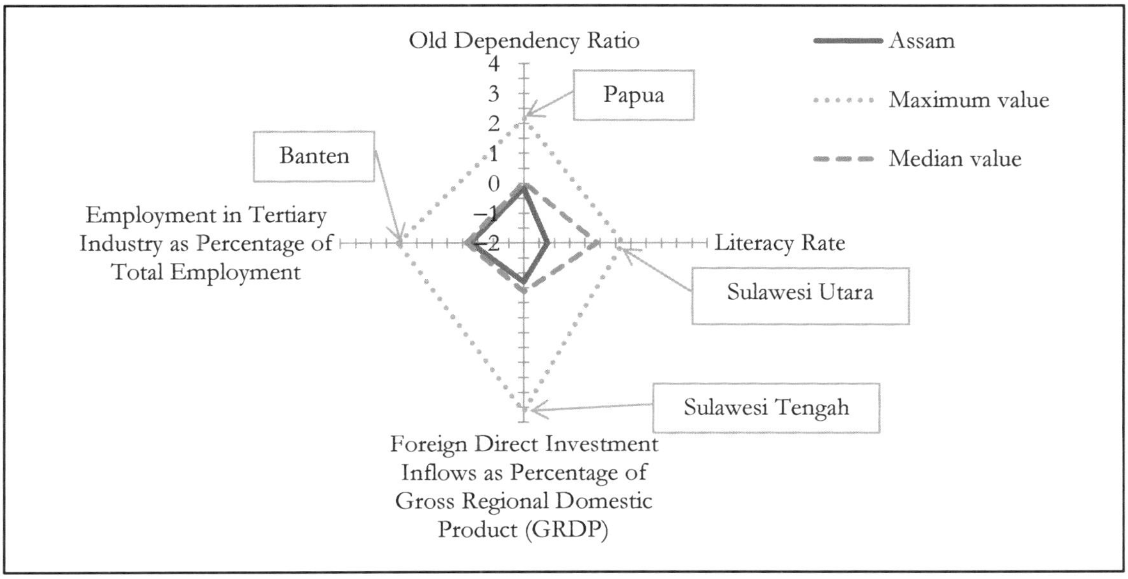

Source: Asia Competitiveness Institute's calculations.

In general, Assam's scores for old dependency ratio, foreign direct investment inflows as percentage of GRDP and employment in tertiary industry as percentage of total employment were close to the median scores for the lower-middle-income group. However, as shown in Figure 4.9, Assam's score for literacy rate lagged far behind other economies in the same income group. Thus, more should be done to improve access to basic education.

Bihar

Low-Income Economy

Figure 4.10 shows the relative strengths and weaknesses of Bihar which was a low-income economy in 2012 according to the income classification we adopt. As discussed in Section 4.6.1, we found three determinants which are associated with growth slowdown in this particular income group, namely length of road per capita, literacy rate and foreign direct investment inflows as percentage of GRDP. The solid line shows the standardised score for Bihar. The dashed line represents the median score for all economies in the low-income group across ASEAN, Greater China, India, and Indonesia, while the dotted line denotes the maximum score for those economies.

Bihar performed well in foreign direct investment inflows as percentage of GRDP, as its score for this determinant was close the median of the lower-middle-income group. However, it lagged

Figure 4.10: Bihar's Strengths and Weaknesses

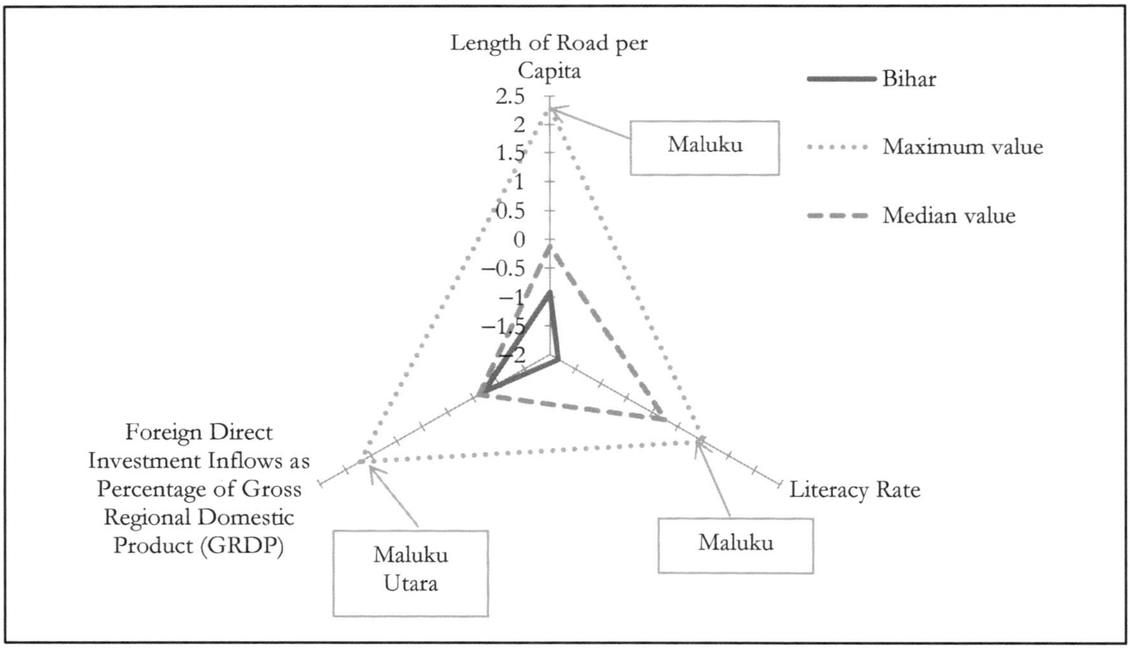

Source: Asia Competitiveness Institute's calculations.

behind other economies in terms of length of road per capita and particularly literacy rate. More should be done to improve access to basic education. Furthermore, Bihar might also look to leverage on foreign direct investment to invest more in infrastructure, especially roads, so as to strengthen intra-state and inter-state connectivity.

Chandigarh

Upper-Middle-Income Economy

Figure 4.11 shows the relative strengths and weaknesses of Chandigarh which was an upper-middle-income economy in 2012 according to the income classification we adopt. As mentioned in Section 4.4.2, due to data constraint, we have combined the analysis of high-income economies with that of the upper-middle-income economies. As discussed in Section 4.6.1, we found four determinants which are associated with growth slowdown in this combined group of upper-middle-income and high-income economies, namely openness to trade, literacy rate, secondary industry value added per worker and employment in tertiary industry as percentage of total employment. The solid line shows the standardised score for Chandigarh. The dashed line represents the median score for all economies in the combined group of upper-middle-income and high-income economies across ASEAN, Greater China, India, and Indonesia, while the dotted line denotes the maximum score for those economies.

Figure 4.11: Chandigarh's Strengths and Weaknesses

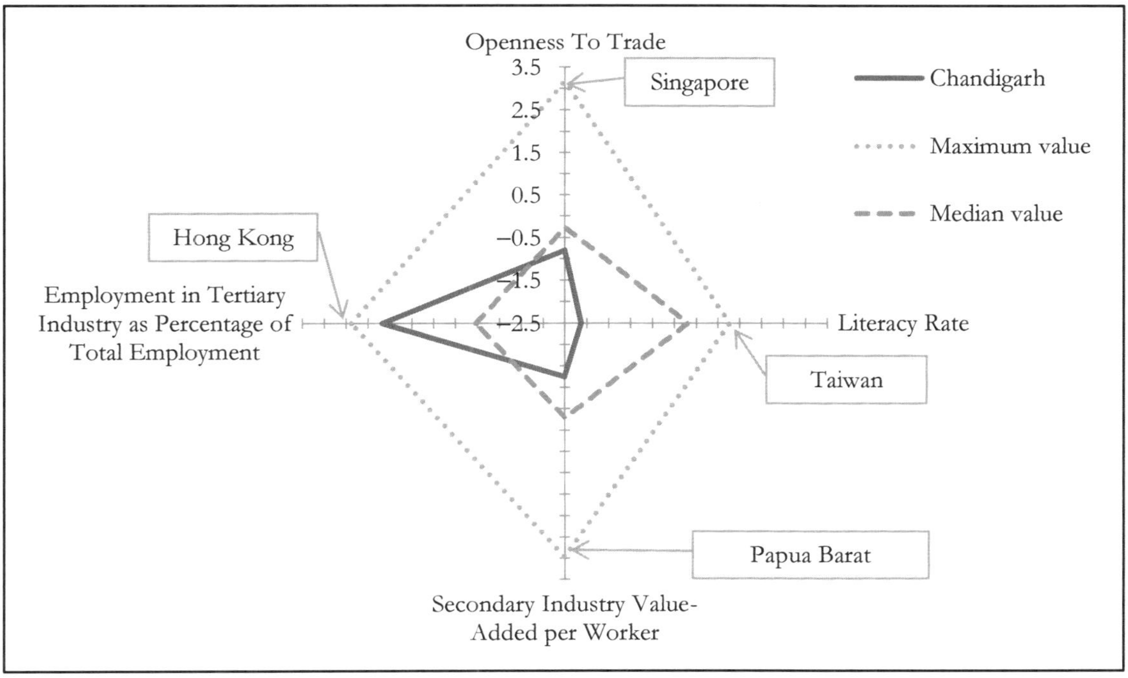

Source: Asia Competitiveness Institute's calculations.

Chandigarh achieved a positive score of 1.6735 for employment in tertiary industry as percentage of total employment while the maximum score of the combined group of upper-middle-income and high-income economies was 3.1663 which was obtained by Hong Kong. However, it lagged behind in the other three determinants, especially in terms of literacy rate. Going forward, Chandigarh may need to improve access to basic education and the development of its human capital in general. It may also look to boost productivity in its secondary sector.

Chhattisgarh

Lower-Middle-Income Economy

Figure 4.12 shows the relative strengths and weaknesses of Chhattisgarh which was a lower-middle-income economy in 2012 according to the income classification we adopt. As discussed in Section 4.6.1, we found four determinants which are associated with growth slowdown in this particular income group, namely old dependency ratio, literacy rate, foreign direct investment inflows as percentage of GRDP and employment in tertiary industry as percentage of total employment. The solid line shows the standardised score for Chhattisgarh. The dashed line represents the median score for all economies in the lower-middle-income group across ASEAN, Greater China, India, and Indonesia, while the dotted line denotes the maximum score for those economies.

Figure 4.12: Chhattisgarh's Strengths and Weaknesses

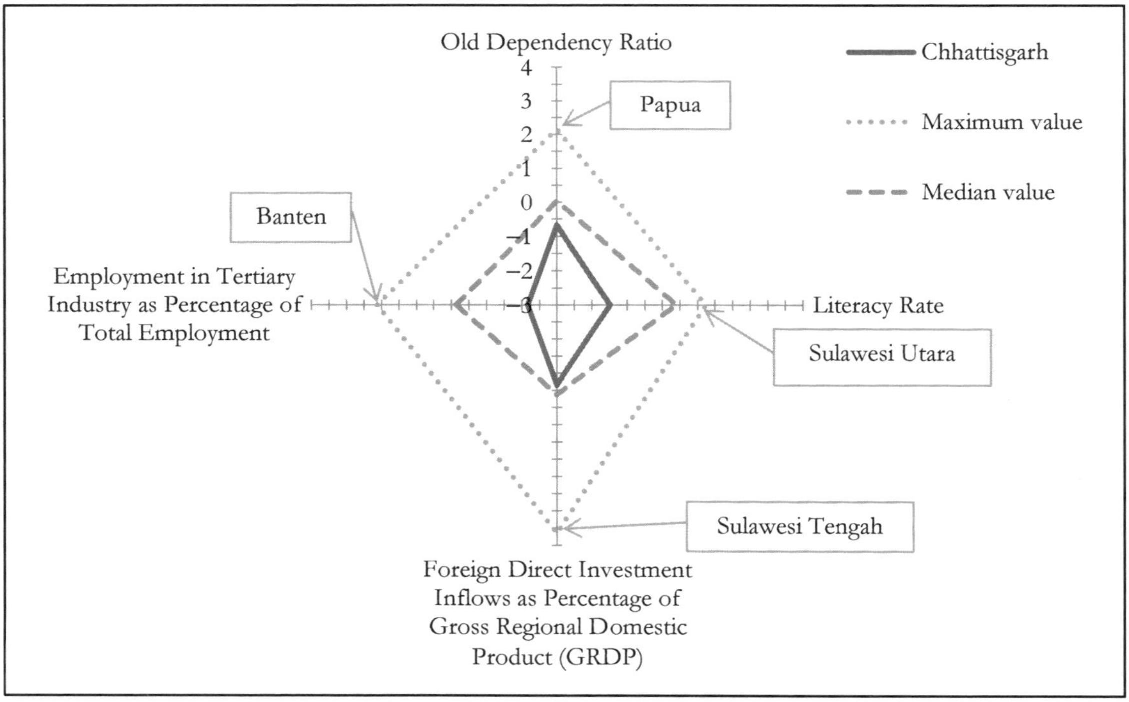

Source: Asia Competitiveness Institute's calculations.

In general, Chhattisgarh's scores were lower than the median scores of the lower-middle-income group in all four determinants. Its performance in old dependency ratio and foreign direct investment inflows as percentage of GRDP was most encouraging as the gaps between Chhattisgarh's scores and the median scores were relatively close. However, more should be done to improve access to basic education and develop Chhattisgarh's human capital in general as Chhattisgarh's score in literacy rate lagged behind other lower-middle-income economies a lot.

Delhi

Upper-Middle-Income Economy

Figure 4.13 shows the relative strengths and weaknesses of Delhi which was an upper-middle-income economy in 2012 according to the income classification we adopt. As mentioned in Section 4.4.2, due to data constraint, we have combined the analysis of high-income economies with that of the upper-middle-income economies. As discussed in Section 4.6.1, we found four determinants which are associated with growth slowdown in this combined group of upper-middle-income and high-income economies, namely openness to trade, literacy rate, secondary industry value added per worker and employment in tertiary industry as percentage of total employment. The solid line shows the standardised score for Delhi. The dashed line represents

Figure 4.13: Delhi's Strengths and Weaknesses

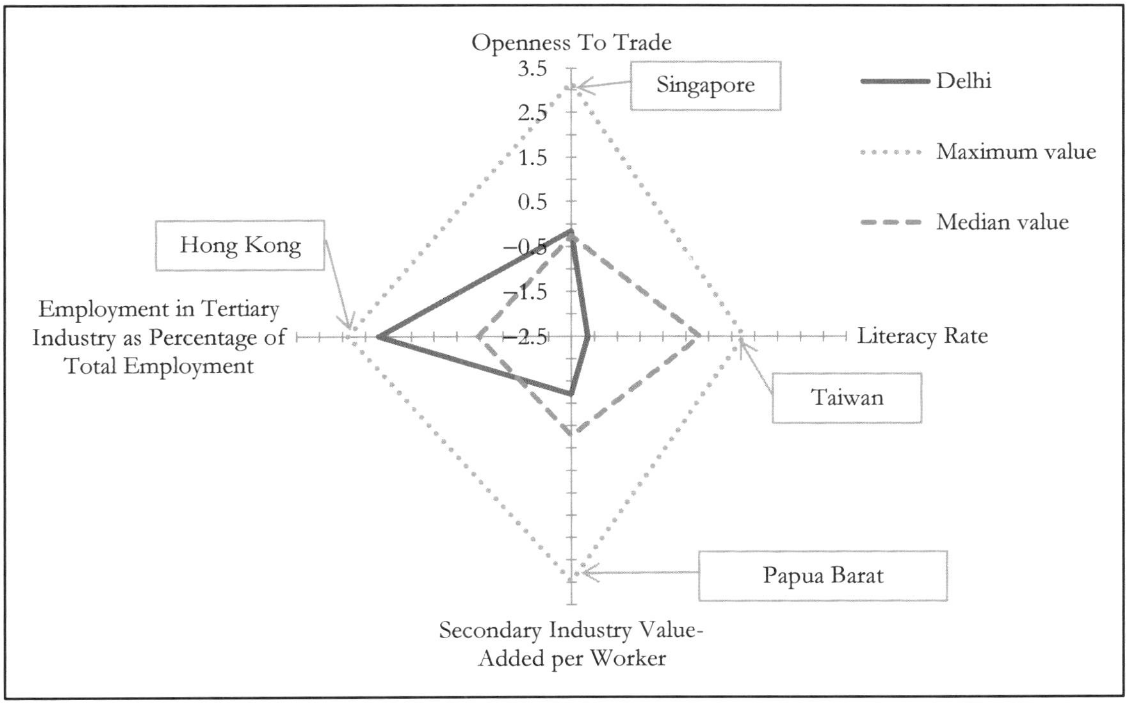

Source: Asia Competitiveness Institute's calculations.

the median score for all economies in the combined group of upper-middle-income and high-income economies across ASEAN, Greater China, India, and Indonesia, while the dotted line denotes the maximum score for those economies.

As the capital of the country, Delhi performed quite well in terms of employment in tertiary industry as percentage of total employment, as reflected in Figure 4.13. Besides, its score for openness to trade also exceeded the median score for the combined group of upper-middle-income and high-income economies. However, Delhi lagged behind its counterparts in terms of literacy rate and secondary industry value added per worker. Developing human capital and improving productivity will be the major challenges for policymakers in order to mitigate Delhi's risk of growth slowdown.

Goa

High-Income Economy

Figure 4.14 shows the relative strengths and weaknesses of Goa which was a high-income economy in 2012 according to the income classification we adopt. As mentioned in Section 4.4.2, due to data constraint, we have combined the analysis of high-income economies with that of the upper-middle-income economies. As discussed in Section 4.6.1, we found four determinants

Figure 4.14: Goa's Strengths and Weaknesses

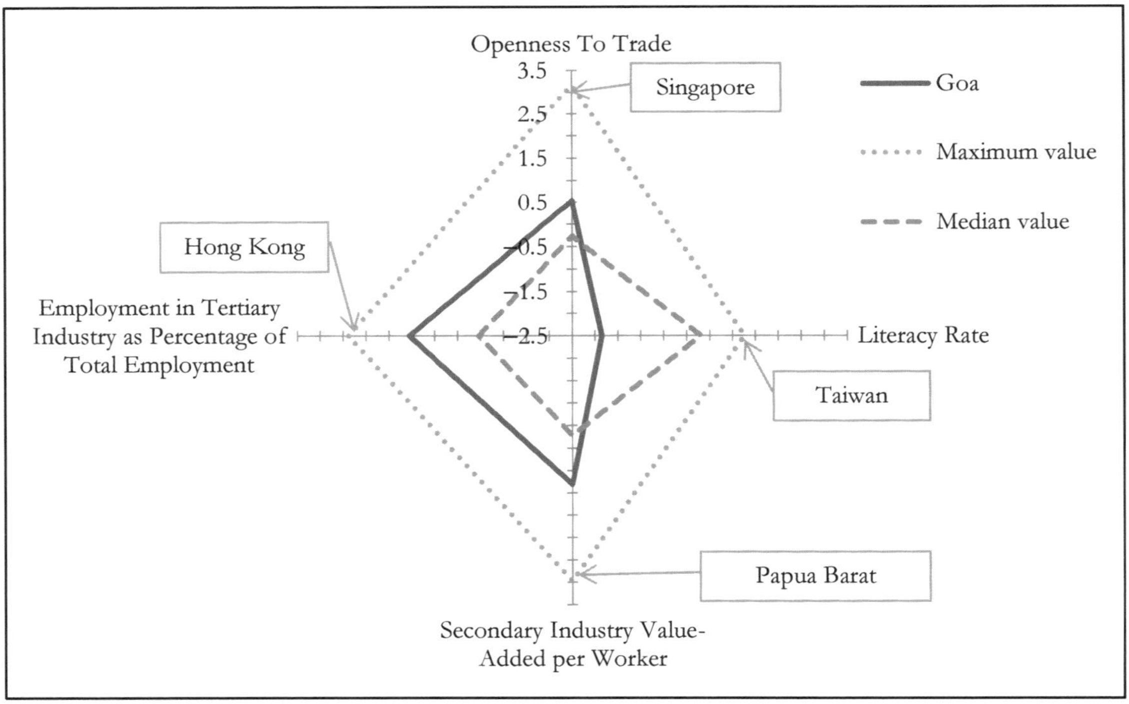

Source: Asia Competitiveness Institute's calculations.

which are associated with growth slowdown in this combined group of upper-middle-income and high-income economies, namely openness to trade, literacy rate, secondary industry value added per worker and employment in tertiary industry as percentage of total employment. The solid line shows the standardised score for Goa. The dashed line represents the median score for all economies in the combined group of upper-middle-income and high-income economies across ASEAN, Greater China, India, and Indonesia, while the dotted line denotes the maximum score for those economies.

Goa was the only high-income sub-national economy in India in 2012. Its scores for openness to trade, secondary industry value added per worker and employment in tertiary industry as percentage of total employment outperformed the median scores for the combined group of upper-middle-income and high-income economies. However, Goa lagged behind its peers in terms of literacy rate. More should be done to improve basic access to education and develop human capital in general. Goa may also look to further develop its tertiary industry, especially high value-added services in order to achieve sustainable growth.

Gujarat

Lower-Middle-Income Economy

Figure 4.15 shows the relative strengths and weaknesses of Gujarat which was a lower-middle-income economy in 2012 according to the income classification we adopt. As discussed in Section 4.6.1, we found four determinants which are associated with growth slowdown in this

Figure 4.15: Gujarat's Strengths and Weaknesses

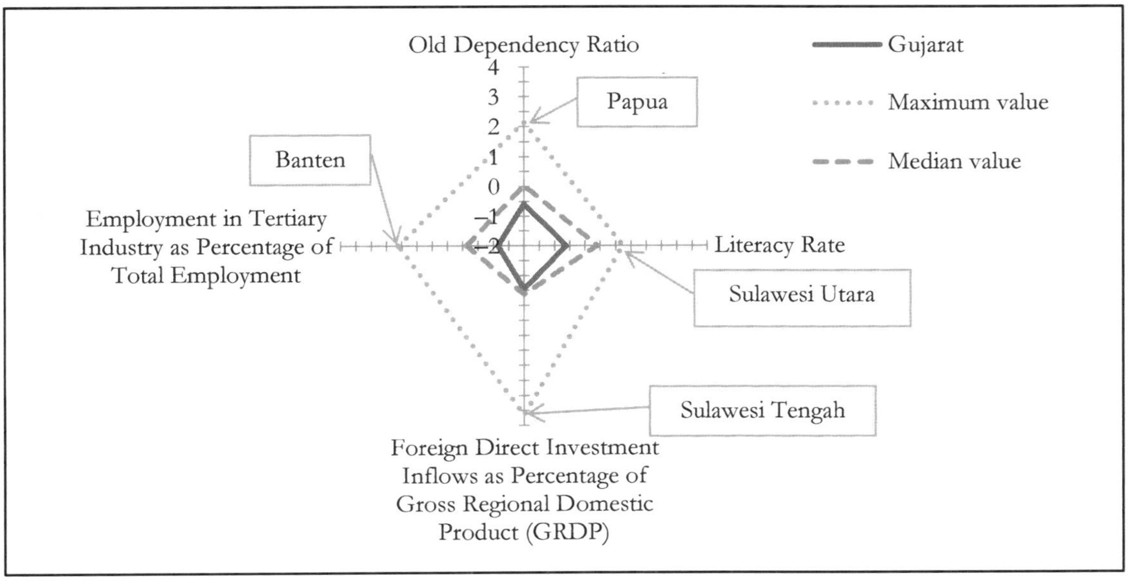

Source: Asia Competitiveness Institute's calculations.

particular income group, namely old dependency ratio, literacy rate, foreign direct investment inflows as percentage of GRDP and employment in tertiary industry as percentage of total employment. The solid line shows the standardised score for Gujarat. The dashed line represents the median score for all economies in the lower-middle-income group across ASEAN, Greater China, India, and Indonesia, while the dotted line denotes the maximum score for those economies.

In general, Gujarat's scores lagged behind the median for the lower-middle-income groups in all four determinants. The economy's performance in terms of foreign direct investment inflows as percentage of GRDP is most encouraging as its score is the closest to the median. As such, Gujarat may look to intensify its effort to attract foreign direct investment. At the same time, it should also develop its human capital, especially improving access to basic education.

Haryana

Lower-Middle-Income Economy

Figure 4.16 shows the relative strengths and weaknesses of Haryana which was a lower-middle-income economy in 2012 according to the income classification we adopt. As discussed in Section 4.6.1, we found four determinants which are associated with growth slowdown in this particular income group, namely old dependency ratio, literacy rate, foreign direct investment inflows as percentage of GRDP and employment in tertiary industry as percentage of total

Figure 4.16: Haryana's Strengths and Weaknesses

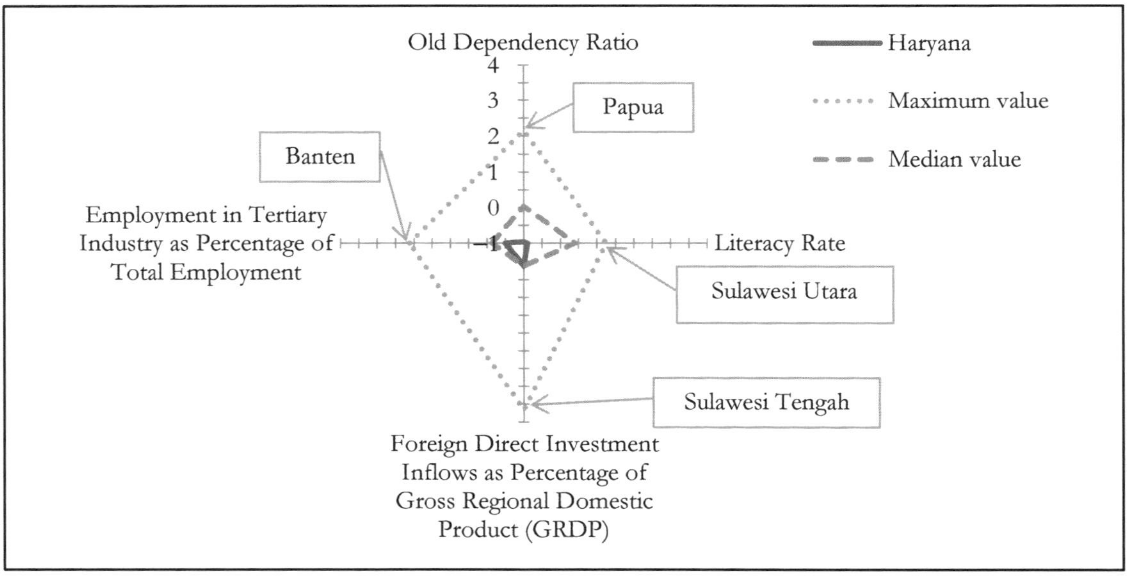

Source: Asia Competitiveness Institute's calculations.

employment. The solid line shows the standardised score for Haryana. The dashed line represents the median score for all economies in the lower-middle-income group across ASEAN, Greater China, India, and Indonesia, while the dotted line denotes the maximum score for those economies.

Except for foreign direct investment inflows as percentage of GRDP where Haryana's score was the same as the median for the lower-middle-income group, the economy's scores for all other determinants lagged far behind the respective median scores. There are thus much to be done in terms of developing tertiary industry and upgrading the labour force through training and education if Haryana is to avoid growth slowdown and meet the challenges of its ageing population.

Himachal Pradesh

Lower-Middle-Income Economy

Figure 4.17 shows the relative strengths and weaknesses of Himachal Pradesh which was a lower-middle-income economy in 2012 according to the income classification we adopt. As discussed in Section 4.6.1, we found four determinants which are associated with growth slowdown in this particular income group, namely old dependency ratio, literacy rate, foreign direct investment inflows as percentage of GRDP and employment in tertiary industry as percentage of total employment. The solid line shows the standardised score for Himachal Pradesh. The dashed line represents the median score for all economies in the lower-middle-income group

Figure 4.17: Himachal Pradesh's Strengths and Weaknesses

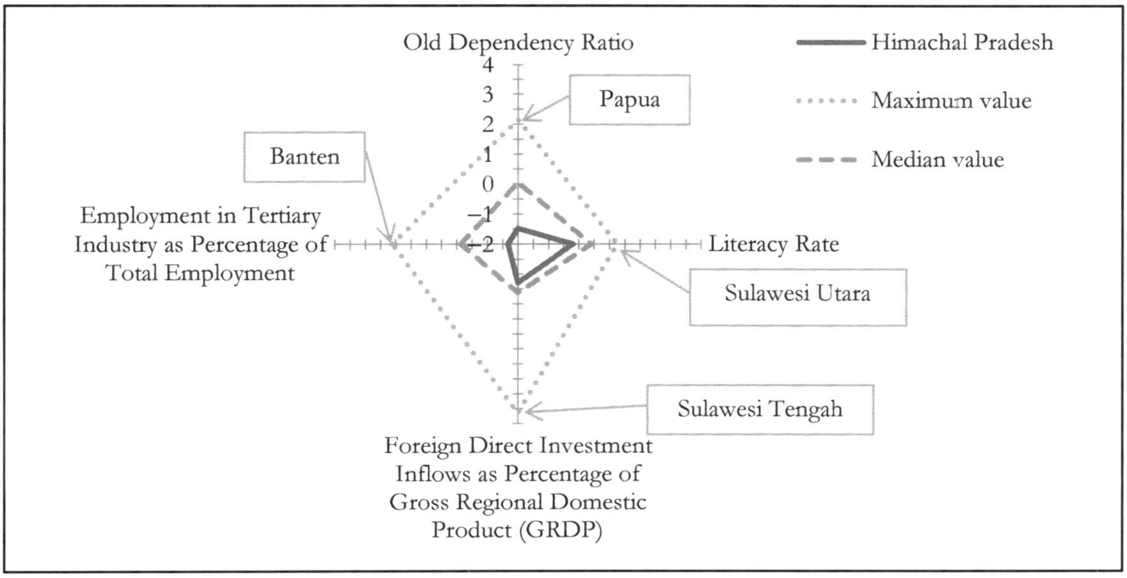

Source: Asia Competitiveness Institute's calculations.

across ASEAN, Greater China, India, and Indonesia, while the dotted line denotes the maximum score for those economies.

In general, Himachal Pradesh's scores for all four determinants lagged behind the median score for the lower-middle-income group. The economy's scores for literacy rate and foreign direct investment inflows as percentage of GRDP were closer to the respective medians than its scores for old dependency ratio and employment in tertiary industry as percentage of total employment. Thus, the underdevelopment of the tertiary sector and ageing population seem to be the most major challenges for Himachal Pradesh.

Jammu and Kashmir

Lower-Middle-Income Economy

Figure 4.18 shows the relative strengths and weaknesses of Jammu and Kashmir which was a lower-middle-income economy in 2012 according to the income classification we adopt. As discussed in Section 4.6.1, we found four determinants which are associated with growth slow-down in this particular income group, namely old dependency ratio, literacy rate, foreign direct investment inflows as percentage of GRDP and employment in tertiary industry as percentage of total employment. The solid line shows the standardised score for Jammu and Kashmir. The dashed line represents the median score for all economies in the lower-middle-income group across ASEAN, Greater China, India, and Indonesia, while the dotted line denotes the maximum score for those economies.

Figure 4.18: Jammu and Kashmir's Strengths and Weaknesses

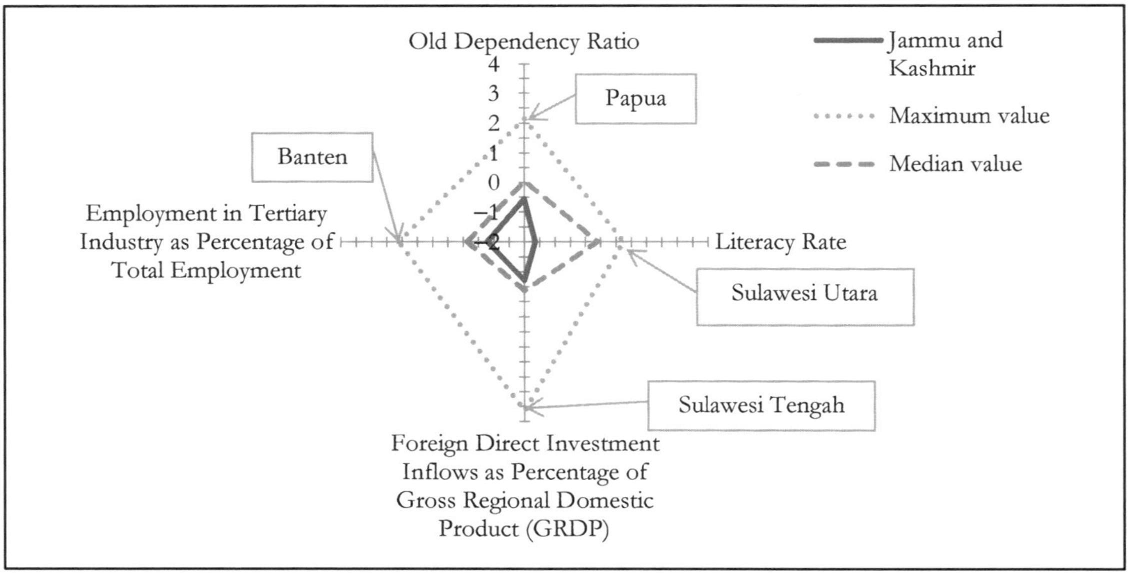

Source: Asia Competitiveness Institute's calculations.

Jammu and Kashmir's scores fell behind the median scores for the lower-middle-income groups in all four determinants, especially in terms of literacy rate. Thus, improving access to basic education and developing human capital in general is paramount if the economy is to avoid the risk of growth slowdown in the future.

Jharkhand

Lower-Middle-Income Economy

Figure 4.19 shows the relative strengths and weaknesses of Jharkhand which was a lower-middle-income economy in 2012 according to the income classification we adopt. As discussed in Section 4.6.1, we found four determinants which are associated with growth slowdown in this particular income group, namely old dependency ratio, literacy rate, foreign direct investment inflows as percentage of GRDP and employment in tertiary industry as percentage of total employment. The solid line shows the standardised score for Jharkhand. The dashed line represents the median score for all economies in the lower-middle-income group across ASEAN, Greater China, India, and Indonesia, while the dotted line denotes the maximum score for those economies.

Jharkhand's scores for old dependency ratio and foreign direct investment inflows as percentage of GRDP were slightly below the median scores for the lower-middle-income group, whereas the scores of literacy rate and employment in tertiary industry as percentage of total employment still lagged far behind the median. Consequently, Jharkhand may consider fully

Figure 4.19: Jharkhand's Strengths and Weaknesses

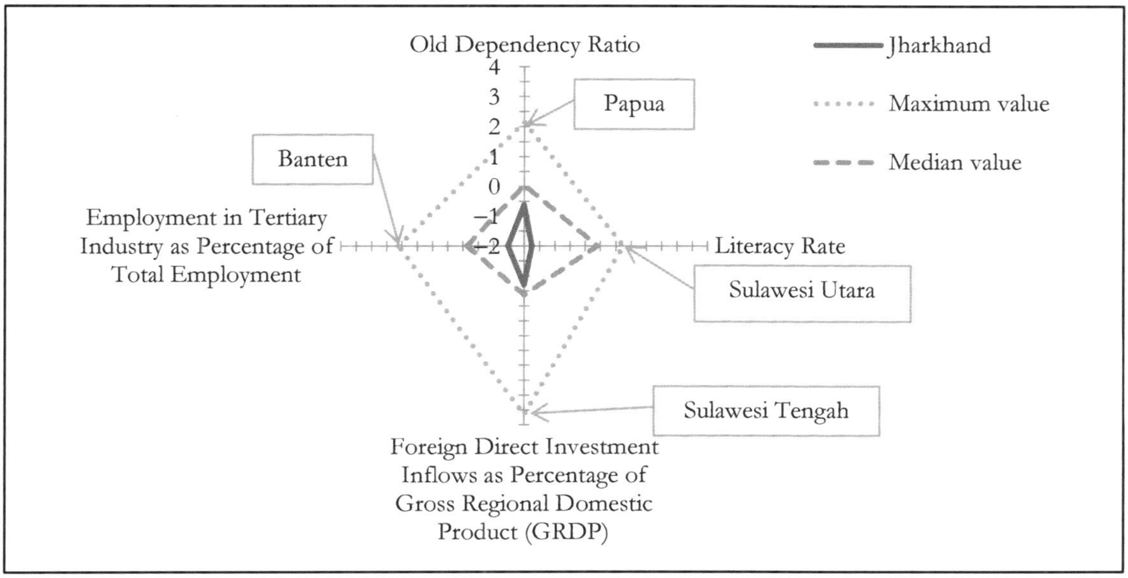

Source: Asia Competitiveness Institute's calculations.

utilising its fund from foreign direct investment inflows to develop its tertiary industry and hence provide more job opportunities for labour forces. Besides, the government of Jharkhand should look to improve access to basic education.

Karnataka

Lower-Middle-Income Economy

Figure 4.20 shows the relative strengths and weaknesses of Karnataka which was a lower-middle-income economy in 2012 according to the income classification we adopt. As discussed in Section 4.6.1, we found four determinants which are associated with growth slowdown in this particular income group, namely old dependency ratio, literacy rate, foreign direct investment inflows as percentage of GRDP and employment in tertiary industry as percentage of total employment. The solid line shows the standardised score for Karnataka. The dashed line represents the median score for all economies in the lower-middle-income group across ASEAN, Greater China, India, and Indonesia, while the dotted line denotes the maximum score for those economies.

Karnataka's scores for employment in tertiary industry as percentage of total employment and foreign direct investment inflows as percentage of GRDP were close to the median of the lower-middle-income group. However, as shown in Figure 4.20, the economy lagged behind its peers in terms of literacy rate and old dependency ratio. Going forward, Karnataka can leverage on its

Figure 4.20: Karnataka's Strengths and Weaknesses

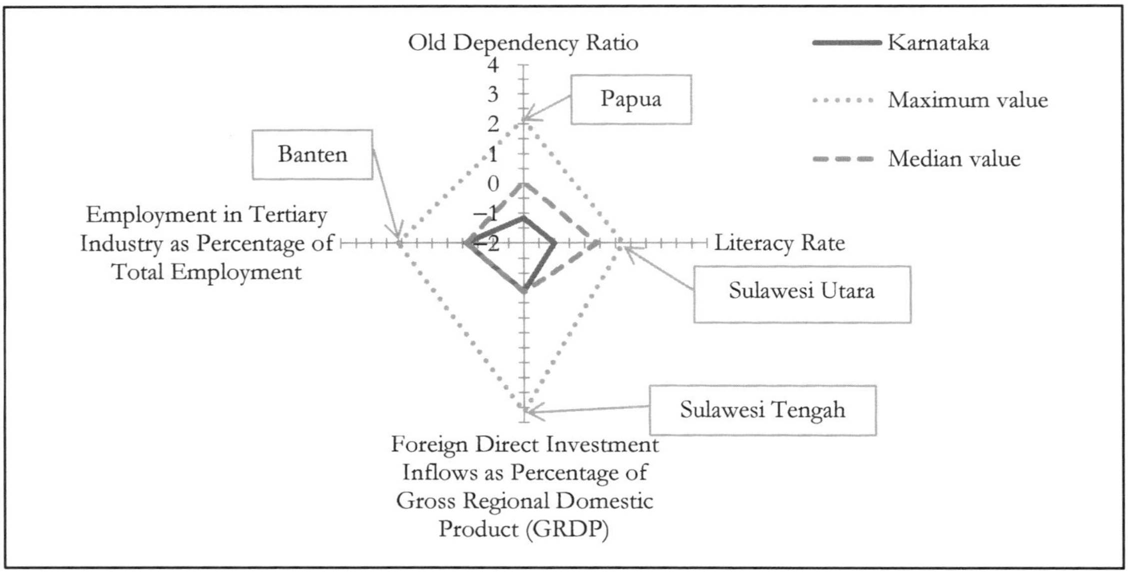

Source: Asia Competitiveness Institute's calculations.

existing strengths to attract more foreign direct investment and further develop the tertiary sector to create more good jobs for its workforce. However, improving access to basic education is paramount if Karnataka is to upgrade its workforce in order to ensure that growth is sustained.

Kerala

Lower-Middle-Income Economy

Figure 4.21 shows the relative strengths and weaknesses of Kerala which was a lower-middle-income economy in 2012 according to the income classification we adopt. As discussed in Section 4.6.1, we found four determinants which are associated with growth slowdown in this particular income group, namely old dependency ratio, literacy rate, foreign direct investment inflows as percentage of GRDP and employment in tertiary industry as percentage of total employment. The solid line shows the standardised score for Kerala. The dashed line represents the median score for all economies in the lower-middle-income group across ASEAN, Greater China, India, and Indonesia, while the dotted line denotes the maximum score for those economies.

Kerala showed strong performance in terms of literacy rate and employment in tertiary industry as percentage of total employment, as its standardised scores for these determinants were above the median scores for the lower-middle-income group. However, the large gap between Kerala's score for old dependency ratio and the median score indicates that ageing population is

Figure 4.21: Kerala's Strengths and Weaknesses

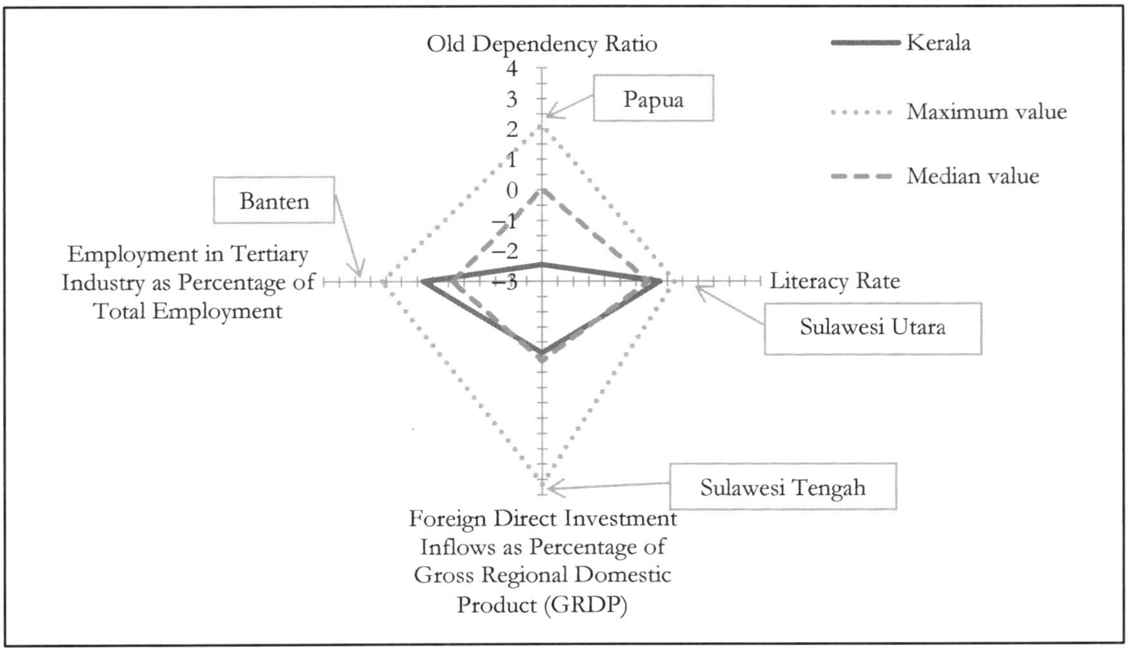

Source: Asia Competitiveness Institute's calculations.

the major challenge for the economy. Going forward, Kerala may look to leverage on its existing strengths to attract more foreign direct investment and further develop its tertiary industry to create more job opportunities. This will help attract and retain the young workforce, which mitigates the challenges of ageing population.

Madhya Pradesh

Lower-Middle-Income Economy

Figure 4.22 shows the relative strengths and weaknesses of Madhya Pradesh which was a lower-middle-income economy in 2012 according to the income classification we adopt. As discussed in Section 4.6.1, we found four determinants which are associated with growth slowdown in this particular income group, namely old dependency ratio, literacy rate, foreign direct investment inflows as percentage of GRDP and employment in tertiary industry as percentage of total employment. The solid line shows the standardised score for Madhya Pradesh. The dashed line represents the median score for all economies in the lower-middle-income group across ASEAN, Greater China, India, and Indonesia, while the dotted line denotes the maximum score for those economies.

Madhya Pradesh's score for foreign direct investment inflows as percentage of GRDP was close to the median of the lower-middle-income group, but its scores for the other determinants lagged behind the respective median scores. Going forward, policymakers in Madhya Pradesh

Figure 4.22: Madhya Pradesh's Strengths and Weaknesses

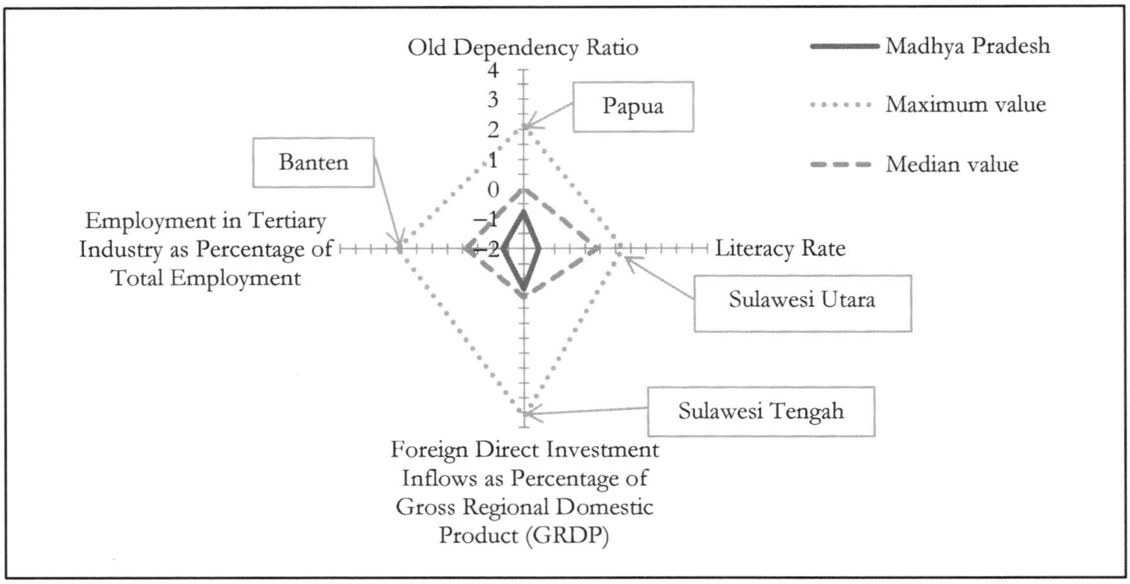

Source: Asia Competitiveness Institute's calculations.

should look to improve basic access to education. They may also seek to leverage on foreign direct investment to develop the economy's tertiary industry as an engine of growth.

Maharashtra

Lower-Middle-Income Economy

Figure 4.23 shows the relative strengths and weaknesses of Maharashtra which was a lower-middle-income economy in 2012 according to the income classification we adopt. As discussed in Section 4.6.1, we found four determinants which are associated with growth slowdown in this particular income group, namely old dependency ratio, literacy rate, foreign direct investment inflows as percentage of GRDP and employment in tertiary industry as percentage of total employment. The solid line shows the standardised score for Maharashtra. The dashed line represents the median score for all economies in the lower-middle-income group across ASEAN, Greater China, India, and Indonesia, while the dotted line denotes the maximum score for those economies.

As shown in Figure 4.23, Maharashtra's score for foreign direct investment inflows as percentage of GRDP exceeded the median of the lower-middle-income group and its score for employment in tertiary industry as percentage of total employment was close to the median. However, it lagged behind its peers in terms of literacy rate and especially old dependency ratio. Thus, improving access to basic education and developing human capital in general is a priority if Maharashtra is to mitigate the risk of growth slowdown. Furthermore, policymakers in Maharashtra may also

Figure 4.23: Maharashtra's Strengths and Weaknesses

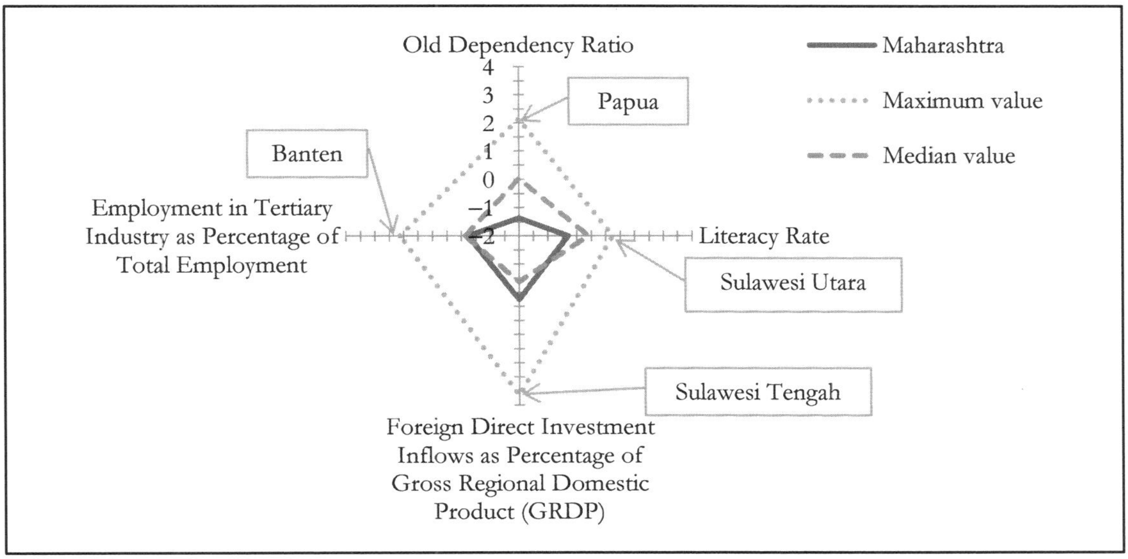

Source: Asia Competitiveness Institute's calculations.

leverage on its existing strength to attract more foreign direct investment and further develop its tertiary industry to create more job opportunities. This will attract and retain the young workforce, which helps Maharashtra to cope with the challenges brought about by its ageing population.

Manipur

Lower-Middle-Income Economy

Figure 4.24 shows the relative strengths and weaknesses of Manipur which was a lower-middle-income economy in 2012 according to the income classification we adopt. As discussed in Section 4.6.1, we found four determinants which are associated with growth slowdown in this particular income group, namely old dependency ratio, literacy rate, foreign direct investment inflows as percentage of GRDP and employment in tertiary industry as percentage of total employment. The solid line shows the standardised score for Manipur. The dashed line represents the median score for all economies in the lower-middle-income group across ASEAN, Greater China, India, and Indonesia, while the dotted line denotes the maximum score for those economies.

In general, Manipur's score for old dependency ratio was close to the median for the lower-middle-income group, but its scores for the other three determinants were below the respective median scores. In particular, Manipur lagged far behind its peers in terms of literacy rate. Thus, more should be done to improve basic access to education and develop the economy's human capital in general.

Figure 4.24: Manipur's Strengths and Weaknesses

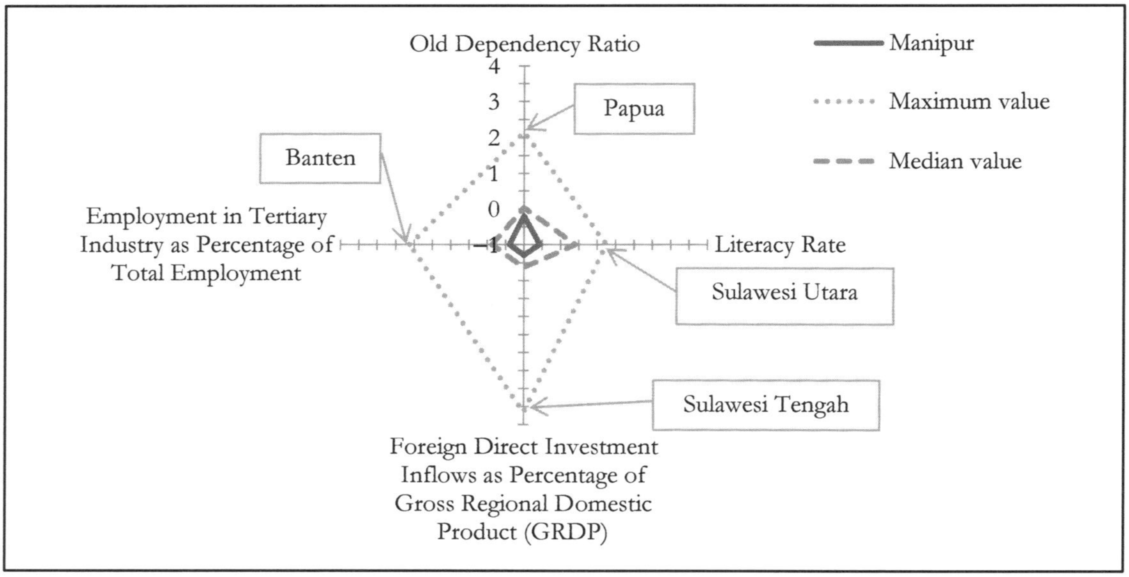

Source: Asia Competitiveness Institute's calculations.

Meghalaya

Lower-Middle-Income Economy

Figure 4.25 shows the relative strengths and weaknesses of Meghalaya which was a lower-middle-income economy in 2012 according to the income classification we adopt. As discussed in Section 4.6.1, we found four determinants which are associated with growth slowdown in this particular income group, namely old dependency ratio, literacy rate, foreign direct investment inflows as percentage of GRDP and employment in tertiary industry as percentage of total employment. The solid line shows the standardised score for Meghalaya. The dashed line represents the median score for all economies in the lower-middle-income group across ASEAN, Greater China, India, and Indonesia, while the dotted line denotes the maximum score for those economies.

Meghalaya's performance in terms of old dependency ratio and employment in tertiary industry as percentage of total employment was encouraging as its scores for these determinants were higher than the median scores of the lower-middle-income group. However, Meghalaya's score for foreign direct investment inflows as percentage of GRDP was below the median. The economy also lagged far behind its peers in terms of literacy rate. Going forward, Meghalaya should intensify the effort to attract foreign direct investment. More should also be done to improve access to basic education and develop human capital in general to ensure that growth can be sustained.

Figure 4.25: Meghalaya's Strengths and Weaknesses

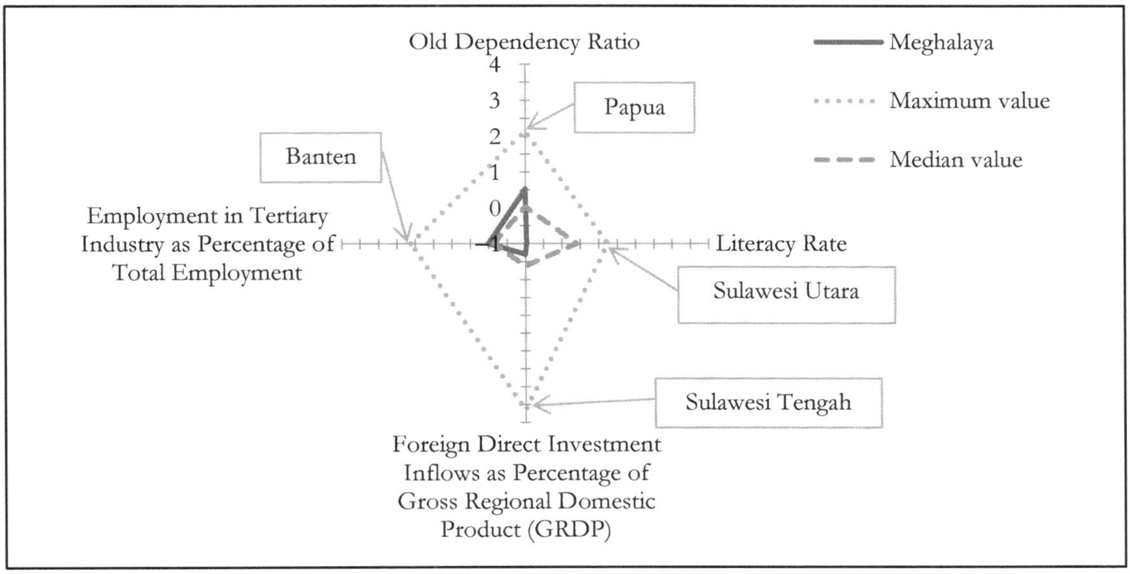

Source: Asia Competitiveness Institute's calculations.

Mizoram

Lower-Middle-Income Economy

Figure 4.26 shows the relative strengths and weaknesses of Mizoram which was a lower-middle-income economy in 2012 according to the income classification we adopt. As discussed in Section 4.6.1, we found four determinants which are associated with growth slowdown in this particular income group, namely old dependency ratio, literacy rate, foreign direct investment inflows as percentage of GRDP and employment in tertiary industry as percentage of total employment. The solid line shows the standardised score for Mizoram. The dashed line represents the median score for all economies in the lower-middle-income group across ASEAN, Greater China, India, and Indonesia, while the dotted line denotes the maximum score for those economies.

Overall, Mizoram's scores for all four determinants are close to the respective median scores of the lower-middle-income group. However, Mizoram's score for foreign direct investment inflows as percentage of GRDP lagged slightly behind the median. Going forward, Mizoram could intensify its effort to attract foreign direct investment. It may also make use of its advantage in employment in tertiary industry as percentage of total employment to further develop the tertiary sector, especially high value-added services.

Figure 4.26: Mizoram's Strengths and Weaknesses

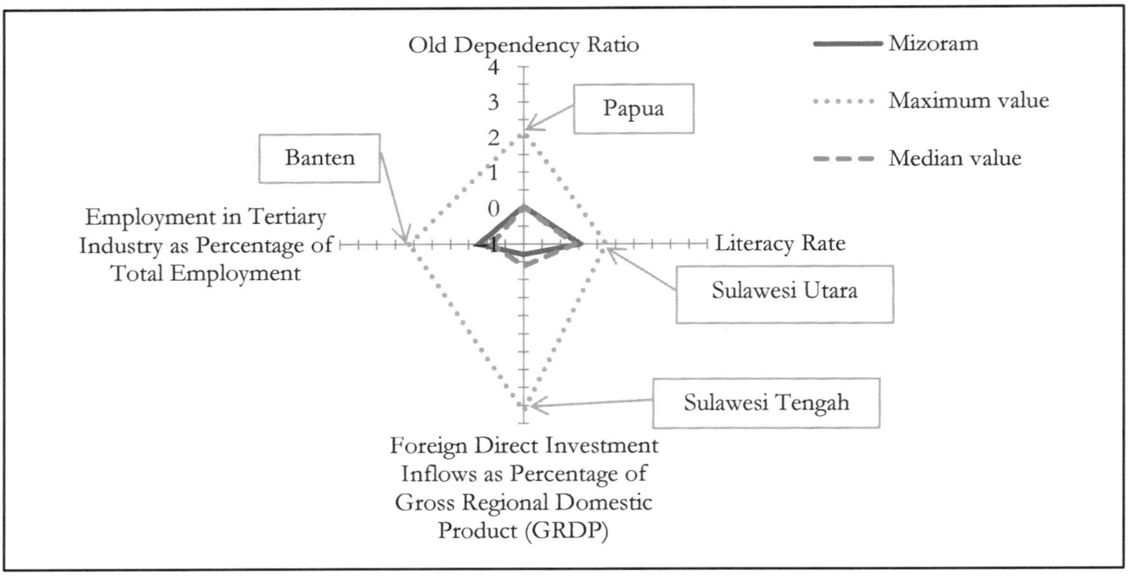

Source: Asia Competitiveness Institute's calculations.

Nagaland

Lower-Middle-Income Economy

Figure 4.27 shows the relative strengths and weaknesses of Nagaland which was a lower-middle-income economy in 2012 according to the income classification we adopt. As discussed in Section 4.6.1, we found four determinants which are associated with growth slowdown in this particular income group, namely old dependency ratio, literacy rate, foreign direct investment inflows as percentage of GRDP and employment in tertiary industry as percentage of total employment. The solid line shows the standardised score for Nagaland. The dashed line represents the median score for all economies in the lower-middle-income group across ASEAN, Greater China, India, and Indonesia, while the dotted line denotes the maximum score for those economies.

Nagaland's scores for old dependency ratio and employment in tertiary industry as percentage of total employment were above the respective median scores of the lower-middle-income group. However, the economy lagged behind its peers in terms of literacy rate and foreign direct investment inflows as percentage of GRDP. Thus, more should be done to improve access to basic education and to develop human capital in general. At the same time, policymakers should step up their effort to attract foreign direct investment.

Figure 4.27: Nagaland's Strengths and Weaknesses

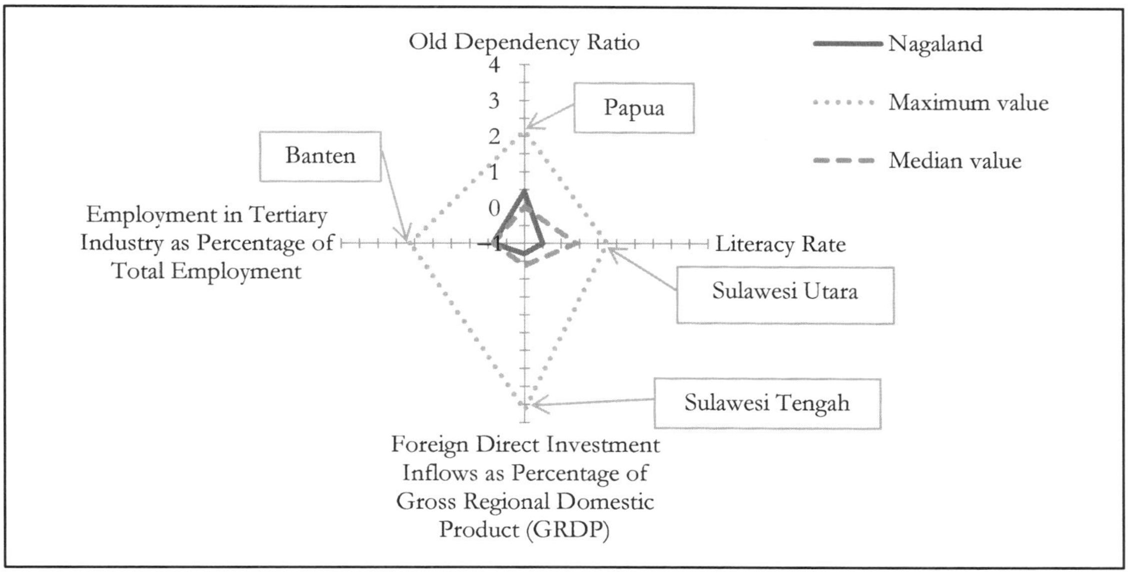

Source: Asia Competitiveness Institute's calculations.

Odisha

Lower-Middle-Income Economy

Figure 4.28 shows the relative strengths and weaknesses of Odisha which was a lower-middle-income economy in 2012 according to the income classification we adopt. As discussed in Section 4.6.1, we found four determinants which are associated with growth slowdown in this particular income group, namely old dependency ratio, literacy rate, foreign direct investment inflows as percentage of GRDP and employment in tertiary industry as percentage of total employment. The solid line shows the standardised score for Odisha. The dashed line represents the median score for all economies in the lower-middle-income group across ASEAN, Greater China, India, and Indonesia, while the dotted line denotes the maximum score for those economies.

Odisha's scores for all four determinants were below the median scores for the lower-middle-income group. However, its score for foreign direct investment inflows as percentage of GRDP was relatively closer to the median than its scores for employment in tertiary industry as percentage of total employment, old dependency ratio, and literacy rate. Going forward, more should be done to improve access to basic education and in general, develop Odisha's human capital. Moreover, Odisha may look to leverage on foreign direct investment to further develop its tertiary industry. This will help create more job opportunities, which helps attract and retain the young workforce.

Figure 4.28: Odisha's Strengths and Weaknesses

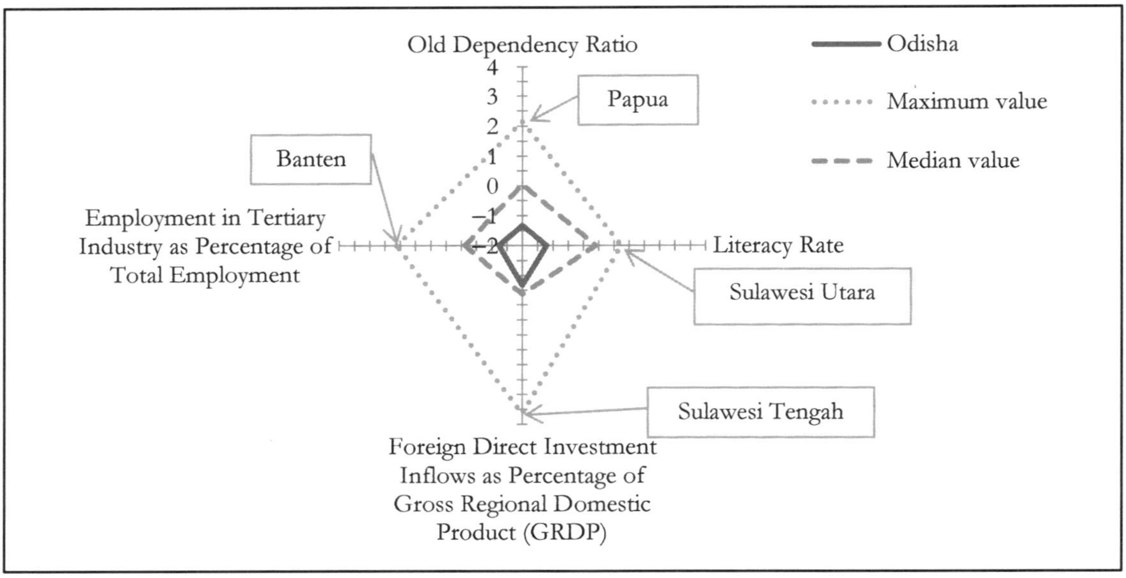

Source: Asia Competitiveness Institute's calculations.

Puducherry

Lower-Middle-Income Economy

Figure 4.29 shows the relative strengths and weaknesses of Puducherry which was a lower-middle-income economy in 2012 according to the income classification we adopt. As discussed in Section 4.6.1, we found four determinants which are associated with growth slowdown in this particular income group, namely old dependency ratio, literacy rate, foreign direct investment inflows as percentage of GRDP and employment in tertiary industry as percentage of total employment. The solid line shows the standardised score for Puducherry. The dashed line represents the median score for all economies in the lower-middle-income group across ASEAN, Greater China, India, and Indonesia, while the dotted line denotes the maximum score for those economies.

Puducherry performed very well in terms of employment in tertiary industry as percentage of total employment, as its score for this determinant at 1.7407 was far above the median of the lower-middle-income group and close to the maximum score of the group (2.1165) as obtained by Banten. In terms of literacy rate and foreign direct investment inflows as percentage of GRDP, Puducherry's scores were close to the median. However, Puducherry's score for old dependency ratio was below the median, indicating that ageing population is the most major challenge for the economy. Going forward, Puducherry may seek to intensify the effort to attract foreign direct investment. It may also leverage on existing strengths to further develop the tertiary sector. This will create more job opportunities, which will help attract and retain the young workforce.

Figure 4.29: Puducherry's Strengths and Weaknesses

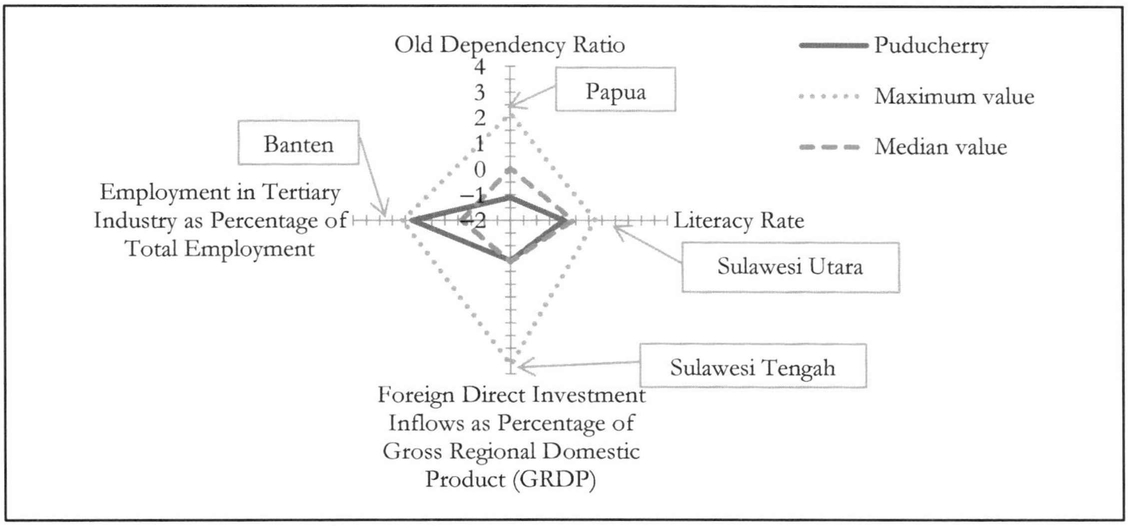

Source: Asia Competitiveness Institute's calculations.

Punjab

Lower-Middle-Income Economy

Figure 4.30 shows the relative strengths and weaknesses of Punjab which was a lower-middle-income economy in 2012 according to the income classification we adopt. As discussed in Section 4.6.1, we found four determinants which are associated with growth slowdown in this particular income group, namely old dependency ratio, literacy rate, foreign direct investment inflows as percentage of GRDP and employment in tertiary industry as percentage of total employment. The solid line shows the standardised score for Punjab. The dashed line represents the median score for all economies in the lower-middle-income group across ASEAN, Greater China, India, and Indonesia, while the dotted line denotes the maximum score for those economies.

Punjab's score for employment in tertiary industry as percentage of total employment was also the median score for the lower-middle-income group. However, for the rest of the determinants, Punjab performed below the median. In particular, literacy rate and old dependency ratio seem to be the economy's most significant weaknesses. Going forward, improving access to basic education and developing human capital in general is paramount if Punjab is to avoid growth slowdown.

Figure 4.30: Punjab's Strengths and Weaknesses

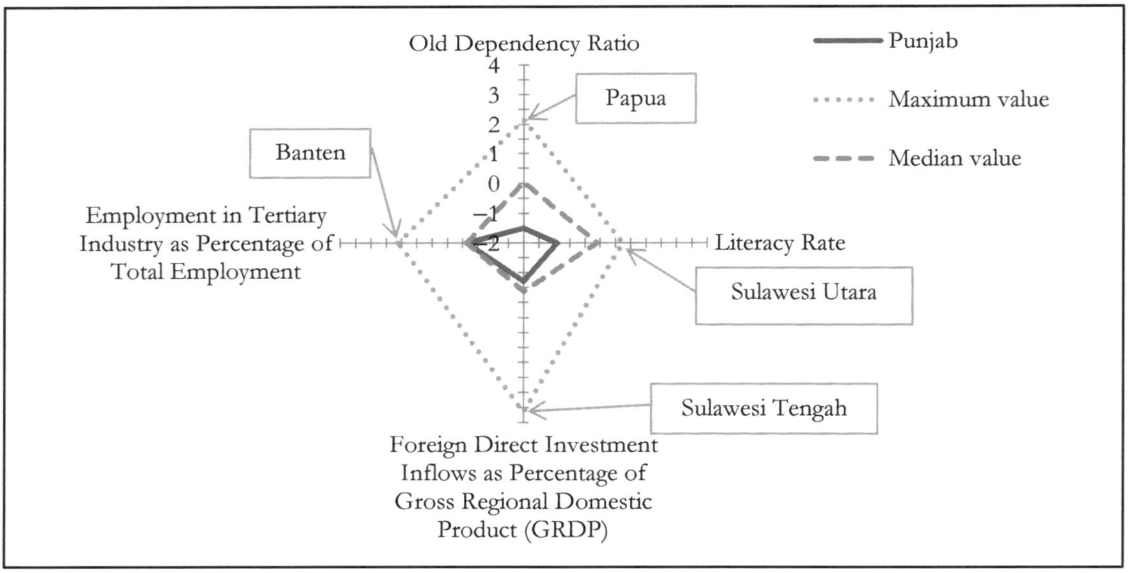

Source: Asia Competitiveness Institute's calculations.

Rajasthan

Lower-Middle-Income Economy

Figure 4.31 shows the relative strengths and weaknesses of Rajasthan which was a lower-middle-income economy in 2012 according to the income classification we adopt. As discussed in Section 4.6.1, we found four determinants which are associated with growth slowdown in this particular income group, namely old dependency ratio, literacy rate, foreign direct investment inflows as percentage of GRDP and employment in tertiary industry as percentage of total employment. The solid line shows the standardised score for Rajasthan. The dashed line represents the median score for all economies in the lower-middle-income group across ASEAN, Greater China, India, and Indonesia, while the dotted line denotes the maximum score for those economies.

In general, Rajasthan's scores for all four determinants were all below the median scores of the lower-middle-income group. Rajasthan's scores for old dependency ratio and foreign direct investment inflows were relatively close to the median. On the other hand, Rajasthan lagged far behind its peers in terms of employment in tertiary industry as percentage of total employment and literacy rate. In order to ensure that growth is sustained, Rajasthan must look to improve access to basic education and develop human capital. Furthermore, Rajasthan can develop tertiary industry, especially high value-added services.

Figure 4.31: Rajasthan's Strengths and Weaknesses

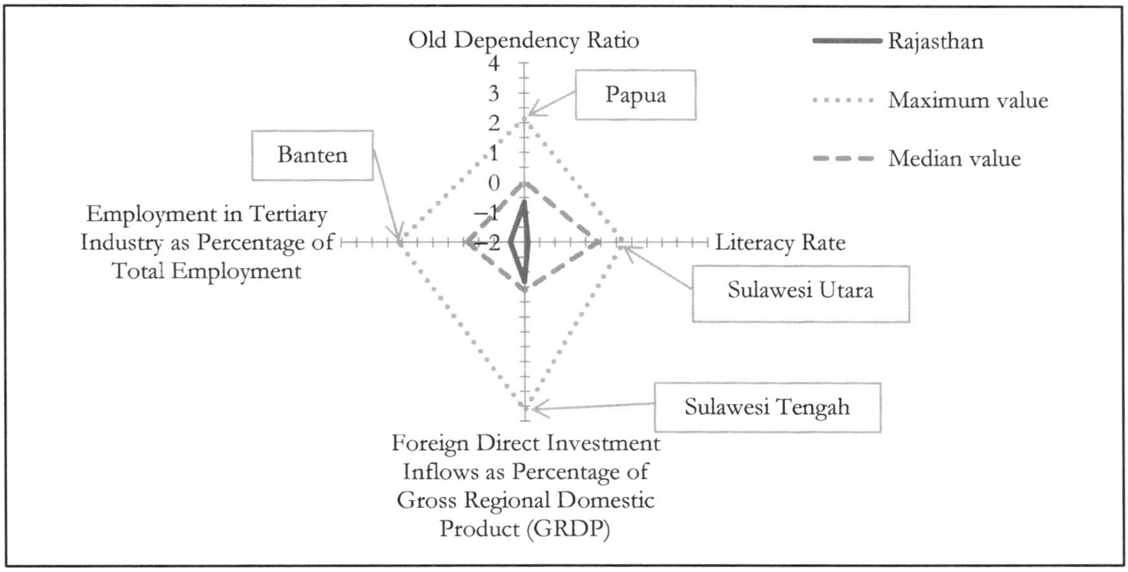

Source: Asia Competitiveness Institute's calculations.

Sikkim

Upper-Middle-Income Economy

Figure 4.32 shows the relative strengths and weaknesses of Sikkim which was an upper-middle-income economy in 2012 according to the income classification we adopt. As mentioned in Section 4.4.2, due to data constraint, we have combined the analysis of high-income economies with that of the upper-middle-income economies. As discussed in Section 4.6.1, we found four determinants which are associated with growth slowdown in this combined group of upper-middle-income and high-income economies, namely openness to trade, literacy rate, secondary industry value added per worker and employment in tertiary industry as percentage of total employment. The solid line shows the standardised score for Sikkim. The dashed line represents the median score for all economies in the combined group of upper-middle-income and high-income economies across ASEAN, Greater China, India, and Indonesia, while the dotted line denotes the maximum score for those economies.

Sikkim's attainment of upper-middle-income status was by and large due to the small population of the economy. Similarly, Sikkim's small workforce helps it to achieve a relatively high standardised score of 1.8166 for secondary industry value added per worker. However, in terms

Figure 4.32: Sikkim's Strengths and Weaknesses

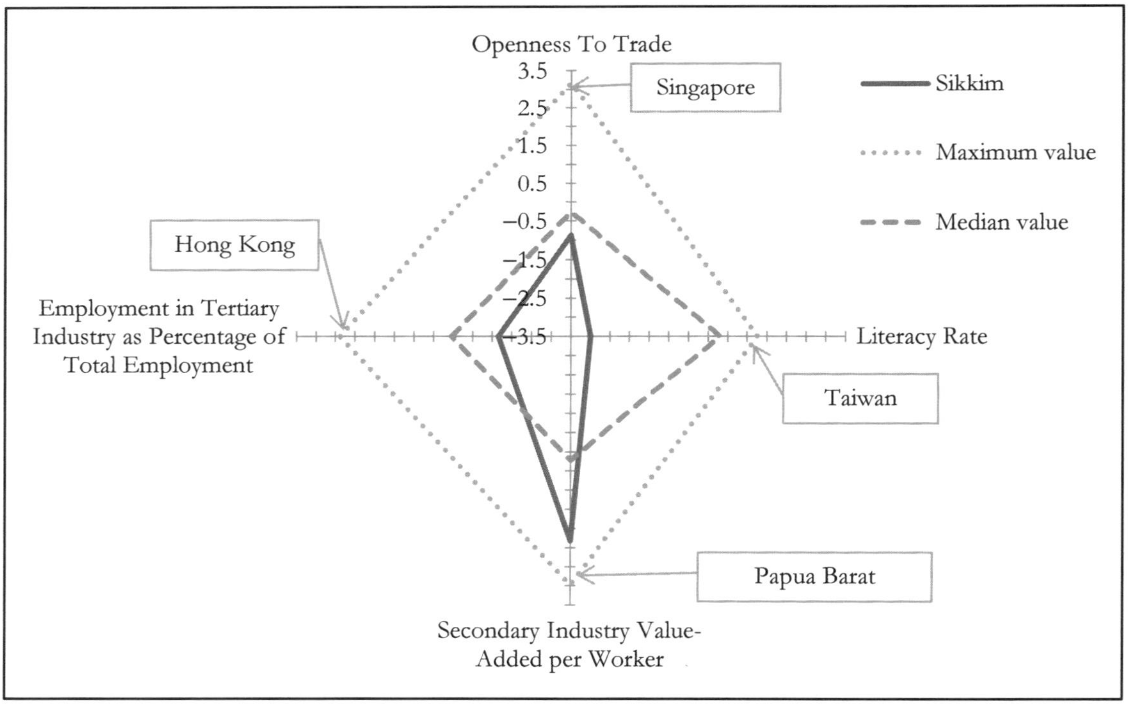

Source: Asia Competitiveness Institute's calculations.

of the other determinants, namely openness to trade, employment in tertiary industry as percentage of total employment and literacy rate, Sikkim lagged behind its peers. In particular, literacy rate seems to be Sikkim's most major weakness as its score for this determinant fell far behind the median of the combined group of upper-middle-income and high-income economies. Going forward, it is crucial that Sikkim improves access to basic education and develop its human capital in general in order to sustain growth.

Tamil Nadu

Lower-Middle-Income Economy

Figure 4.33 shows the relative strengths and weaknesses of Tamil Nadu which was a lower-middle-income economy in 2012 according to the income classification we adopt. As discussed in Section 4.6.1, we found four determinants which are associated with growth slowdown in this particular income group, namely old dependency ratio, literacy rate, foreign direct investment inflows as percentage of GRDP and employment in tertiary industry as percentage of total employment. The solid line shows the standardised score for Tamil Nadu. The dashed line represents the median score for all economies in the lower-middle-income group across ASEAN, Greater China, India, and Indonesia, while the dotted line denotes the maximum score for those economies.

Figure 4.33: Tamil Nadu's Strengths and Weaknesses

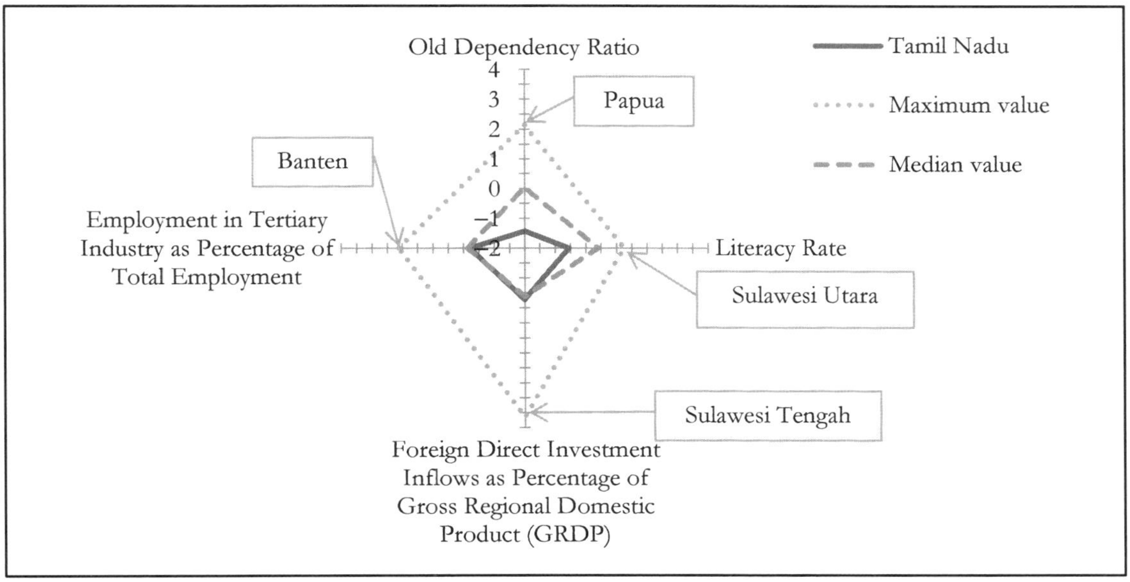

Source: Asia Competitiveness Institute's calculations.

Tamil Nadu's score for employment in tertiary industry as percentage of total employment was close to the median of the lower-middle-income group while its score for foreign direct investment inflows as percentage of GRDP was slightly above the median. However, the economy fell behind its peers in terms of literacy rate and especially old dependency ratio. Going forward, Tamil Nadu may seek to leverage on its strength in attracting foreign direct investment to further develop the tertiary sector. This will create more job opportunities which will help attract and retain the young workforce.

Tripura

Lower-Middle-Income Economy

Figure 4.34 shows the relative strengths and weaknesses of Tripura which was a lower-middle-income economy in 2012 according to the income classification we adopt. As discussed in Section 4.6.1, we found four determinants which are associated with growth slowdown in this particular income group, namely old dependency ratio, literacy rate, foreign direct investment inflows as percentage of GRDP and employment in tertiary industry as percentage of total employment. The solid line shows the standardised score for Tripura. The dashed line represents the median score for all economies in the lower-middle-income group across ASEAN, Greater China, India, and Indonesia, while the dotted line denotes the maximum score for those economies.

In general, Tripura's scores for all four determinants were below the respective median scores of the lower-middle-income group. As shown in Figure 4.34, the tertiary sector in Tripura remains

Figure 4.34: Tripura's Strengths and Weaknesses

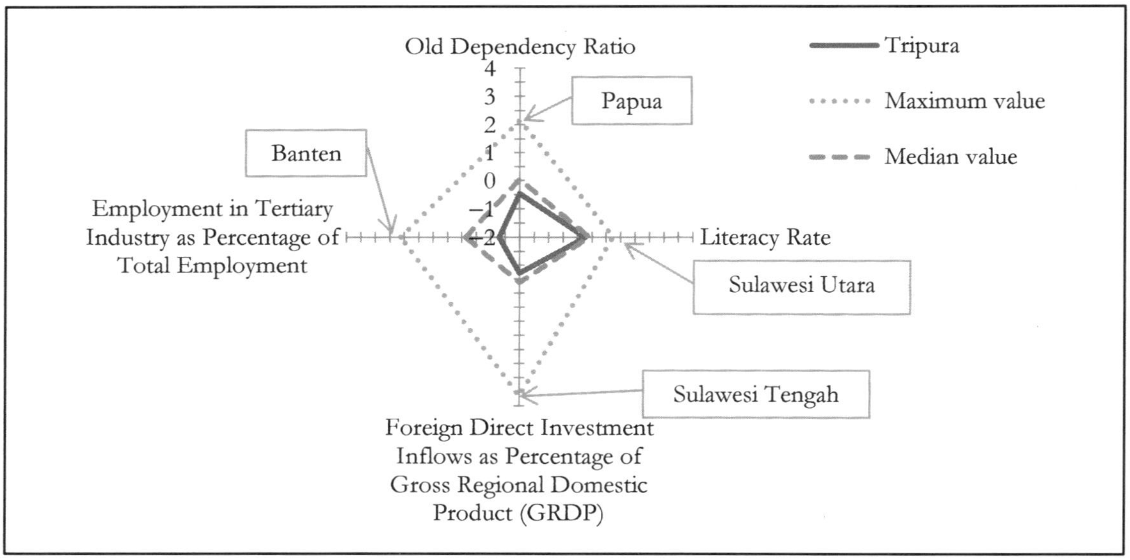

Source: Asia Competitiveness Institute's calculations.

underdeveloped as Tripura's score for employment in tertiary industry as percentage of total employment lagged far behind the median. In comparison, Tripura performed better in terms of literacy rate as its score for this determinant was close to the median. Going forward, Tripura may seek to leverage on its educated workforce to develop tertiary sector as an engine of growth.

Uttar Pradesh

Low-Income Economy

Figure 4.35 shows the relative strengths and weaknesses of Uttar Pradesh which was a low-income economy in 2012 according to the income classification we adopt. As discussed in Section 4.6.1, we found three determinants which are associated with growth slowdown in this particular income group, namely length of road per capita, literacy rate and foreign direct investment inflows as percentage of GRDP. The solid line shows the standardised score for Uttar Pradesh. The dashed line represents the median score for all economies in the low-income group across ASEAN, Greater China, India, and Indonesia, while the dotted line denotes the maximum score for those economies.

Figure 4.35: Uttar Pradesh's Strengths and Weaknesses

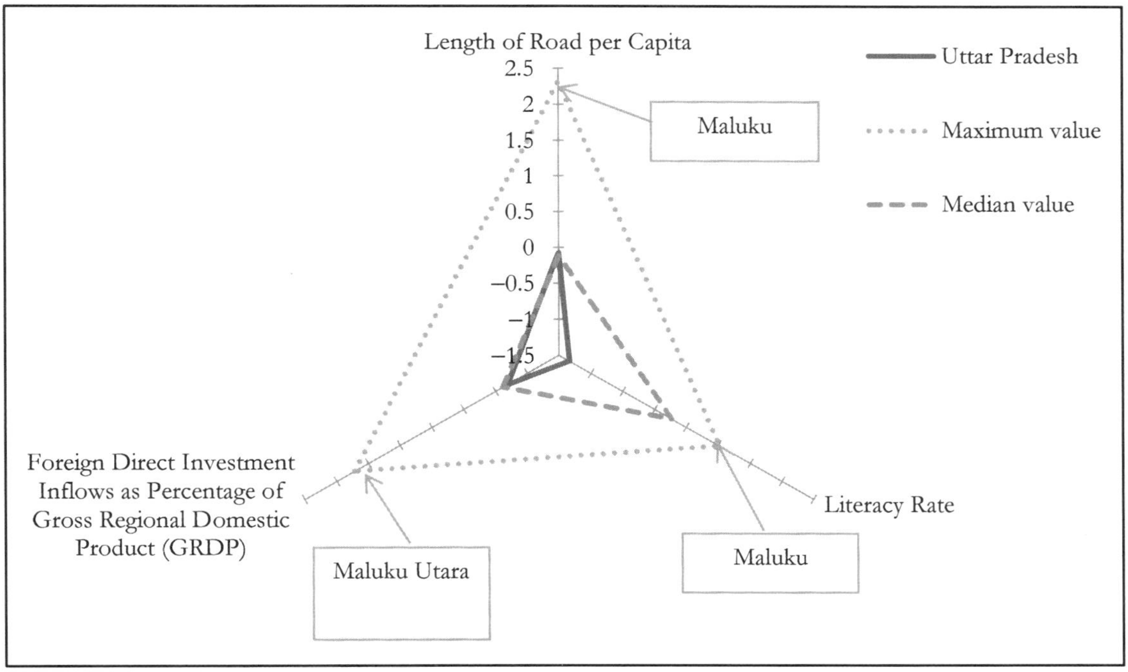

Source: Asia Competitiveness Institute's calculations.

As shown in Figure 4.35, Uttar Pradesh's scores for length of road per capita and foreign direct investment inflows as percentage of GRDP were close to the respective median scores of the low-income group. However, Uttar Pradesh lagged far behind its peers in terms of literacy rate. Going forward, improving access to basic education and developing human capital in general is key for Uttar Pradesh to generate and sustain economic growth so that the economy can break out from the low-income group.

Uttarakhand

Lower-Middle-Income Economy

Figure 4.36 shows the relative strengths and weaknesses of Uttarakhand which was a lower-middle-income economy in 2012 according to the income classification we adopt. As discussed in Section 4.6.1, we found four determinants which are associated with growth slowdown in this particular income group, namely old dependency ratio, literacy rate, foreign direct investment inflows as percentage of GRDP and employment in tertiary industry as percentage of total employment. The solid line shows the standardised score for Uttarakhand. The dashed line represents the median score for all economies in the lower-middle-income group across ASEAN, Greater China, India, and Indonesia, while the dotted line denotes the maximum score for those economies.

In general, Uttarakhand's scores are all below the median scores of the lower-middle-income group for all four determinants. However, the gaps between Uttarakhand's scores for foreign

Figure 4.36: Uttarakhand's Strengths and Weaknesses

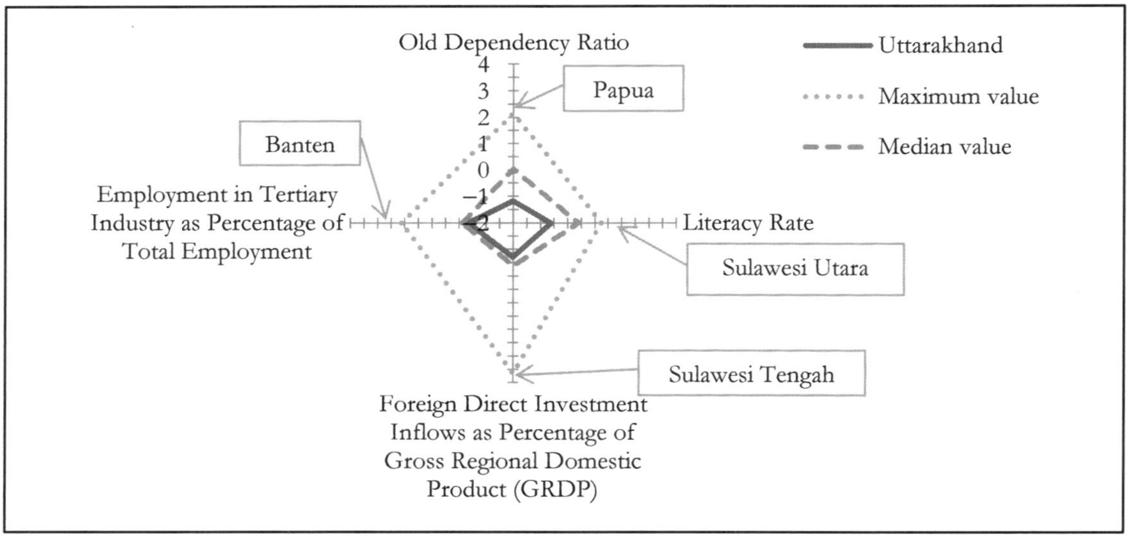

Source: Asia Competitiveness Institute's calculations.

direct investment inflows as percentage of GRDP and employment in tertiary industry as percentage of total employment and the respective median for these determinants were relatively small. In comparison, Uttarakhand lagged far behind other lower-middle-income economies in terms of literacy rate and old dependency ratio. Going forward, Uttarakhand must look to improve access to basic education. In addition, it may also seek to attract more foreign direct investment and develop the tertiary sector. This will create more job opportunities, which will help attract and retain the young workforce.

West Bengal

Lower-Middle-Income Economy

Figure 4.37 shows the relative strengths and weaknesses of West Bengal which was a lower-middle-income economy in 2012 according to the income classification we adopt. As discussed in Section 4.6.1, we found four determinants which are associated with growth slowdown in this particular income group, namely old dependency ratio, literacy rate, foreign direct investment inflows as percentage of GRDP and employment in tertiary industry as percentage of total employment. The solid line shows the standardised score for West Bengal. The dashed line represents the median score for all economies in the lower-middle-income group across ASEAN, Greater China, India, and Indonesia, while the dotted line denotes the maximum score for those economies.

Figure 4.37: West Bengal's Strengths and Weaknesses

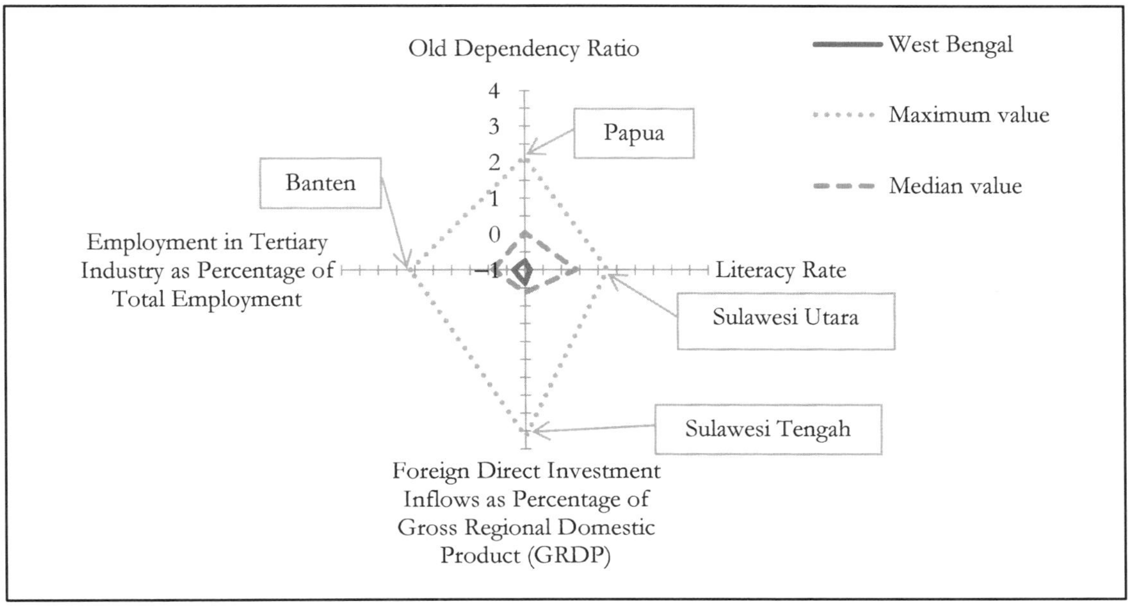

Source: Asia Competitiveness Institute's calculations.

As shown in Figure 4.37, West Bengal lagged far behind other lower-middle-income economies in our sample in all four determinants. In particular, Literacy Rate seems to be West Bengal's most major weakness. As such, going forward, improving access to basic education and developing human capital must be the priority for West Bengal if the economy is to avoid growth slowdown. At the same time, more should also be done to attract foreign direct investment.

4.8 Policy Implications and Concluding Notes

In the 12th Five-Year Plan (2012–2017), the government of India has put across a series of measures aiming at achieving a rapid, sustainable and inclusive growth. The official growth target set by the government is 8 percent over the five-year period. It is heartening to see that quality economic growth is the top priority for the plan as 25 core indicators are identified and will be tracked, each with well-defined target, reflecting the various areas of focus for further improvement. The indicators range from economic growth, poverty and employment, education, health, infrastructure, environment and sustainability to service delivery.[28]

In this context, our research differs from existing literature on middle-income trap and growth slowdown in India by studying this issue at the sub-national level rather than that at the macro level. Despite steady increase in level of GRDP per capita for the sub-national economies of India since we start to track them in 1993, disparity still exists across economies. According to the income thresholds classification we adopted, there was only one economy in the high-income group by 2013 which was Goa, while three sub-national economies attained the upper-middle-income status, namely Chandigarh, Delhi, and Sikkim. Conversely, Bihar and Uttar Pradesh were still stuck in the low-income group. The rest of the 26 sub-national economies were in the lower-middle-income group as of 2013.

By conducting both logistic and probit estimations as well as employing the Bayesian Model Averaging (BMA) techniques, we found that growth slowdown in various income groups tend to be associated with different sets of determinants. Growth slowdown in low-income group is mainly associated with high level of GRDP per capita, low literacy rate, low foreign direct investment inflows as percentage of GRDP and short length of road per capita. On the other hand, lower-middle-income economies are more likely to experience growth slowdown when they have higher level of GRDP per capita, lower foreign direct investment inflows as percentage of GRDP, higher old dependency ratio, lower employment in tertiary industry as percentage of total employment and lower literacy rate. As for the combined group of upper-middle-income and high-income economies, growth slowdown for economies in this group is associated with high GRDP per capita, low openness to trade, low literacy rate, low employment in tertiary industry as percentage of total employment, and low secondary industry value added per worker.

---

[28] For more information on the 12th Five-Year Plan (2012–2017) of India, refer to http://planningcommission.gov.in/plans/planrel/12thplan/pdf/12fyp_vol1.pdf (last accessed on 16 February 2017) (Planning Commission (Government of India) 2013).

Having identified the underlying drivers of growth slowdown in each income group, we assessed whether each sub-national economy of India is prone to experience growth deceleration. Overall, we discovered that the near-future prospects of the sub-national economies of India is less worrying than that of Greater China economies but bleaker than the outlook for economies in ASEAN and Indonesia. Sub-national economies of India have a 43 percent chance of experiencing growth slowdown in the 2012–2017 period on average.[29] However, by looking specifically at each sub-national economy, we find that their probability of experiencing growth slowdown differ significantly from each other depending on the income group they are in. The average probability for the low-income economies is only 0.20057 while the average for the combined group of India's upper-middle-income and high-income economies is much higher at 0.61294. The average for the lower-middle-income economies is 0.42038, close to the overall average. Although the risk of slowdown stemmed largely from the weaknesses of certain dimensions only for some of the sub-national economies in India, others are vulnerable in all aspects considered. For instance, Andhra Pradesh, Assam, Chhattisgarh, Gujarat, Haryana, Himachal Pradesh, Jammu and Kashmir, Jharkhand, Madhya Pradesh, Manipur, Odisha, Punjab, Rajasthan, Uttarakhand, and West Bengal perform worse than the median scores of the lower-middle-income group in all determinants considered.

In general, the chief policy implication of our study lies in the variables identified as significant by our income group specific models. Peer-learning is important in formulating policies to combat the growth slowdown. The sub-national economies of India can benchmark their performances in the relevant policy dimensions against other Asian developing economies to identify their relative strengths and weaknesses and promote necessary reforms to mitigate the risk of growth slowdown.

References

Abbas, Ali, S., Nazim Belhocine, Asmaa El Ganainy and Mark Horton. 2010. "A Historical Public Debt Database." IMF Working Paper 10/425, International Monetary Fund (IMF), Washington D.C.

Agenor, Pierre-Richard. 2015. "Caught in the Middle? The Economics of Middle-Income Trap", FERDI Working Paper 142. Fondation pour les études et recherches sur le développement international (FERDI), Clermont-Ferrand.

Aiyar, Shekhar, Romain Duval, Damien Puy, Yiqun Wu and Longmei, Zhang. 2013. "Growth Slowdowns and the Middle-Income Trap." IMF Working Paper 13/71, International Monetary Fund (IMF), Washington D.C.

Azariadis, Costas and John Stachurski. 2005. "Poverty Traps." in *Handbook of Economic Growth*, edited by Philippe Aghion and Steven N. Durlauf, 1A:295–384. Amsterdam: Elsevier.

Barro, Robert J. and Jong Wha Lee. 2013. "A New Data Set of Educational Attainment in the World, 1950–2010." *Journal of Development Economics*, 104(C): 184–198.

[29] The average predictive probabilities of ASEAN, Greater China, and Indonesia are 0.20890, 0.56872, and 0.10264, respectively.

Benkovskis, Konstantins, Marcel Bluhm, Elena Bobeica, Chiara Osbat and Stefan Zeugner. 2015. "An Empirical Analysis of Competitiveness Drivers Using Bayesian Model Averaging." Mimeo.

Bloom, David E., David Canning and Jaypee Sevilla. 2003. "Geography and Poverty Traps." *Journal of Economic Growth*, 8(4): 355–378.

Bluedorn, John, Rupa Duttagupta, Jaime Guajardo and Petia Topalova. 2013. "Capital Flows Are Fickle: Anytime, Anywhere." IMF Working Paper 13/183, International Monetary Fund (IMF), Washington D.C.

Brock, William. A. 2001. "What Have We Learned from a Decade of Empirical Research on Growth? Growth Empirics and Reality." *The World Bank Economic Review*, 15(2): 229–272.

Bulman, David, Maya Eden and Ha Nguyen. 2014. "Transitioning from Low-Income Growth to High-Income Growth: Is There a Middle Income Trap?" 7104. The World Bank Policy Research Working Paper 7104, The World Bank, Washington D.C.

Dehn, Jan. 2014. "The High Income Trap." *The Emerging View*. https://www.ashmoregroup.com/sites/default/files/article-docs/June 14 High Income trap.pdf.

Eichengreen, Barry, Donghyun Park and Kwanho Shin. 2012. "When Fast-Growing Economies Slow Down: International Evidence and Implications for China." *Asian Economic Papers*, 11: 42–87.

Eichengreen, Barry, Donghyun Park and Kwanho Shin. 2013. "Growth Slowdowns Redux: New Evidence on the Middle-Income Trap." NBER Economic Research Paper Series 18673, National Bureau of Economic Research (NBER), Massachusetts.

Felipe, Jesus. 2012a. "Tracking the Middle-Income Trap: What Is It, Who Is in It, and Why? Part 1." ADB Working Paper 306, Asian Development Bank (ADB), Manila.

Felipe, Jesus. 2012b. "Tracking the Middle-Income Trap: What Is It, Who Is in It, and Why? Part 2." ADB Working Paper 307, Asian Development Bank (ADB), Manila.

Flaaen, Aaron, Ejaz Ghani and Saurabh Mishra. 2013. "How to Avoid Middle Income Traps? Evidence from Malaysia." The World Bank Policy Research Working Paper 6427, The World Bank, Washington D.C.

Gill, Indermit Singh and Homi Kharas. 2007. *An East Asian Renaissance: Ideas for Economic Growth*. Washington D.C.: The World Bank.

Gill, Indermit Singh and Homi Kharas. 2015. "The Middle-Income Trap Turns Ten." The World Bank Policy Research Working Paper 7403, The World Bank, Washington D.C.

González-Aguado, Carlos and Enrique Moral-Benito. 2013. "Determinants of Corporate Default: A BMA Approach." *Applied Economics Letters,* 20(6): 511–514.

Hausmann, Ricardo, Lant Pritchett and Dani Rodrik. 2005a. "Growth Accelerations. Journal of Economic Growth." *Journal of Economic Growth,* 10(4): 303–329.

Hausmann, Ricardo, Jason Hwang and Dani Rodrik. 2005b. "What You Export Matters." NBER Economic Research Paper Series 11905, National Bureau of Economic Research (NBER), Massachusetts.

Hausmann, Ricardo, Francisco Rodríguez and Rodrigo Wagner. 2006. "Growth Collapses." 136. CID Working Paper 146, Center for International Development (CID), Harvard University, Massachusetts.

Im, Fernando Gabriel and David Rosenblatt. 2013. "Middle-Income Traps: A Conceptual and Empirical Survey." The World Bank Policy Research Working Paper 6594, The World Bank, Washington D.C.

International Monetary Fund. 2015. "World Economic Outlook: Adjusting to Lower Commodity Prices." Available from http://www.imf.org/external/pubs/ft/weo/2015/02/pdf/text.pdf (last accessed on February 25, 2016).

Jalan, Jyotsna and Martin Ravallion. 2002. "Geographic Poverty Traps? A Micro Model of Consumption Growth in Rural China." *Journal of Applied Econometrics*, 17(4): 329–346.

Jerzmanowski, Michal. 2006. "Empirics of Hills, Plateaus, Mountains and Plains: A Markov-Switching Approach to Growth." *Journal of Development Economics*, 81(2): 357–385.

Kasenda, Daniel. 2015. "Can Asian Developing Countries Stuck In A "Middle-Income Trap" Learn From South Korea's Economic Development Experience?" GDN Working Paper No. 86, Global Development Network (GDN), Washington D.C.

Maddison, James. 2010. "Statistics on World Population, GDP and Per Capita GDP, 1-2008AD." Available from http://www.ggdc.net/maddison/oriindex.htm (last accessed on August 11, 2015).

Neumann, Frederic. 2015. "Time to Talk about the High Income Trap." *Nikkei Asian Review*, May 24. Available from http://asia.nikkei.com/Viewpoints/Economeister/Time-to-talk-about-the-high-income-trap (last accessed on February 23, 2016).

Petroff, Alanna. 2016. "India Primed for 9 Percent Growth, Says Finance Minister." *CNN*, January 21. Available at http://money.cnn.com/2016/01/20/news/economy/india-economy-growth-davos/ (last accessed on February 25, 2016).

Planning Commission (Government of India). 2013. "Twelfth Five Year Plan (2012–2017): Faster, More Inclusive and Sustainable Growth. New Delhi." Available at http://planningcommission.gov.in/plans/planrel/12thplan/pdf/12fyp_vol1.pdf (last accessed on February 25, 2016).

Pritchett, Lant. 2000. "Understanding Patterns of Economic Growth: Searching for Hills among Plateaus, Mountains, and Plains." *The World Bank Economic Review*, 14(2): 221–250.

Pritchett, Lant and Lawrence H. Summers. 2014. "Asiaphoria Meets Regression to the Mean." NBER Working Paper 20573, National Bureau Economic Research (NBER), Massachusetts.

Quah, Danny T. 1993. "Empirical Cross-Section Dynamics in Economic Growth." *European Economic Review*, 37(2–3): 426–434.

Ranjan, Rajiv, Sujan Hajra and Narendra Jadhav. 2005. *Re-Emerging India: A Global Perspective*. Hyderabad: ICFAI University Press.

Reddy, Sanjay and Camelia Minoiu. 2008. "Real Income Stagnation of Countries 1960–2001." *The Journal of Development Studies*, 45(1): 1–23.

Rodrik, Dani and Arvind Subramanian. 2004. "From 'Hindu Growth' to Productivity Surge: The Mystery of the Indian Growth Transition." IMF Working Paper 04/77, International Monetary Fund (IMF), Washington D.C.

Shrinivasan, Rukmini. 2010. "World's Poor Move with India into Middle-Income Bracket", The Times of India, December 26. Available from http://timesofindia.indiatimes.com/india/Worlds-poor-move-with-India-into-middle-income-bracket/articleshow/7165089.cms (last accessed on February 24, 2016).

Tan, Khee Giap, Linda Low, Kartik Rao and Kong Yam Tan. 2015. "*2014 Regional Competitiveness Analysis and a Master Plan on Regional Development Strategies for India: Annual Competitiveness Update and Evidence on Economic Development Model for Selected States of India*". Singapore: World Scientific.

Tan, Khee Giap, Nguyen Trieu Duong Luu and Sangiita Wei Cher Yoong. 2016a. "An Empirical Investigation of Growth Slowdown Analysis for India's Sub-National Economies". ACI Technical Working Paper #06-2016, Asia Competitiveness Institute, Lee Kuan Yew School of Public Policy, National University of Singapore, June.

Tan, Khee Giap, Lian Xiao and Xie Teleixi. 2016b. "Growth Slowdown Analysis for Greater China Economies." *Journal of Economics and Development Studies*, 4(2): 129–144, June 2016.

Tan, Khee Giap, Nursyahida Binte Ahmad and Sasidaran Gopalan. 2016c. "Indonesian Sub-National Economies and Growth Slowdown: An Empirical Analysis." ACI Technical Working Paper #07-2016, Asia Competitiveness Institute, Lee Kuan Yew School of Public Policy, National University of Singapore, June.

Tan, Khee Giap, Nguyen Trieu Duong Luu and Lian Xiao. 2017. "Empirical Analysis of Growth Slowdown in ASEAN." *The Journal of Developing Areas*, 51(3): 363–376.

The Conference Board, 2015. "Output, Labor and Labor Productivity, 1950–2015, Total Economy Database, May 2015 Version." Available from https://www.conference-board.org/data/economydatabase/index.cfm?id=27762 (last accessed on August 11, 2015).

Tsounta, Evridiki. 2014. "Slowdown in Emerging Markets: Sign of a Bumpy Road Ahead?" IMF Working Paper 14/205, International Monetary Fund (IMF), Washington D.C.

Woo, Wing Thye. 2012. "China Meets the Middle-Income Trap: The Large Potholes in the Road to Catching-Up." *Journal of Chinese Economic and Business Studies*, 10(4): 313–336.

Ye, Longfeng and Peter Robertson. 2016. "Identifying Prisoners of the Middle-Income Trap." Available from http://www.voxeu.org/article/identifying-prisoners-middle-income-trap (last accessed on April 29, 2016).

Yusuf, Shahid and Kaoru Nabeshima. 2009. "Can Malaysia Escape the Middle-Income Trap? A Strategy for Penang." The World Bank Policy Research Working Paper 4971, The World Bank, Washington D.C.

Zhang, Derong. 2014. "The Mechanism of the Middle Income Trap and the Potential Factors Influencing China's Economic Growth." *Frontiers of Economics in China*, 9(3): 499–528.

Zhang, Longmei and Damien Puy. 2015. "Growth Slowdown: Are Frontier and Developing Asian Economies Different?" in *Frontier and Developing Asia: The Next Generation of Emerging Markets*, edited by Alfred Schipke. Washington D.C.: International Monetary Fund.

Discussant Note 4.1

Comments on "Growth Slowdown Analysis by Income Thresholds for India's Sub-National Economies"

Professor Pulapre Balakrishnan
Ashoka University, India

The study is valuable for there are several that analyse the slowdown at the macro level this one must be among the few that studies sub-national economies of the second and third largest economies of the world (in PPP terms). It opens by presenting some the stylised facts on India and China. Notable among these are that in China "most of the graduation from lower-middle-income to upper-middle -income group took place between "2010–2014" which is after the slowing of the world economy following the Global Financial Crisis commencing 2007. By contrast the most populous states of India — Uttar Pradesh and Bihar — have remained low income economies. Only one Indian sub-national economy, namely Goa, is in the upper income bracket as opposed to several in China. However, we are told, by 2025 India is expected to overtake China's population!

The Middle Income Trap

The authors consider the idea of the 'Middle Income Trap' — originating in the World Bank and the IMF — but do not adopt it, preferring to take the view that slowdown can occur at any level. This is a correct view. It is also supported by the data presented in this study.

The Methodology for Identification of Slowdowns

- The authors adopt Felipe's (2012) classification of economies by income level but do not tell us why. This is unsatisfactory as they discuss four methods possible.
- The methodology used is that of Eichengreen, Park and Shin (2012).

It may be said that the criteria used for identification — that growth ought to have exceeded 3.5 percent before 2012 and the slowdown ought to be at least by 2 percentage points — reflects the Asian experience. In Asia, there has been high growth for the past three decades. This is not true of much of the rest of the world.

Predictive Probability of a Slowdown

It is not clear what is meant by the suggestion that a country with a 5 percent growth rate runs the risk of falling into a trap (in this case, the MIT). Surely it only means that it will take the country longer to transit to the high income group. Further, the study identifies "the main drivers of growth in China: investment, consumption and export", but these three components (almost) exhaust income. So the statement does not contain much information or analytical content. Does consumption have an autonomous status, for we write consumption as a dunction of income (Y) expressed as $C = c(Y)$? Of course, the interest rate can affect consumption, but has this shown a secular movement in China? We are not told.

Growth Slowdown Analysis: The Greater China Economies

The study correctly identifies challenges to growth posed by declining competitiveness due to an appreciating *renminbi* and the bursting of a likely real estate bubble. But it also refers to consumption having dropped to "less than 40 percent of the economy". As already said, it is not clear why this may have happened. Has income dropped or could investment have increased? If so, this may bode well for growth in the future!

Determinants of the Growth Slowdown

This is the most significant part of the study. There is considerable work but the interpretation of the results is not obvious. I remain sceptical of almost all the variables the authors use, despite their statistical significance, as the underlying theory is missing. Consider, for example, the resort to 'openness to trade'. How am I to believe that openness to trade reduces the probability of a growth slowdown when I find that China, which is the more open economy, has slowed more than India has since 2007? India too has slowed precisely as it has got increasingly integrated into the world economy.

It would of course be correct to say that roads, literacy and the dependency ratio are all important drivers of long-term growth. But they are unlikely to prevent a slowdown in an integrated economy when the world trade slows. Finally, there is something counterintuitive in arguing that productivity ("value added per worker") in manufacturing ("secondary sector") reduces the risk of a slowdown while at the same time saying that a higher share of the tertiary sector in the economy also reduces the same.

Strengths and Weaknesses of Economies

A very useful comparative perspective is provided. For instance, I am now able to see how the Indian state of Bihar fares in relation to its Asian peers. However, I would have been interested in seeing how the low-income Indian state of Uttar Pradesh fares in a pan-Asian comparison as the study by Tan *et al.* (2017) ranks it very high in terms of 'attractiveness to FDI'.

Concluding Comments

The study is very strong on the empirics. But a more analytical and critical approach to both the methodology adopted and the interpretation would have been appropriate. Moreover, having estimated the predictive probability of slowdown it would have been interesting to compare the prediction with actual outcome. This would also serve as an evaluation of the procedure adopted in the study.

While concluding, two general comments would be in order. First, the authors appear to accept uncritically the likely positive consequences of some of the recent policy announcements of the Indian government. Some, at least preliminary, analysis of the progress made under 'Make in India' could have been attempted. Secondly, surprisingly the study does not recommend what can be done to restore the rate of growth in China, or do the authors accept the view of that country's leadership whom they quote? This would be a matter of interest to much of the world concerned with slowing growth in China!

References

Eichengreen, Barry, Donghyun Park and Kwanho Shin. 2012. "When Fast-Growing Economies Slow Down: International Evidence and Implications for China." *Asian Economic Papers*, 11: 42–87.

Felipe, Jesus. 2012a. "Tracking the Middle-Income Trap: What Is It, Who Is in It, and Why? Part 1." ADB Working Paper 306, Asian Development Bank (ADB), Manila.

Felipe, Jesus. 2012b. "Tracking the Middle-Income Trap: What Is It, Who Is in It, and Why? Part 2." ADB Working Paper 307, Asian Development Bank (ADB), Manila.

Tan, Khee Giap, Sasidaran Gopalan, Anuja Tandon and Kong Yam Tan. 2017. "*2016 Annual Competitiveness and Growth Slowdown Analysis for the Sub-National Economies of India*." (Forthcoming).

Discussant Note 4.2

Comments on "Growth Slowdown Analysis by Income Thresholds for Greater China Economies and India's Sub-National Economies"

Dr Sun Jingying
Assistant Professor, Institute of World Economics and Politics, Chinese Academy of Social Sciences

First, I would like to express my great appreciation to our host. Thank you for the opportunity to comment on this very exciting topic on the comparison of how India and China perform on the potential slowdown issues at the sub-national level. Yesterday when I was here, I visited the National Museum of Singapore which gave me very interesting lessons on how Singapore has developed. I have gained a different understanding about Singapore and its very unique position. Our seminar today on China and India is not held in these countries, but in Singapore which provides a third-party perspective. As such, we can come together and freely exchange our ideas. Also, I am reminded of the former Singapore Prime Minister, Mr Lee Kuan Yew. He spoke about managing globalisation and the rises of India and China way back in 2005. It is interesting that these are also the themes for our seminar today.

I like the growth slowdown research by the ACI very much. I don't think I have seen any similar Chinese research on the topic, especially at the sub-national level. In China, we predicted that we would bounce back from the downturn. When it did not happen, we switched to assuming that China's growth followed a U-shaped pattern. Later, we observed that the Chinese economy did bounce back for a short time and then resumed to be in slow growth, so we suspected that it might be an L-shaped pattern. However, someone who was more pessimistic thought there was a possibility that the pattern could be I-shaped! Here, the ACI used very solid macro-level foundation data to assess the Chinese economy, which is good.

There are four points I like about this research. First, it is a pioneering work which used the provincial data covering ASEAN, China, India and Indonesia to group the sub-national economies into three income categories as the study's starting point. Based on that, the second point is that the study allows us to compare the economies and how they performed over the study period. Thirdly, this research offers a very solid database. It also sheds light on important policy implications which are presented in a very graphical manner for both central and local policymakers to use as a policy reference tool. Finally, I also like the tests applied in the paper.

Having said that, I have some technical issues that I would like to discuss with the authors. First, the empirical findings on determinants of growth slowdown in the different income groups was based on a pooled sample. In other words, the determinants were identified using data not only for China and India but also for ASEAN and Indonesia. However, if we are discussing specifically about China and India, ASEAN and Indonesia are out of context. If you had excluded ASEAN and Indonesia from the analysis, the determinants might have been different from what you had identified. In its current state, the study provides an insightful but not direct comparison between China and India. Secondly, the impact of the 2008 Financial Crisis was not taken into consideration. For future research, there can be a financial crisis dummy to represent this period.

I like the Bayesian Model Averaging (BMA) analysis because it is a novel technique. However, I am a little bit confused about the results and probably I need further explanations. For the upper-middle-income and high-income groups, I do not understand why you dropped "road density" and "overall productivity". I think that road density gave really good results, instead of the other determinants. At the same time, you selected "secondary industry value-added per worker" as a robust determinant, but left out "tertiary industry value-added per worker" without any further explanation. At the same time, the radar maps showing the strengths and weaknesses of each economy only include four determinants. However, perhaps you need more determinants to fully explain growth slowdown in the sub-national economies.

Next, this is a small point but I also note that while the determinants of growth slowdown for Greater China and India were symmetrical, in the Potentials and Challenges section, you focussed more on country-specific issues. For instance, for China you talked about the Gross Domestic Product (GDP) accounting identity (GDP = Consumption (C) + Investment (I) + Goverment (G) + Net Exports (X)) and for India, you talked about national policies. Perhaps you can incorporate these country-specific characteristics in the analysis of determinants, which will be of great interest for policy-makers.

In conclusion, I like the research. It drew on Eichengreen, Park and Shin (2012), Felipe (2012) and the BMA literature. Interestingly, Eichengreen, Park and Shin (2012) was based on Hausmann, Rodriguez and Wagner (2006) and this latter paper was titled "Growth Acceleration". It is thus an interesting contrast to note that in 2005, we talked about growth acceleration, and now we are talking about growth slowdown instead. In my opinion, the common challenge for China and India is that these countries may slow down before they get rich, and also getting old before getting rich. The academic world should put in more efforts to understand these issues.

Thank you very much.

References

Eichengreen, Barry, Donghyun Park and Kwanho Shin. 2012. "When Fast-Growing Economies Slow Down: International Evidence and Implications for China." *Asian Economic Papers*, 11: 42–87.

Felipe, Jesus. 2012a. "Tracking the Middle-Income Trap: What Is It, Who Is in It, and Why? Part 1." ADB Working Paper 306, Asian Development Bank (ADB), Manila.

Felipe, Jesus. 2012b. "Tracking the Middle-Income Trap: What Is It, Who Is in It, and Why? Part 2." ADB Working Paper 307, Asian Development Bank (ADB), Manila.

Hausmann, Ricardo, Francisco Rodríguez and Rodrigo Wagner. 2006. "Growth Collapses." 136. CID Working Paper 146, Center for International Development (CID), Harvard University, Massachusetts.

Discussant Note 4.3

Comments on "Growth Slowdown Analysis by Income Thresholds for ASEAN Countries and Indonesia's Sub-National Economies"[30]

Dr Darwin Marcelo
Infrastructure Economist, The World Bank

I have two sets of comments, one on the methods and models, and the other one on the results.

First, this is a very interesting research, addresses a very relevant question and includes a huge effort to prepare the data, especially because the numbers are at the sub-regional level. Last year, The World Bank worked together with NUS and ACI to obtain similar information at the national level. This process was very complicated, so what you have achieved here is remarkable.[30]

On the methods and models, the search for slowdown episodes started with a window of five years. The selection of that window is rather arbitrary. A question I would ask to the researchers is what would have happened if you had a longer or shorter window. This is relevant because the number of episodes may change if the window is narrower or wider. When trying to explain the probability of occurrence of a slowdown episode, the window selection may affect the results. This window also has a direct effect on the time series presented. The study used a twenty-year dataset, but with a five-year window, ten years of data are lost. The analysis detected a slowdown only for a period of ten years, from 1998 to 2008. One may think that most slowdowns happened after 2008 and before 1998. Therefore, the selection of this window is very important, because it has two repercussions on the results of the model.

On the results, it would be useful if you can include the classification statistics, given that the whole point of the exercise is to make a prediction and assess the probability of a slowdown episode. Two indicators should have been presented; sensitivity and specificity. Sensitivity means the fraction of events that are correctly classified and specificity means fraction of non-events that correctly classified. This will give the reader an idea of how powerful the model is. Furthermore, given that the suggested probabilistic model is trying to predict the probability of occurrence of a slowdown event, it should also be contrasted against the observed results to give the reader an idea of how powerful the model is.

I also think that it is highly possible that observations are clustered at the country level because the units of observation are at the sub-regional level. This might lead to standard error bias, but more importantly, coefficient bias, which could lead to a wrong conclusion. Therefore, I suggest to perform a test to be completely sure that this kind of phenomenon (clustering at the

[30] These discussant remarks were presented as part of the ACI-World Bank ASEAN Economic Forum held on September 09, 2016, hosted by ACI at LKYSPP, NUS.

country level) is not present. The intuition is that a country is exposed to the same macroeconomic environment. Observations may not be independent because they correspond to sub-regions within a country. All the sub-regions are exposed to the same macroeconomic factors and so they may be clustered.

The results are striking. For a country like Singapore, there is a very high probability of experiencing a slowdown event. And then, when we look at the sub-regional level there are many economies that have about 40 percent probability for facing a slowdown event (Tan *et al.,* 2017).

Results suggest that the richer the sub-national region is, the higher the probability of a slowdown episode is. Again, what happens when you have clustering? You may have a region within a country that is getting richer and that has a high probability of facing a slowdown. But it may happen that all the regions inside a country growth at the same time because they are clustered at the country level. I would not consider the sub-regional levels as micro nations, I would consider the sub-region as a cluster inside a country. Again, regions are similar in terms of legislation, language, trade relations, national government, etc.

Finally, regarding the implications of the model, I have the following question: what is the space that governments have or what are the instruments that governments have to reduce the probability of a slowdown, especially when the country is a middle-income or high-income one? According to the model, one of the determinants of growth slowdown is the literacy rate. Well, increasing the literacy rate is very complicated when the nation is already well educated, as in the case of Singapore.

Reference

Tan, Khee Giap, Nguyen Trieu Duong Luu and Xiao Lian. 2017. "Empirical Analysis of Growth Slowdown in ASEAN". *The Journal of Developing Areas*, 51(3): 363–376.

Chapter 5
Concluding Remarks and Directions for Future Research

5.1 Concluding Remarks: Making "Make in India" Work — Opportunities and Policy Challenges

This book has offered an in-depth analysis of India's competitiveness and growth profile at the sub-national level. The empirical results revealed not only the stark disparities that exist among the sub-national economies in India but also the consistent efforts by various sub-national governments to reduce these disparities. This is best reflected in the patterns of "convergence" we can observe over the years both with respect to income and other competitiveness indicators between the sub-national economies ranked at the bottom and middle *vis-à-vis* those at the top of the table. However, our growth slowdown analysis presented in Chapter 4 also showed that on a relative scale, although the probability of growth slowdown in India's sub-national economies is lower than that of the Greater China economies, the outlook is bleaker compared to the probability of a growth slowdown in Indonesian sub-national economies or the Association of Southeast Asian Nations (ASEAN). Further, our results also suggested that almost a third of the Indian sub-national economies have higher than even odds of slowing down which is a cause for concern, moving forward.

Viewed in totality, our findings on both competitiveness and economic growth slowdown of India's sub-national economies presents some scope for cautious optimism. To be sure, while overall macroeconomic indicators appear to support the optimistic side of the outlook, there are clear downsides in that persistently weak investment environment could increase the country's vulnerability to handle external economic shocks, thereby denting its growth performance.

Such cautious optimism becomes all the more important when the global economic environment is still weak and India is facing a hostile external growth environment. In fact, the world economy seems to have entered turbulent times once again. Nearly eight years have passed since the global financial crisis of 2007–2009 but global economic growth is yet to be back on its rails. The most recent global growth numbers from the International Monetary Fund (IMF)'s World Economic Outlook (WEO) offer no reason for optimism, with growth projections downbeat and downgraded relative to previous years. Specifically, the October 2016 IMF WEO forecasts global growth to be 3.1 percent in 2016, lower not only relative to 2015, but also a far cry from the average global growth rate of 4.5 percent between 2000 and 2007 before the global financial crisis began.

Much of this underwhelming performance in terms of economic growth comes from the continued growth stagnation of the advanced economies who have experienced a notable slowdown in their average growth rate of about 2.7 percent pre-global financial crisis. Fears of 'secular stagnation' in the advanced economies aside, the growth projections of emerging market and developing economies in 2016 was around 4.2 percent which is not impressive either, especially when viewed in historical context where they posted an average growth of about 6.6 percent from the turn of the millennium till the global financial crisis.

Emerging market economies in Asia more generally and countries like India particularly are still better off than their counterparts in the rest of the world and still manage to contribute to the growth of the region on the whole. However, there have been legitimate concerns about the process of 'deglobalisation' of trade and financial flows which could not only potentially reverse the economic gains brought about by global economic interconnectedness so far but also wield a negative influence on the sustainability of growth in Asian economies such as India, moving forward. Indeed, recent data appear to suggest notably sharp and sustained declines in global trade as well as cross-border capital flows (particularly banking flows) in recent years, which are being viewed as the beginning of the process of deglobalisation.

The hostile external environment is beyond the influence of Indian policymakers, but as the discussion in the previous chapters had highlighted, there is immense scope for India to ensure that its growth record does not derail and its efforts to build a robust competitiveness profile is sustained. One of the important ways of achieving this is to focus on flagship policy initiatives that would find ways to remove the slack in the economy and trigger growth and economic development through higher investments.

One such flagship policy that was introduced four months after the Narendra Modi-led government took the reins of power at the Centre in 2014 was the "Make in India" initiative. One of the key stated objectives of the "Make in India" initiative was to transform the country into a global manufacturing hub by getting the manufacturing sector to contribute a quarter of India's economic output by 2025.[1] As remarked by Prime Minister Narendra Modi on November 23, 2016 at a related event, "... we launched the Make in India campaign to create employment and self-employment opportunities for our youth. We are working aggressively towards making India a global manufacturing hub. We want the share of manufacturing in our Gross Domestic Product (GDP) to go up to 25 percent in the near future..."[2]

Aiming to increase the contribution of manufacturing by about 10 percentage points is a tall ask, considering the dominance of services sector to India's output and the several capacity constraints that ail India's manufacturing sector. Keeping this in mind, the government actually came up with a targeted focus by identifying 25 sectors as part of the "Make in India" initiative among which, 13 are in the manufacturing sector and the remaining pertain to services and infrastructure.

While these objectives are laudable, how far along has India progressed in meeting this objective? There have been several mixed opinions about the performance of "Make in India" so far and several critics have dubbed it as a mere branding tool with no tangible reform in sight to

---

[1] For more details of the "Make in India" initiative, see Government of India's Portal on *Make in India*, available from http://www.makeinindia.com/policy/national-manufacturing (last accessed on February 20, 2017).

[2] Prime Minister Narendra Modi's Inauguration Speech at "Make in India" Week, Mumbai, available from http://www.pmindia.gov.in/en/news_updates/prime-ministers-speech-at-inauguration-of-make-in-india-week-mumbai/ (last accessed on February 20, 2017).

transform India's manufacturing sector (The Wire, 2016). While such criticism might be too harsh, as one needs to wait till 2025 to see how this initiative pans out, available data on foreign direct investment (FDI) inflows to India and specifically to the manufacturing sector seem to highlight some areas for concern that must be addressed in order for the country to achieve the tall objectives laid out in "Make in India".

There are two important trends that available FDI data seem to point out which are relevant to understand how "Make in India" is playing out. At the broad national level, as already shown in Chapter 1, India has been doing very well in terms of attracting FDI inflows into the country and the numbers clearly suggest that Prime Minister Modi's efforts to improve the ease of doing business in India's sub-national economies have borne fruit as reflected in the resurgence in FDI inflows in 2015–2016. In particular, there was a jump of over 23 percent in India's reported FDI inflows between 2014–2015 and 2015–2016, with the increase over 45 percent when comparing the FDI inflows between the official launch of "Make in India" in 2014–2015 and 2015–2016 (Rao and Dhar, 2016).

However, to project this increase in FDI as an outcome of the "Make in India" policy appears inaccurate, when we compare the FDI data at the sectoral level. Since a large part of the initiative pertains to manufacturing, sectoral data on manufacturing suggest that after a spike in FDI inflows into manufacturing to close to US$9.6 billion in 2014–2015, inflows dropped to US$8.4 percent in 2015–2016 (Figure 5.1). Further, to provide more perspective, FDI inflows into manufacturing as a proportion of overall FDI inflows which had been hovering around 35–40 percent

Figure 5.1: Annual FDI Inflows to Manufacturing in India (US$ Billion)

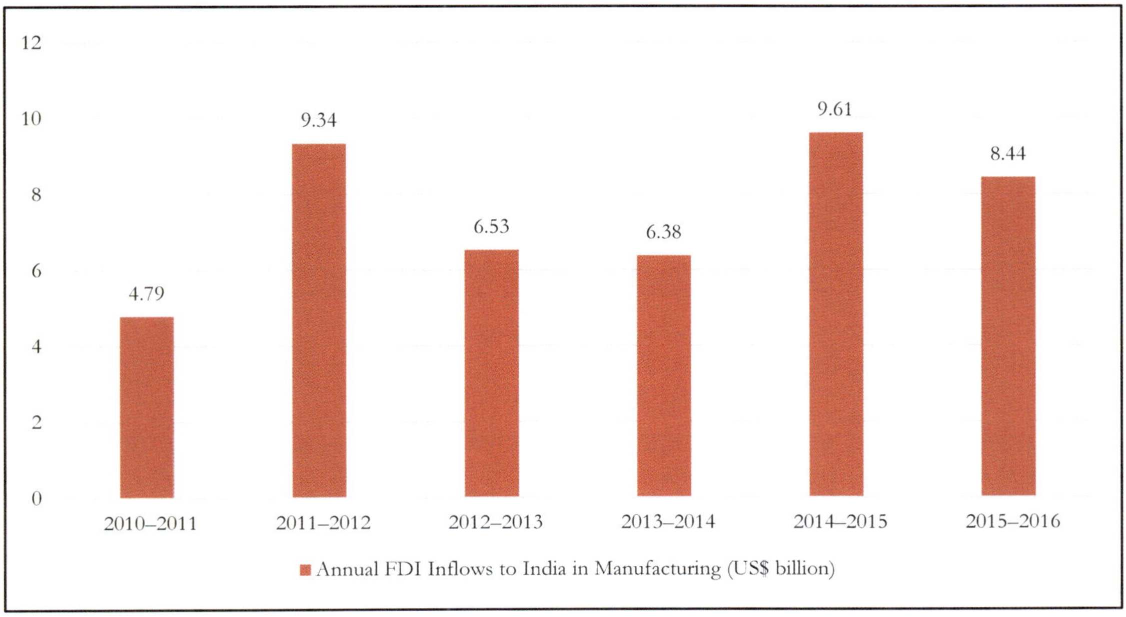

Source: Asia Competitiveness Institute based on Reserve Bank of India Database.

Figure 5.2: FDI in Manufacturing as a Percent of Total Annual FDI Inflows to India

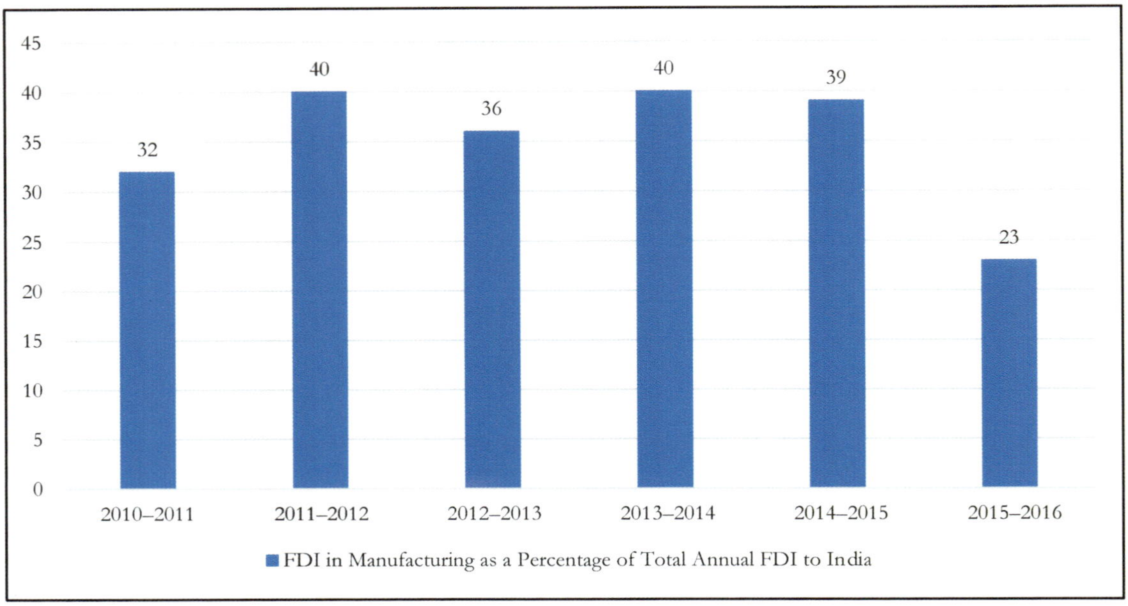

Source: Asia Competitiveness Institute based on Reserve Bank of India Database.

since 2011–2012, declined significantly to about 23 percent in 2015–2016 (Figure 5.2). Since the time the "Make in India" initiative came into force till 2015–2016, it appears as if the services sector accounted for over three-fourths of overall FDI inflows (Rao and Dhar, 2016).

Thus, it is clear from the available data that it is too early and in fact to some degree inappropriate to attribute the resurgence in India's FDI inflows to "Make in India" as FDI into manufacturing has not seen any visibly notable foreign investments. However, beyond the immediate question of attracting foreign investments into manufacturing, the larger question that the government needs to grapple with is whether it is appropriate to treat this whole "Make in India" initiative as merely an attempt to revitalise the manufacturing sector.

In a very interesting take on this issue, the former Reserve Bank of India Governor Dr. Raghuram Rajan argued that it was dangerous to treat "Make in India" as a means of focusing on manufacturing which implicitly implies mimicking China's export-led growth path. The main contention of the argument was that there would not be enough capacity in the advanced world to absorb the additional exports from India that is possible with such an initiative, adding that the export-led growth model that was adapted by several East Asian economies would not be easy to implement for India (Rajan, 2014). Further, he had the following to note:

"India has been extremely successful at carving out its own areas of comparative advantage, and will continue to do so.... I am counselling against an export led strategy that involves subsidizing exporters with cheap inputs as well as an undervalued exchange rate, simply because it is unlikely

to be as effective at this juncture. I am also cautioning against picking a particular sector such as manufacturing for encouragement, simply because it has worked well for China. India is different, and developing at a different time, and we should be agnostic about what will work..." (p. 6).

Such an argument has its merits. What the current government makes of "Make in India" remains to be seen. However, an important point that needs to be emphasised here, which was also highlighted by Rajan (2014), is the role that exchange rates can play in this process. If achieving the stated objectives of "Make in India" entails an explicit policy focus on export-led strategies, following China's footsteps, then an integral part of such a policy toolkit would involve maintaining a competitive exchange rate, undervalued relative to its peers. Whether such a strategy will be undertaken or will yield the desired benefits if India heads in that direction like China is hard to tell. However, the important role played by competitive exchange rates in the grand scheme of things cannot be ignored, which reiterates the importance of understanding the role exchange rates can possibly play in affecting India's growth prospects.

Exchange rates become all the more important when we consider the broad trends in India's real effective exchange rates (REER) which is a widely accepted measure of competitiveness. While bilaterally the Indian rupee depreciated only about 2.7 percent against the US dollar in 2016 and has remained broadly stable, in REER terms, the RBI's 36 country trade based REER index clearly shows that the Indian rupee has appreciated by 13.5 percent since the end of 2013 (Figure 5.3).

Figure 5.3: Trends in Real Effective Exchange Rates

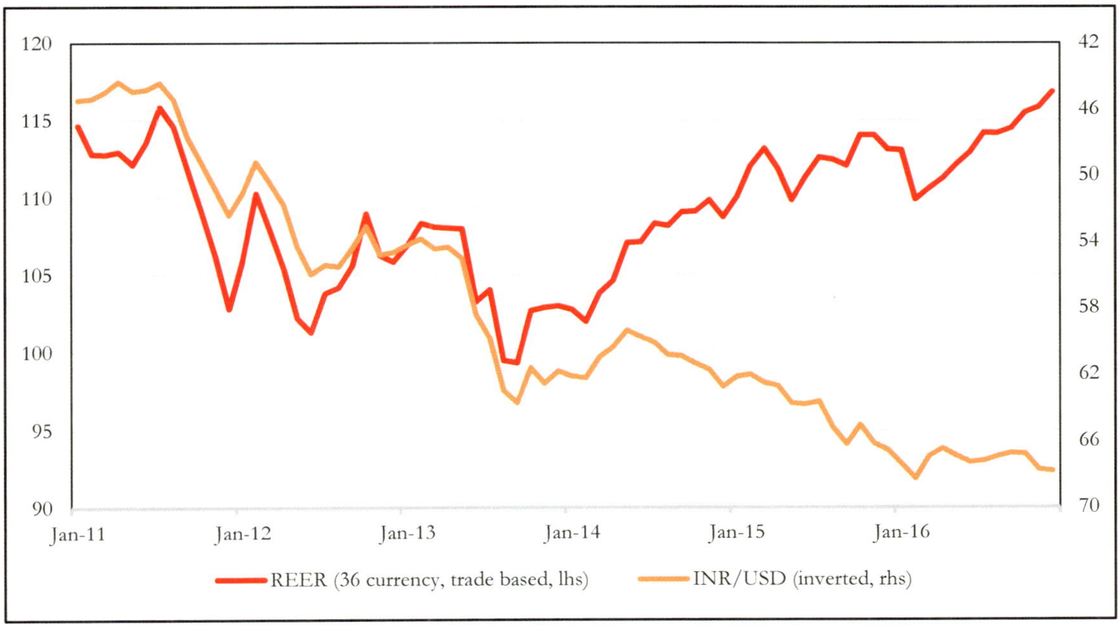

Source: Based on Reserve Bank of India and Pacific Exchange Rate Database.

It is also striking that the pace of REER appreciation was significant towards the end of 2016 and it coincided with the RBI's intervention in the foreign exchange markets to defend a rupee depreciation against the US dollar. A persistent appreciation of India's REER could lead to a loss of export competitiveness, which in turn could affect India's economic growth, moving forward, which makes it important for the policymakers to understand the impact of movements in exchange rates and their volatility. In fact, it is with this objective that Asia Competitiveness Institute (ACI) has planned to undertake future research that involves studying the impact of exchange rates on FDI inflows to India, followed by an analysis of exchange rate impacts on India's trade, both at the sub-national level. The final section concludes with a brief discussion of ACI's proposed future research agenda.

5.2 Agenda for Future Research: Nexus between Exchange Rates and FDI Inflows to Indian Sub-National Economies

The gradual normalisation of the United States (US) monetary policy has begun and consequently has generated fears that there will be a repeat of the 'taper tantrum' that battered countries like India in 2013. Changes in the US monetary policies has always exerted significant spillover effects on countries like India, especially pronounced during the period following the global financial crisis. While ultra-loose monetary policies in the form of quantitative easing resulted in currency appreciations due to massive capital inflows, the tapering of the same through interest rate hikes generated massive capital outflows and consequent currency depreciations. The severity of the impact was more on fragile emerging economies like India with relatively weak macroeconomic fundamentals. Thus, the ebbs and flows of international capital flows sensitive to US monetary policy changes have in general given rise to a variety of policy challenges concerning monetary and exchange rate management in countries like India, which in turn has a significant bearing on its overall macroeconomic and financial stability.

More generally, currency swings in India matter because of the potential macroeconomic implications they can have on its trade and foreign investments. Viewed particularly in the context of the importance of trade and foreign investments to India, one of the most significant challenges for the policymakers is to understand the potential implications of exchange rate volatility on trade flows as well as foreign investments.

There is particularly a large extant academic literature that has well documented the importance of FDI inflows to emerging markets as a source of supplementing domestic capital, technology and skills that in turn help accelerate economic growth. Policymakers also tend to have a preference to attract FDI compared to other types of capital flows (such as portfolio flows), as FDI is considered relatively more stable than the rest.

As noted in Chapter 1 earlier, although India on the whole appears to be receiving significant inflows of FDI, one must not forget the heavily skewed nature of these inflows into India's sub-national economies. For instance, on average between 2001 and 2013, nearly 60 percent of the FDI inflows have been largely directed to five States including Maharashtra, Delhi (National Capital Region), Tamil Nadu, Gujarat, and Karnataka. Maharashtra and Delhi (National Capital

Region) have consistently been the largest recipient of FDI inflows, as a share of India's overall FDI inflows during this period.

Past research suggests that a variety of 'pull' factors ranging from skill endowments to robust institutions to locational advantages (to just name a few) determine the extent of FDI that flows into a country. From this list, an important but underexamined factor relates to the behaviour of exchange rates and how it affects FDI inflows. Thus, one of the many determinants on FDI concerns the movements of exchange rates both in terms of their levels and volatility.

How do we expect exchange rate movements to affect FDI inflows? Let us take the example of a rupee depreciation. In theory, we can expect three different effects through which a weakening of Indian rupee will affect FDI inflows into the country. First, through wealth effects, depreciation of the rupee will make its assets cheap and can encourage FDI inflows.

Second, through the demand effects, a cheaper rupee makes it less attractive for firms to repatriate profits back to home country which will in turn lead to higher reinvestment of retained earnings in India.

Third, through cost-competitiveness effects, when FDI is export-promoting in nature, firms using India as an export platform tend to experience lowering of export costs when the rupee depreciates which will lead to a greater inflow of FDI. If FDI is more domestic market-oriented, then again a depreciation induces FDI because of wealth effects.

While this seemingly looks straightforward, there are three caveats to bear in mind. If the country is part of a supply chain and has low-value-add, then changes in exchange rates (levels) might not have a significant effect. Similarly, if there are strong expectations of sustained and further depreciation of the rupee, it may actually impede further FDI from flowing into India. Finally, expectations of rupee depreciation can also reduce repatriation of retained earnings.

Despite the lack of consensus, theory gives us a broad idea as to what to expect about the relationship between exchange rates and FDI inflows. However, is empirical evidence consistent with theory? Most studies on this issue have focused on advanced economies primarily, with very little empirical work dedicated to understand the dynamics in major emerging markets like India. The broader point that cost competitiveness remains one of the crucial determining variables affecting FDI inflows cannot be ignored and in fact sustaining cost competitiveness has become a prerequisite for countries like India to continue being an attractive destination for global FDI inflows.

Given this context, our future research will attempt to understand the determinants of FDI inflows at the sub-national level in India, with a specific focus on real effective exchange rates (REER) and REER volatility. Given the sparse work that exists to date on one of the important policy issues as to whether exchange rates matter or not in attracting FDI inflows, we investigate how movements in REER (both in levels and volatility) affect FDI inflows to its sub-national economies. Further, given that the world has seen a proliferation of global value chains in the way international trade transactions take place and that India is plugged into this network quite densely, it naturally becomes important to understand what role exchange rate movements both in terms of levels and volatility play on the country's trade flows, which will also be part of our future research agenda.

References

Rajan, Raghuram. 2014. "Make in India, Largely for India." Speech delivered by at the Bharat Ram Memorial Lecture, December 12, 2014, New Delhi, available from https://www.rbi.org.in/scripts/BS_SpeechesView.aspx?Id=930 (last accessed on February 20, 2017).

Rao, K.S. Chalapati and Biswajit Dhar. 2016. "The Tenuous Relationship between Make in India and FDI Inflows." Policy Brief No. 2, Institute for Studies in Industrial Development, New Delhi, India, available from http://isid.org.in/pdf/ISIDpb02.pdf (last accessed on February 20, 2017).

The Wire. 2017. "A Closer Look at Modi's Make in India." available from https://thewire.in/62808/a-closer-look-at-make-in-india/ (last accessed on February 20, 2017).

Appendices

Appendix 1

List of Indicators for 35 Indian Sub-National Economies

No.	Indicator	Unit	Reversed Indicator
1	**MACROECONOMIC STABILITY**		
1.1	Regional Economic Vibrancy		
1.1.01	Gross State Domestic Product (GSDP)	10 Million Rupees (₹), Real GSDP (Base Year 2000)	
1.1.02	Gross State Domestic Product Growth	Percent Change per Annum	
1.1.03	Gross State Domestic Product per Capita	Rupees (₹)	
1.1.04	Primary Industry	10 Million Rupees (₹), Real GSDP (Base Year 2000)	
1.1.05	Secondary Industry	10 Million Rupees (₹), Real GSDP (Base Year 2000)	
1.1.06	Tertiary Industry	10 Million Rupees (₹), Real GSDP (Base Year 2000)	
1.1.07	Gross Capital Formation (Percent)	Percent of GSDP	
1.1.08	Inflation (Consumer Price Index — Rural Labourers)	Percent	R
1.1.09	Inflation (Consumer Price Index — Industrial Labourers)	Percent	R
1.1.10	Domestic Tourists	10,000 Visits	
1.2	Openness to Trade and Services		
1.2.01	Exports of Merchandise Goods	10 Million Rupees (₹), Real Prices (Base Year 2000)	
1.2.02	Openness to Trade	Ratio	
1.2.03	International Tourists	10,000 Visits	
1.3	Attractiveness to Foreign Investors		
1.3.01	Foreign Direct Investment	10 Million Rupees (₹), Real Prices (Base Year 2000)	
1.3.02	Number of Foreign Companies (Percent)	Percent of Total	

(Continued)

(Continued)

No.	Indicator	Unit	Reversed Indicator
2	**GOVERNMENT AND INSTITUTIONAL SETTING**		
2.1	Government Policies and Fiscal Sustainability		
2.1.01	Government Revenue	10 Million Rupees (₹), Real Prices (Base Year 2000)	
2.1.02	Tax Revenue	10 Million Rupees (₹), Real Prices (Base Year 2000)	
2.1.03	Tax Revenue/Government Revenue	Percent of Government Revenue	
2.1.04	Government Consumption Expenditure	Percent of GSDP	
2.1.05	Budget Balance	Percent of GSDP	
2.2	Institutions, Governance and Leadership		
2.2.01	Limited Companies	Number	
2.2.02	Public Limited Companies (Percent)	Percent of Total Limited Companies	
2.2.03	Foreign Companies	Number	
2.2.04	Public Limited Companies	Number	
2.2.05	Private Limited Companies	Number	
2.2.06	Policemen per 100 km^2	Ratio	
2.2.07	Policemen per 100,000 Population	Ratio	
2.2.08	Police Expenditure	10 Million Rupees (₹), Real Prices (Base Year 2000)	
3	**FINANCIAL, BUSINESSES AND MANPOWER CONDITIONS**		
3.1	Financial Deepening and Business Efficiency		
3.1.01	Bank Offices	Number	
3.1.02	Population Served per Bank Office	Ratio	R
3.1.03	Bank Credit	10 Million Rupees (₹), Real Prices (Base Year 2000)	
3.1.04	Bank Deposits	10 Million Rupees (₹), Real Prices (Base Year 2000)	
3.2	Labour Market Flexibility		
3.2.01	Total Workers	Number	
3.2.02	Urban Workers	Percent of Total Workers	
3.2.03	Unemployment Rate (Urban Area)	Percent	R
3.2.04	Wages and Salaries	10 Million Rupees (₹), Real Prices (Base Year 2000)	

(Continued)

(Continued)

No.	Indicator	Unit	Reversed Indicator
3.2.05	Agricultural Wages	Rupees (₹), Real Prices (Base Year 2000)	
3.2.06	Industrial Training Institutes	Number	
3.3	Productivity Performance		
3.3.01	Overall Labour Productivity	Rupees (₹) per Person-Year	
3.3.02	Secondary Industry, Value-Added per Worker	Rupees (₹) per Person-Year	
4	**QUALITY OF LIFE AND INFRASTRUCTURE DEVELOPMENT**		
4.1	Physical Infrastructure		
4.1.01	Population	10,000 Persons	
4.1.02	Urban Population	Percent of Total Population	
4.1.03	Population Density	Persons per km^2	R
4.1.04	Length of Railways in Operation	km	
4.1.05	Length of Roads	km	
4.1.06	Number of Ports	Number	
4.1.07	Total Cargo Handled	1,000 Tonnes	
4.1.08	Consumption of Electricity per Capita	kWh	
4.1.09	Power Generation	Million Units	
4.1.10	Motor Vehicles per Km of Road	Number	R
4.1.11	Total Land Area	km^2	
4.1.12	Cultivated Land	Percent of Geographical Area	
4.2	Technological Infrastructure		
4.2.01	Persons per Internet Subscriber	Number	R
4.2.02	Persons per Mobile Telephone Subscriber	Number	R
4.2.03	Expenditure on Science, Technology and Environment	Percent of GSDP	
4.3	Standard of Living, Education and Social Stability		
4.3.01	Illiteracy Rate	Percent	R
4.3.02	Number of Educational Institutions	Total Units	
4.3.03	Disparity between Primary and Secondary Institutions	Percent	R
4.3.04	Tertiary Institutions	Percent of Total Institutions	

(Continued)

(Continued)

No.	Indicator	Unit	Reversed Indicator
4.3.05	Student–Teacher Ratio (Primary)	Ratio	R
4.3.06	Student–Teacher Ratio (Secondary)	Ratio	R
4.3.07	Student–Teacher Ratio (Tertiary)	Ratio	R
4.3.08	Expenditure on Education	Percent of GSDP	
4.3.09	Health Expenditure	Percent of Total Expenditure	
4.3.10	Per Capita Public Health Expenditure	Rupees (₹), Real Prices (Base Year 2000)	
4.3.11	Urban Population Growth	Percent per Annum	
4.3.12	Air Pollution	Milligram/m^3	R
4.3.13	Ageing Profile	Percent of Population Over 60 Years	R
4.3.14	Old Age Dependency Ratio	Ratio	R
4.3.15	Motor Vehicles per Person	Number	
4.3.16	Death Rate	Per 1,000 Persons	R
4.3.17	Adequacy of Hospitals	Per 10,000 Persons per Hospital	R
4.3.18	Population per Hospital Bed	Per 10,000 Persons	R
4.3.19	Population per Medical Personnel	Per 10,000 Persons	R
4.3.20	Infant Mortality Rate	Number of Persons	R

Appendix 2
Computation of Rankings — The Algorithm

A step-by-step description of the ranking process is described below for N regions, M practical indicators and C environments, with each environment comprising S sub-environments.

Algorithm: Ranking Methodology

(1) Compute the mean value of practical indicator j ($j = 1, \ldots , M$),

$$\bar{X}_j = \frac{1}{N} \sum_{i=1}^{N} X_{ij}$$

where X_{ij} represents the value that region i ($i = 1, \ldots , N$) takes for practical indicator j.

(2) For each practical indicator j ($j = 1, \ldots , M$), calculate its standard deviation (SD),

$$SD_j = \sqrt{\frac{1}{N} \sum_{i=1}^{N} \left(X_{ij} - \bar{X}_j\right)^2}$$

(3) Compute the standardised value of indicator (SVI) that each region i ($i = 1, \ldots , N$) takes under each of the practical indicators j ($j =1, \ldots , M$),

$$SVI_{ij} = \frac{X_{ij} - \bar{X}_j}{SD_j}$$

(4) Compute the 'ranked' standardised value of indicator (RSVI) that each region i ($i = 1, \ldots , N$) takes under each of the practical indicators j ($j = 1, \ldots , M$),

$$RSVI_{ij} = \begin{cases} SVI_{ij}, & \textit{if a higher value is better} \\ -SVI_{ij}, & \textit{if a lower value is better} \end{cases}$$

(5) For each practical indicator j ($j = 1, \ldots , M$), a ranking can be obtained for regions. Regions with a higher value of RSVI for indicator j are ranked ahead of those with a lower value.

(6) For each region i ($i = 1, \ldots, N$), calculate the RSVI for each sub-environment k ($k = 1, \ldots, S$) belonging to environment l ($l = 1, \ldots, C$),

$$Raw\_RSVI_{i,lk} = \frac{1}{y_{lk}} \sum_{p=1}^{y_{lk}} RSVI_{i,j_{lk,p}}$$

$$Mean\_RSVI_{lk} = \frac{1}{N} \sum_{i=1}^{N} Raw\_RSVI_{i,lk}$$

$$SD\_RSVI_{lk} = \sqrt{\frac{1}{N} \sum_{i=1}^{N} \left(Raw\_RSVI_{i,lk} - Mean\_RSVI_{lk}\right)^2}$$

$$RSVI_{i,lk} = \frac{Raw\_RSVI_{i,lk} - Mean\_RSVI_{lk}}{SD\_RSVI_{lk}}$$

where y_{lk} is the total number of practical indicators under sub-environment k of environment l and (*RSVIi,jlk,*1, ... , *RSVIi,jlk,ylk*) are the RSVIs for region i that make up sub-environment k of environment l.

(7) For each region i ($i = 1, \ldots, N$), calculate the RSVI for each environment l ($l = 1, \ldots, C$),

$$Raw\_RSVI_{i,l} = \frac{1}{S_l} \sum_{k=1}^{S_l} RSVI_{i,lk}$$

$$Mean\_RSVI_{l} = \frac{1}{N} \sum_{i=1}^{N} Raw\_RSVI_{i,l}$$

$$SD\_RSVI_{l} = \sqrt{\frac{1}{N} \sum_{i=1}^{N} \left(Raw\_RSVI_{i,l} - Mean\_RSVI_{l}\right)^2}$$

$$RSVI_{i,l} = \frac{Raw\_RSVI_{i,l} - Mean\_RSVI_{l}}{SD\_RSVI_{l}}$$

where (*RSVIi,l*1, . . . , *RSVIi,lS*) are the RSVIs for the S sub-environments under each environment l.

(8) Overall rank score of region i ($i = 1, \ldots, N$),

$$Raw\_R_i = \frac{1}{C}\sum_{l=1}^{C} RSVI_{i,l}$$

$$Mean\_R = \frac{1}{N}\sum_{i=1}^{N} Raw\_R_i$$

$$SD\_R = \sqrt{\frac{1}{N}\sum_{i=1}^{N}\left(Raw\_R_i - Mean\_R\right)^2}$$

$$R_i = \frac{Raw\_R_i - Mean\_R}{SD\_R}$$

Regions with a higher R_i are ranked ahead of those with a lower R_i, and the region with the highest R_i is the most competitive region.

Step (5) provides the ranking of each region for each individual practical indicator. To achieve this ranking, Step (4) adjusts the value of the SVIs so that a higher value will lead to a better ranking in terms of 'competitiveness'. Depending on the nature of the indicator in question, a higher or lower value may reflect a more 'competitive' region. Take, for instance, the practical sub-indicators 'Gross Regional Domestic Product (GRDP)' and 'unemployment rate (urban area)'. Having a higher GRDP but a lower unemployment rate suggests better economic performance, which makes a region more 'competitive'. In most cases where a higher value is better (e.g. GRDP), the SVIs of regions are considered, and those with a higher SVI value will have a better ranking. However, for indicators where the inverse is true (e.g. unemployment rate (urban area)), the 'negative SVI' values are compared between regions and a lower SVI value will lead to a better ranking. Step (4) thus seeks to make the standardised values of all practical indicators consistent for ranking purposes.

Step (6) determines the sub-environment rankings of each region. The average RSVI of all the indicators in the sub-environment are calculated, re-standardised across all the regions and compared to other regions. Regions with a higher average RSVI rank better in the sub-environment.

To arrive at the ranking for each environment, the RSVIs of the sub-environments are averaged and re-standardised across all the regions as detailed by Step (7). Finally, Step (8) requires the RSVI values of each environment to be averaged and re-standardised across all the regions to determine the overall ranking of the region. Regions with a higher RSVI are ranked ahead of those with a lower RSVI.

Although the number of sub-environments and indicators varies for each main environment, the aggregate score for each main environment is given an equal weight: 25% of the Indian

Regional Overall Competitiveness Index. An identical weight is assigned to each environment as they present equal significance to the computation of the index. This method is repeated and applied consistently across all the regions to ensure precision of the rankings. Mathematically, this can be illustrated as follows:

$$
\begin{aligned}
\text{India Regional Overall Competitiveness Index} \\
&= 25\% \times (\text{Macroeconomic Stability}) \\
&\quad + 25\% \times (\text{Government and Institutional Setting}) \\
&\quad + 25\% \times (\text{Financial, Businesses and Manpower Conditions}) \\
&\quad + 25\% \times (\text{Quality of Life and Infrastructure Development}).
\end{aligned}
$$

Appendix 3
Notes on Data Aggregation for Computation of Regional Rankings

No.	Indicator	Unit	Reversed Indicator	Aggregation Method
1	**MACROECONOMIC STABILITY**			
1.1	Regional Economic Vibrancy			
1.1.01	Gross Regional Domestic Product (GRDP)	10 Million Rupees (₹), Real GRDP (Base Year 2000)		Method 1
1.1.02	Gross Regional Domestic Product Growth	Percent Change per Annum		Method 2
1.1.03	Gross Regional Domestic Product per Capita	Rupees (₹)		Method 2
1.1.04	Primary Industry	10 Million Rupees (₹), Real GRDP (Base Year 2000)		Method 1
1.1.05	Secondary Industry	10 Million Rupees (₹), Real GRDP (Base Year 2000)		Method 1
1.1.06	Tertiary Industry	10 Million Rupees (₹), Real GRDP (Base Year 2000)		Method 1
1.1.07	Gross Capital Formation (Percent)	Percent of GRDP		Method 2
1.1.08	Inflation (Consumer Price Index — Rural Labourers)	Percent	R	Method 3
1.1.09	Inflation (Consumer Price Index — Industrial Labourers)	Percent	R	Method 3
1.1.10	Domestic Tourists	10,000 Visits		Method 1
1.2	Openness to Trade and Services			
1.2.01	Exports of Merchandise Goods	10 Million Rupees (₹), Real Prices (Base Year 2000)		Method 1
1.2.02	Openness to Trade	Ratio		Method 2
1.2.03	International Tourists	10,000 Visits		Method 1
1.3	Attractiveness to Foreign Investors			
1.3.01	Foreign Direct Investment	10 Million Rupees (₹), Real Prices (Base Year 2000)		Method 1
1.3.02	Number of Foreign Companies (Percent)	Percent of Total		Method 2

(Continued)

(Continued)

No.	Indicator	Unit	Reversed Indicator	Aggregation Method
2	**GOVERNMENT AND INSTITUTIONAL SETTING**			
2.1	Government Policies and Fiscal Sustainability			
2.1.01	Government Revenue	10 Million Rupees (₹), Real Prices (Base Year 2000)		Method 1
2.1.02	Tax Revenue	10 Million Rupees (₹), Real Prices (Base Year 2000)		Method 1
2.1.03	Tax Revenue/Government Revenue	Percent of Government Revenue		Method 2
2.1.04	Government Consumption Expenditure	Percent of GRDP		Method 2
2.1.05	Budget Balance	Percent of GRDP		Method 2
2.2	Institutions, Governance and Leadership			
2.2.01	Limited Companies	Number		Method 1
2.2.02	Public Limited Companies (Percent)	Percent of Total Limited Companies		Method 2
2.2.03	Foreign Companies	Number		Method 1
2.2.04	Public Limited Companies	Number		Method 1
2.2.05	Private Limited Companies	Number		Method 1
2.2.06	Policemen per 100 km^2	Ratio		Method 2
2.2.07	Policemen per 100,000 Population	Ratio		Method 2
2.2.08	Police Expenditure	10 Million Rupees (₹), Real Prices (Base Year 2000)		Method 1
3	**FINANCIAL, BUSINESSES AND MANPOWER CONDITIONS**			
3.1	Financial Deepening and Business Efficiency			
3.1.01	Bank Offices	Number		Method 1
3.1.02	Population Served per Bank Office	Ratio	R	Method 2
3.1.03	Bank Credit	10 Million Rupees (₹), Real Prices (Base Year 2000)		Method 1
3.1.04	Bank Deposits	10 Million Rupees (₹), Real Prices (Base Year 2000)		Method 1
3.2	Labour Market Flexibility			
3.2.01	Total Workers	Number		Method 1
3.2.02	Urban Workers	Percent of Total Workers		Method 2

(Continued)

(*Continued*)

No.	Indicator	Unit	Reversed Indicator	Aggregation Method
3.2.03	Unemployment Rate (Urban Area)	Percent	R	Method 3
3.2.04	Wages and Salaries	10 Million Rupees (₹), Real Prices (Base Year 2000)		Method 1
3.2.05	Agricultural Wages	Rupees (₹), Real Prices (Base Year 2000)		Method 1
3.2.06	Industrial Training Institutes	Number		Method 1
3.3	Productivity Performance			
3.3.01	Overall Labour Productivity	Rupees (₹) per Person-Year		Method 3
3.3.02	Secondary Industry, Value-Added per Worker	Rupees (₹) per Person-Year		Method 3
4	**QUALITY OF LIFE AND INFRASTRUCTURE DEVELOPMENT**			
4.1	Physical Infrastructure			
4.1.01	Population	10,000 Persons		Method 1
4.1.02	Urban Population	Percent of Total Population		Method 2
4.1.03	Population Density	Persons per km^2	R	Method 2
4.1.04	Length of Railways	km		Method 1
4.1.05	Length of Roads	km		Method 1
4.1.06	Number of Ports	Number		Method 1
4.1.07	Total Cargo Handled	1,000 Tonnes		Method 1
4.1.08	Consumption of Electricity per Capita	kWh		Method 3
4.1.09	Power Generation	Million Units		Method 1
4.1.10	Motor Vehicles per Km of Road	Number	R	Method 2
4.1.11	Total Land Area	km^2		Method 1
4.1.12	Cultivated Land	Percent of Geographical Area		Method 3
4.2	Technological Infrastructure			
4.2.01	Persons per Internet Subscriber	Number	R	Method 2
4.2.02	Persons per Mobile Telephone Subscriber	Number	R	Method 2
4.2.03	Expenditure on Science, Technology and Environment	Percent of GRDP		Method 2
4.3	Standard of Living, Education and Social Stability			
4.3.01	Illiteracy Rate	Percent	R	Method 2

(*Continued*)

(Continued)

No.	Indicator	Unit	Reversed Indicator	Aggregation Method
4.3.02	Number of Educational Institutions	Total Units		Method 1
4.3.03	Disparity between Primary and Secondary Institutions	Percent	R	Method 3
4.3.04	Tertiary Institutions	Percent of Total Institutions		Method 3
4.3.05	Student–Teacher Ratio (Primary)	Ratio	R	Method 3
4.3.06	Student–Teacher Ratio (Secondary)	Ratio	R	Method 3
4.3.07	Student–Teacher Ratio (Tertiary)	Ratio	R	Method 3
4.3.08	Expenditure on Education	Percent of GRDP		Method 2
4.3.09	Health Expenditure	Percent of Total Expenditure		Method 2
4.3.10	Per Capita Public Health Expenditure	Rupees (₹), Real Prices (Base Year 2000)		Method 2
4.3.11	Urban Population Growth	Percent per Annum		Method 2
4.3.12	Air Pollution	Milligram/m^3	R	Method 3
4.3.13	Ageing Profile	Percent of Population Over 60 Years	R	Method 2
4.3.14	Old Age Dependency Ratio	Ratio	R	Method 2
4.3.15	Motor Vehicles per Person	Number		Method 2
4.3.16	Death Rate	Per 1,000 Persons	R	Method 3
4.3.17	Adequacy of Hospitals	Per 10,000 Persons per Hospital	R	Method 2
4.3.18	Population per Hospital Bed	Per 10,000 Persons	R	Method 2
4.3.19	Population per Medical Personnel	Per 10,000 Persons	R	Method 2
4.3.20	Infant Mortality Rate	Number of Persons	R	Method 3

Appendix 4

Table A-4.1: Determinants of Growth Slowdown for the Low-Income Group, Lower-Middle-Income Group and Combined Group of Upper-Middle-Income and High-Income Economies (Based on Probit Specification)

	Growth Slowdown Models		
	Low-Income	**Lower-Middle-Income**	**Combined Group of Upper-Middle-Income and High-Income Economies**
GRDP per Capita	0.0007** (0.0003)	0.0003*** (0.0001)	0.0002*** (0.00004)
Literacy Rate	–0.0171** (0.0069)	–0.0124* (0.0065)	–0.0937*** (0.0364)
Foreign Direct Investment Inflows as Percent of GRDP	–0.2135** (0.1010)	–0.0997*** (0.0266)	
Length of Road per Capita	–0.0068* (0.0039)		
Employment in Tertiary Industry as Percent of Total Employment		–0.0165** (0.0065)	–0.0263** (0.0103)
Old Dependency Ratio		0.0378** (0.0164)	
Openness to Trade			–0.0057*** (0.0018)
Secondary Industry Value-Added per Worker			–0.00001** ($4.72e^{-6}$)
Constant	–0.5704 (0.5692)	–0.4116 (0.6006)	9.1347*** (3.3867)
No. of observations	358	667	147
Pseudo R^2	0.0660	0.0857	0.1234

Notes:
(i) Numbers in the parentheses are standard errors.
(ii) *, ** and *** denote the significance of coefficients at the 10 percent, 5 percent and 1 percent levels, respectively.

Source: Asia Competitiveness Institute's calculations.

Appendix 5

Table A-5.1: Predictive Probabilities of Growth Slowdown for India's Sub-National Economies for 2012–2017 (Results Using Probit Specification of Income Group Specific Growth Slowdown Models)

Economy	Income Group in 2012	Probability of Experiencing Growth Slowdown during 2012–2017
Andaman and Nicobar Islands	Lower-middle-income	0.52701
Andhra Pradesh	Lower-middle-income	0.50333
Arunachal Pradesh	Lower-middle-income	0.41192
Assam	Lower-middle-income	0.20231
Bihar	Low-income	0.17474
Chandigarh	Upper-middle-income	0.69017
Chhattisgarh	Lower-middle-income	0.43120
Delhi	Upper-middle-income	0.44944
Goa	High-income	0.46122
Gujarat	Lower-middle-income	0.54436
Haryana	Lower-middle-income	0.64855
Himachal Pradesh	Lower-middle-income	0.62179
Jammu and Kashmir	Lower-middle-income	0.33898
Jharkhand	Lower-middle-income	0.30969
Karnataka	Lower-middle-income	0.38779
Kerala	Lower-middle-income	0.44919
Madhya Pradesh	Lower-middle-income	0.31331
Maharashtra	Lower-middle-income	0.45791
Manipur	Lower-middle-income	0.19588
Meghalaya	Lower-middle-income	0.22811
Mizoram	Lower-middle-income	0.23262
Nagaland	Lower-middle-income	0.29179
Odisha	Lower-middle-income	0.37779
Puducherry	Lower-middle-income	0.47617

(Continued)

(Continued)

Economy	Income Group in 2012	Probability of Experiencing Growth Slowdown during 2012–2017
Punjab	Lower-middle-income	0.53845
Rajasthan	Lower-middle-income	0.43249
Sikkim	Upper-middle-income	0.87471
Tamil Nadu	Lower-middle-income	0.46365
Tripura	Lower-middle-income	0.28183
Uttar Pradesh	Low-income	0.22128
Uttarakhand	Lower-middle-income	0.54118
West Bengal	Lower-middle-income	0.32345
	Average	0.41882

Notes:

(i) Average reported is simple average.

(ii) Predictive probabilities for Dadra and Nagar Haveli, Daman and Diu and Lakshadweep are not generated. This is because Gross Regional Domestic Product (GRDP) per capita for these economies are not available throughout the study period.

Source: Asia Competitiveness Institute's calculations.

Asia Competitiveness Institute - World Scientific Series

(Continued from page vi)

2015 Estimation of Agricultural Productivity and Annual Update of Competitiveness Analysis for Greater China: Optimising Agricultural Productivity and Promoting Innovation Driven Growth
by Tan Khee Giap, Yuan Randong & Xie Teleixi (Lee Kuan Yew School of Public Policy, NUS, Singapore)

2015 Agricultural Total Factor Productivity and Competitiveness Analysis for States and Federal Territories and Five Regions of India: Annual Competitiveness Update and Evidence on the Agricultural Development Models for Selected Indian States
by Tan Khee Giap, Sasidaran Gopalan & Anuja Tandon (Lee Kuan Yew School of Public Policy, NUS, Singapore)

2015 Agricultural Productivity, Decentralisation, and Competitiveness Analysis for Provinces and Regions of Indonesia
by Tan Khee Giap, Nurina Merdikawati, Mulya Amri & Tan Kong Yam (Lee Kuan Yew School of Public Policy, NUS, Singapore)

2015 Annual Competitiveness Analysis and Development Strategies for Indonesian Provinces
by Tan Khee Giap, Mulya Amri, Nurina Merdikawati & Nursyahida Ahmad (Lee Kuan Yew School of Public Policy, NUS, Singapore)

2014

2014 Annual Competitiveness Ranking and Simulation Study for ASEAN-10 and Development Strategies to Enhance Asia Economic Connectivity
by Tan Khee Giap, Sangiita Yoong Wei Cher, Sasidaran Gopalan & Nguyen Le Phuong Anh (Lee Kuan Yew School of Public Policy, NUS, Singapore)

2014 Annual Provincial and Regional Competitiveness Analysis for Greater China Economies: Development Strategies under the New Normal
by Tan Khee Giap, Yuan Randong & Sangiita Yoong Wei Cher (Lee Kuan Yew School of Public Policy, NUS, Singapore)

2014 Regional Competitiveness Analysis and a Master Plan on Regional Development Strategies for India: Annual Competitiveness Update and Evidence on Economic Development Model for Selected States of India
by Tan Khee Giap, Linda Low, Kartik Rao & Tan Kong Yam (Lee Kuan Yew School of Public Policy, NUS, Singapore)

2014 Provincial and Inaugural Regional Competitiveness Analysis: Safeguarding Indonesia's Growth Momentum
by Tan Khee Giap, Nurina Merdikawati, Mulya Amri & Tan Kong Yam (Lee Kuan Yew School of Public Policy, NUS, Singapore)

2014 Annual Competitiveness Analysis and Development Strategies for Indonesian Provinces
by Tan Khee Giap, Nurina Merdikawati, Mulya Amri & Blake Harley Berger (Lee Kuan Yew School of Public Policy, NUS, Singapore)

2013

Annual Analysis of Competitiveness, Simulation Studies and Development Perspective for 34 Greater China Economies: 2000–2010
by Tan Khee Giap, Yuan Randong, Sangiita Yoong Wei Cher & Yang Mu (Lee Kuan Yew School of Public Policy, NUS, Singapore)

Annual Analysis of Competitiveness, Simulation Studies and Development Perspective for 35 States and Federal Territories of India: 2000–2010
by Tan Khee Giap, Linda Low, Tan Kong Yam & Kartik Rao (Lee Kuan Yew School of Public Policy, NUS, Singapore)

Competitiveness Analysis and Development Strategies for 33 Indonesian Provinces
by Tan Khee Giap, Mulya Amri, Linda Low & Tan Kong Yam (Lee Kuan Yew School of Public Policy, NUS, Singapore)